Out of Sorts

MATERIAL TEXTS

Out of Sorts

On Typography and Print Culture

ᴔ ᴔ ᴔ

Joseph A. Dane

PENN

UNIVERSITY OF PENNSYLVANIA PRESS

PHILADELPHIA · OXFORD

Published by
University of Pennsylvania Press
Philadelphia, Pennsylvania 19104-4112
www.upenn.edu/pennpress

Printed in the United States of America on acid-free paper
10 9 8 7 6 5 4 3 2 1

Library of Congress Cataloging-in-Publication Data
Dane, Joseph A.
    Out of sorts : on typography and modern theories of
print culture / Joseph A. Dane.
        p.   cm. — (Material texts)
    ISBN 978-0-8122-4294-2 (acid-free paper)
    Includes bibliographical references and index.
    1. Bibliography—Methodology.   2. Bibliography—
Methodology—History.   3. Type and type-founding—
History.   4. Type and type-founding—Historiography.
5. Printing—History.   6. Printing—Historiography.
7. Incunabula—Bibliography—Methodology.   8. Early
printed books—Bibliography—Methodology.   9. Bibliography, Critical.   10. Transmission of texts.   I. Title
Z1001 .D225   2011
002'.09—dc22   2010017942

P. lectori

CONTENTS

❧

PART II. IMAGES AND TEXTS

ABBREVIATIONS

AK: *Astronomical Calendar*, now *Planeten-Tafel, sive Ephemerides 1448* (Mainz, 1458) ISTC ip00749500

B36:   36-line Bible (printed in DK type). [Bamberg, not after 1460] Goff B527.

B42:   42-line Bible = Gutenberg Bible. [Mainz: Gutenberg and Johannes Fust, ca. 1455] Goff B526.

BMC: *Catalogue of Books Printed in the XVth Century now in the British Museum.* 13 vols. London: British Museum, 1908–.

DK type: type used in the production of Donatus texts and Calendars = "Type of the 36-line Bible"

EETS: Early English Text Society

ESTC: English Short Title Catalogue. www.bl.uk

Goff: Frederick R. Goff, *Incunabula in American Libraries: A Third Census of American Collections.* 2 vols. New York: Bibliographical Society of America, 1972.

GW: *Gesamtkatalog der Wiegendrucke.* 10 vols. Stuttgart: Hiersemann, 1928–. www.gesamtkatalogderwiegendrucke.de

ISTC: Incunabula Short Title Catalogue. British Library. istc.bl.uk/catalogues/istc/

STC: A. W. Pollard, G. R. Redgrave, W. A. Jackson, F. S. Ferguson, and Katherine F. Pantzer, eds., *A Short-Title Catalogue of Books Printed in England, Scotland and Ireland, and of English Books Printed Abroad, 1475–1640.* 3 vols. 2nd ed. London: Bibliographical Society, 1976–91.

VGG: Veröffentlichungen der Gutenberg Gesellschaft

ILLUSTRATIONS

❧

INTRODUCTION

At some point in the mid-fifteenth century, several technicians worked on the problem of an *ars artificialiter scribendi*. Such work is often referred to in early documents, but the language is too vague to clarify exactly what procedures or techniques might have been involved. The so-called Strasbourg documents of the late 1430s, recording a suit involving Gutenberg, refer to the work of a press ("drucken") and a device dismantled by Gutenberg so that its use and function would not be apparent (a hand-mold?).[1] The colophon to the 1457 Mainz Psalter by Johann Fust and Peter Schoeffer refers to the "adinventio artificiosa imprimendi ac caracterizandi absque calami ulla exaratione" [an artificial device for printing without any use of the pen]; the colophon to the *Catholicon* (1460? perhaps by Gutenberg) speaks of its printing as "non calami, stili, aut pennae suffragio, sed mira patronarum formarumque concordia, proporcione, ac modulo" [not by the aid of pen or quill, but by a miraculous concordance of punches and letters].[2] The colophon to the 1470 Sallust (by Da Spira) celebrates the efficiency of printing:

> Quadringenta dedit formata volumina Crispi
> Nunc, lector, venetis spirea vindelinus
> Et calamo libros audes spectare notatos
> Aere magis quando littera ducta nitet.
>
> [To Venice Wendelin, who from Speier comes
> Has given of Sallust twice two hundred tomes,
> And who dare glorify the pen-made book,
> When so much fairer brass-stamped letters look?][3]

The vague reference to brass letters (which may not be brass at all) is omitted from the 1471 second edition.

Similar statements are found Caxton's Epilogue to the *Recuyell of the Historyes of Troye* (ca. 1473–74), the first book printed in English.

> Therefore I haue practysed & lerned at my grete charge and dispense to ordeyne this said book in prynte after the maner & forme as ye may here see / and is not wreton with penne and ynke as other bokes ben / to thende that euery man may haue them attones / ffor all the bookes of this storye named the recule of the historyes of troyes thus empryntid as ye here see were begonne in oon day / and also fynys-hid in oon day.[4]

Caxton's words, written perhaps two decades after the commercial introduction of printing, are as vague as earlier references. Perhaps he means that each of the "books" (that is, sections) in this book-copy and other copies like it were begun in one day and finished also in one day, or perhaps that all of these books were begun and finished at the same time by printing them concurrently. But it is more likely a hyperbole for the speed of printing generally. There is no conventional written language available to describe the nature of this invention.

References such as these, even through the later fifteenth century, are imprecise, perhaps conveniently so from the standpoint of histories of early printing. As was amply demonstrated at the end of the nineteenth century, evidence like this could support multiple and conflicting versions of both the origins and the technology of printing.[5] For material and what might be called internal evidence, we are left with the books themselves: early Donatus grammars from Mainz, or fragments of them, Dutch blockbooks, most now dated to the 1470s, early Dutch grammars, now dated in the 1460s and once considered products of the 1430s, the *Astronomical Calendar* printed in (Gutenberg's?) DK type, once dated with absolute certainty as 1447, now dated a decade later, and of course the Gutenberg Bible, which some scholars claim is not by Gutenberg, or, as it is now known by scholars deferring to this skepticism, the 42-line Bible (or "B42"), even though some of its most significant page-settings are in 40 or 41 lines.

It is difficult even to list these things without the deliberately cumbersome qualifications in the above sentence. We do not know with certainty when they were produced; we do not know with certainty who produced them; and we do not know with certainty how they were produced. They are all related to the origins of printing, but whether they should be described as the key products, the most important collectibles, the best evidence, the earliest monuments—on that there is no consensus. Should they be described as halting, failed attempts, inefficient trials, tentative steps (using sand-cast typesorts?), or should printing be defined as born almost in a state of perfection, and the Gutenberg Bible as produced by procedures unchanged through the eighteenth century? These questions are unlikely to be answered based on simple research or discovery: the answers depend, rather, on the way scholars formulate questions, define their allegiances, and view their own scholarly being and direction.

No Leaners

Whatever we think printing is, printing seems to involve something different from writing. How that difference is to be defined, by what statement printing is to be distinguished from this "something different" (writing? script? manuscript production?)—on that, again, and again, there is little agreement. The distinctive being or essence of printing lies not in the exact reproduction of words or images, not in mass production, and certainly not in some grand thing like the Rise of Humanism. Rather, certain continuities characteristic of writing, both in its history and in its production, seem to be broken by this thing we call print. The typesetter's hand operates in a series of discrete movements, selecting unique sorts from the finite number of compartments in a typecase. Typesetters may reconceive the nature of their task or reimagine the text as they work, but the individual choices they face are defined from the beginning: for each letter, the typesetter chooses among the same 50 or 300 compartments. Scribes, by contrast, produce their lines in a continuum; they do not produce the final stroke of the line under the same conditions as the first stroke of the line; even an individual letterform is begun and completed under different conditions. They can change handwriting styles and handwriting conventions at will.

Figure 2 shows a page from the familiar fourteenth-century *Gawain* manuscript. This is not a professional production. The physical evidence, or the image of that evidence, seems to contradict our modern veneration for it, whether we think of "it" as the text or the manuscript that contains that text. This presumed "masterpiece of English literature" exists in only one copy. There is no reference to it or evidence that it was ever read before the nineteenth century. The drawings, often reproduced, are amateurish; if the text

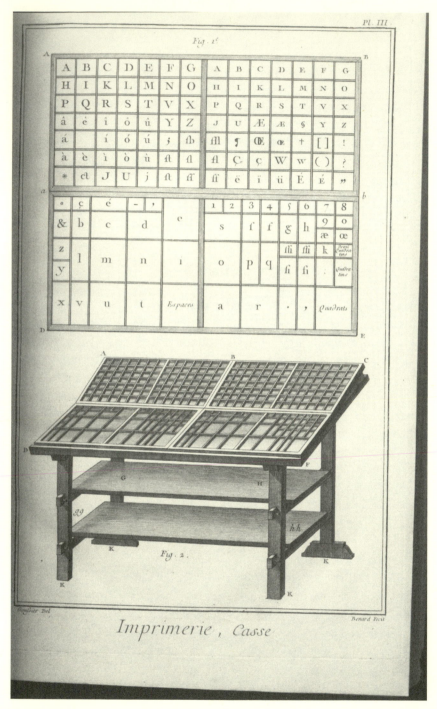

Figure 1. Typecase. From *Encyclopédie, ou dictionnaire raisonné des sciences, des arts et des métiers*; *Recueil de Planches sur les sciences, les arts libéraux, et les arts méchaniques*, vol. 7 (Paris, 1769), Pl. III. Courtesy of the University of Southern California, on behalf of USC Libraries.

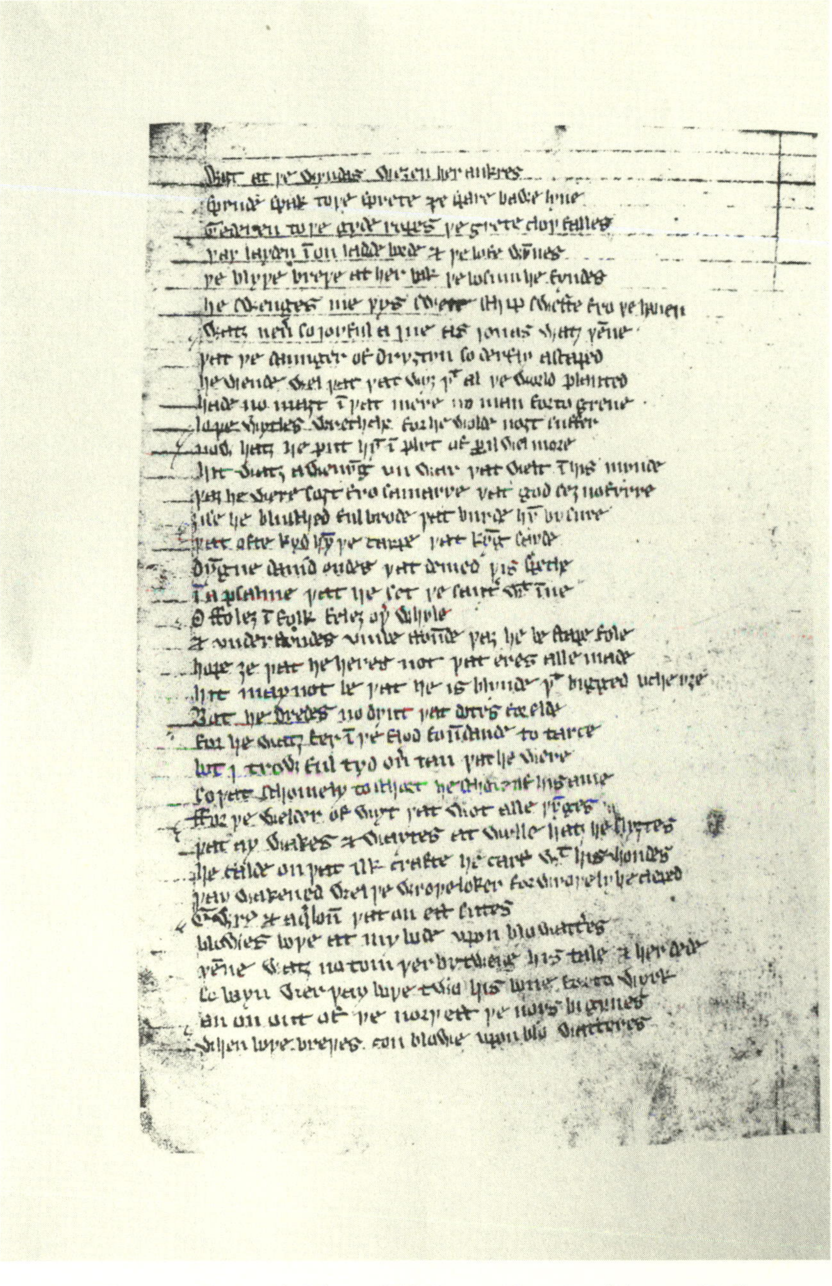

Figure 2. Gawain MS, British Library MS Cotton Nero A.x, fol. 108r. (Gollanz facsimile). Courtesy of the British Library.

were not defined in conventional English literary histories as being of such
great importance, no one would look twice at these things. Anyone who has
even glanced at the doodlings and scribblings of early books has seen better.

The page shown here is curious. In some lines, the words lie on the
formatted line; in others, the words lie between the formatted lines (see lines
1 and 3).[6] A scribe could write on the line; the same scribe could also write
between the lines. Professional scribes of course do not routinely do both,
not because there is anything wrong with doing so aesthetically, but rather
because such decisions as "where to place the letters" are not worth even the
minimal energy that would be expended on them. When I once typed student papers for a living, I quickly developed a set of unchangeable and numb-
ingly inflexible conventions. Deciding whether to hyphenate "be-cause"
before or after the c, whether to capitalize "The" in "The Bible," whether to
add a space between footnotes—there was no point in making such decisions
more than once: I created an arbitrary rule, memorized it, and followed it as
if with conviction. But the *Gawain* scribe, or poet-scribe, has no such obses-
sion with efficiency, and blurs one style into another. Now above the line,
now on the line. And now, perhaps, pausing to display (for himself?) an
example of his drawing skills.

Such a manuscript might seem to reveal what it means to write and to
compose and to copy by hand. Thus, we might theorize, when the scribe's
text is translated into a printed text, these particular and revealing characteristics disappear, or at least it seems as if they should disappear. A typesort
cannot be modified capriciously as it creates an impression on paper. Its
history is fixed with each impression on the page. It can deteriorate, but the
evidence for that will always be discrete—another unique impression on another unique page. There can be no blurring. Our typecase, with its finite
and separate compartments, is a model of discreteness. A typesort can be,
and often is, placed in the wrong type compartment. But it either is or is not
in that wrong compartment. There are, in typecases, no leaners. Surely that
will distinguish print from whatever it may be that print is not.

Yet even here, as I articulate a controlling assumption in much bibliographical thinking, the historical facts are not quite in accord with my
scheme. I examine the earliest European type, or what is now said to be the
earliest—DK type, so carefully and professionally set in its later examples
such as the (now redated) *Astronomical Calendar* or the 36-line Bible of Pfister
(B36) (see Chapter 2, Figures 10 and 11); in the 27-line Donatus from Paris,
by contrast, one of the earliest examples of this type, it "dances" on the line,

now above, now below. I reproduce a facsimile of a facsimile in Figure 3; this image, from Gottfried Zedler's *Die älteste Gutenbergtype* (1902), is likely the source of much of the early twentieth-century discussion of the most primitive state of this type.[7] The carelessness of the amateur, or the presumed amateur, emerges in these early efforts; only later is early type professionalized in the rigidity of B42, later Donatuses, or the *Astronomical Calendar* now dated 1457. And the gap between the continuous and the discrete that seemed to oppose the Scribal to Print reappears in the history of print itself. Perhaps the true gap is between the objects of my thinking (evidence) and my own too simplistic abstractions.

Whenever we examine printing in detail, we are confronted with the discreteness characteristic of the typecase and the individual copy, the differences between our speaking about them, even in the simplest instances, and what the evidence provides. One reason that writing about printing and studying printing is so interesting is that the persistent errors that are the consequence of these differences are everywhere apparent. Analytical bibliographers write about the history of particular editions by filling in the gaps. They imagine the production of an edition of 1,000 copies where only five material book-copies still exist. They chart the deterioration of type where only a finite number of type impressions exist, often made by different types-orts. And they chart the fluid history of a typecase from the discrete fragments of a Donatus text printed, one of many? but how many? in the mid-fifteenth century.[8] Even those texts must be counted: they either exist or do not exist, and the nature and logic of bibliographical identity (is this a book? or is it not?) seems not to permit the existence of leaners even though book history provides many such examples.[9]

Type Classification

One of the central problems here, addressed particularly in Part I, concerns basic classifications of type. Such classifications are borrowed from paleography, even though a scribe was not bound to one style, and as even our one example shows, could shift styles, blur styles, or invent styles at will.[10] The typographical version of the implied distinctions in paleography has a long history. Modern typographers generally recognize schemes such as the Daniel Updike's "three great classes" of type:[11] italic, roman, and gothic (on the meaning of this term, see Chapters 3 and 4 below). Among the subdivisions

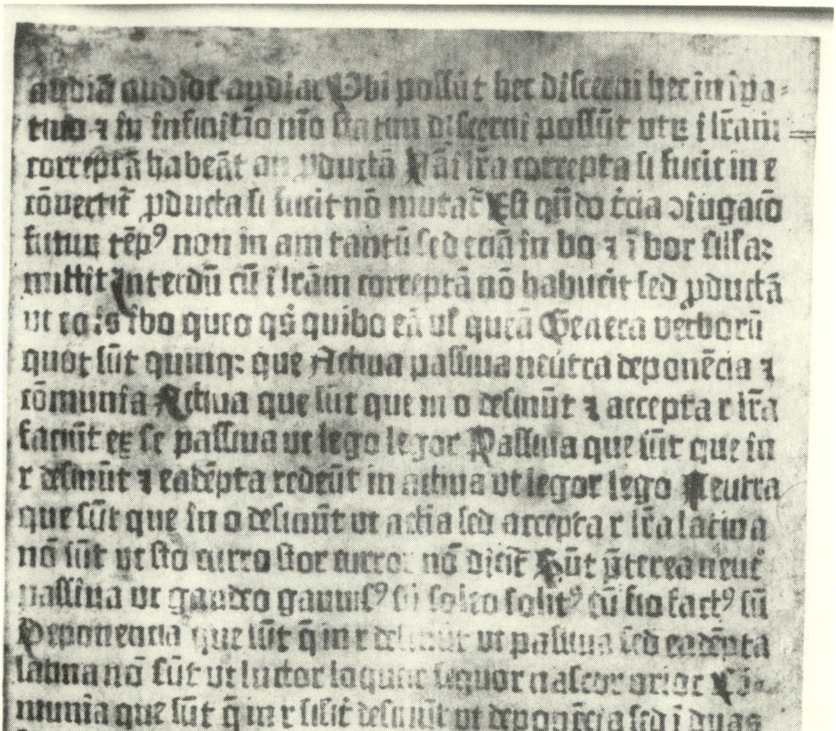

Figure 3. DK type, 27-line Donatus (Paris fragment). From Zedler, *Die älteste Gutenbergtype*, Taf. II.

of gothic are textura, rotunda, bastarda. Under bastarda are the vernacular forms peculiar to a region (Schwabacher, Fraktur); England is exceptional in not developing such a regional typeface.[12] Even the more general of modern classifications of type respond to real situations, both on the printed page and in the printing press. Conveniently selected early books will often show that the oppositions of type are functional, as are the differences between roman, italic, and blackletter in the 1602 Chaucer. These different typefaces are compartmentalized in a way that is analogous to the compartmentalization of the typecase. When used together, different typefaces mean different things. The question is whether these oppositions, these polarities, necessarily have or are meant to invoke a particular content.

Typographical categories and their conventional associations are challenged by much of the evidence they are supposed to describe. What functions as textura in most regions becomes finally in seventeenth-century England "blackletter"—the zero degree of a typeface that opposes roman.[13] The category "rotunda" combines a large rotunda used by Ratdolt (one derived from Bolognese script) with the smaller and generically unrelated "round" type called in French "lettre de somme" after its use in theological "Summae." Furthermore, in the earliest types of the fifteenth century, there is the taxonomically irritating "fere-humanistica" or "Gotico-roman"—a typeface that combines elements of gothic and roman, but not in any well-defined or quantifiable way.[14]

In addition, the abstract classifications by scholars are not the same as the classifications by contemporary readers, nor do any of these necessarily reflect what a typesetter or printer might do. A scribe can vary between two writing styles; printers, by contrast, are limited to the typefonts and sizes in their typecases. A typefont cannot be made larger by a typesetter; nor can it be used if it has insufficient typesorts for the job required. A look at sixteenth-century books from England and France will show this clearly: distinctions even between major families of type (textura versus bastarda) do not operate in the folio works of Chaucer and Gower printed in 1532–1555. Despite their obvious relation (all are double-column folios), these are printed variously in all three typefaces. The 1532 Chaucer is printed in bastarda, the 1532 Gower in rotunda. All re-editions to 1555 are printed in textura.[15]

The distinction between roman and bastarda is also challenged by productions of Rabelais; in the sixteenth century, Rabelais was printed first in bastarda, then in roman. This reflected no great change in the way Rabelais was read, but rather the more banal change in typographical conventions.

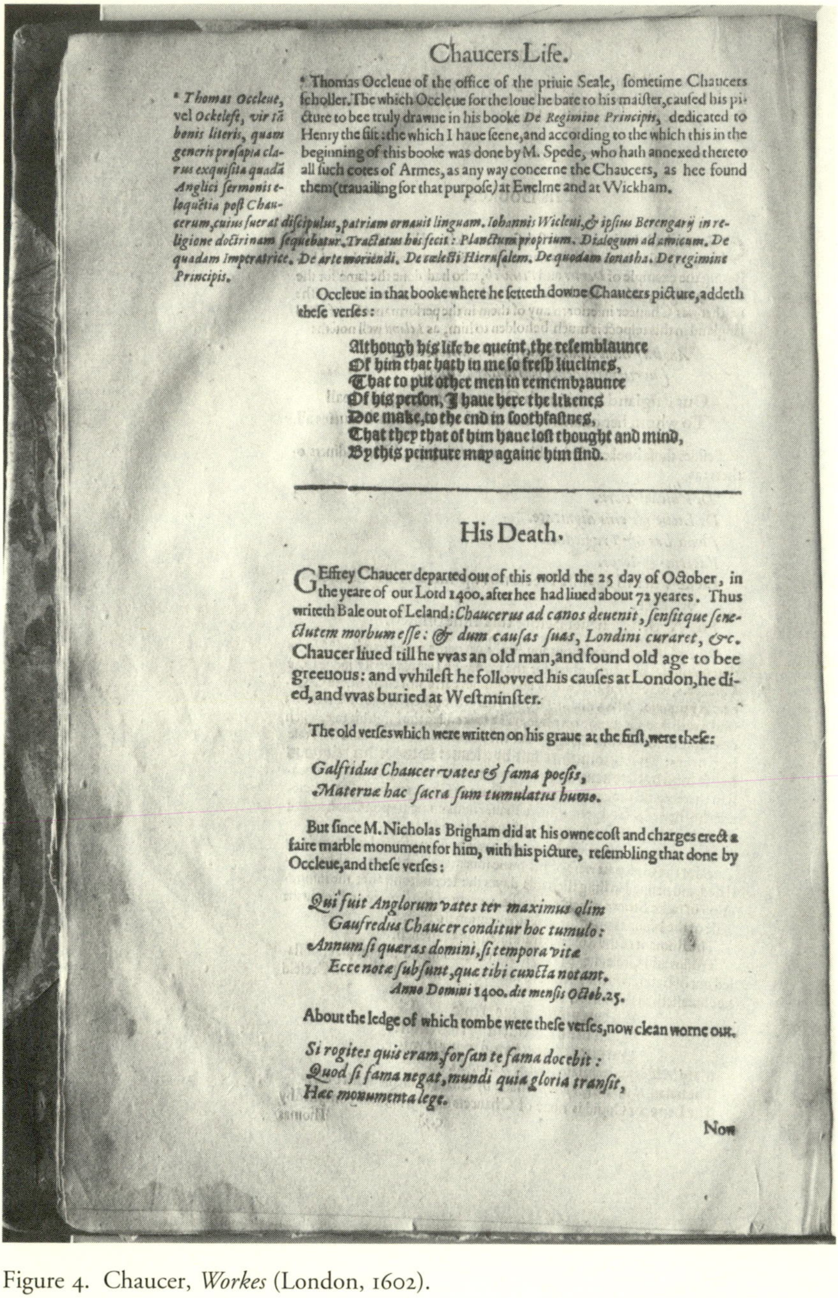

ᵃ *Thomas Occleue, vel Ockeleste, vir tā bonis literis, quam generis prosapia clarus exquisita quadā Anglici sermonis eloquētia post Chaucerum, cuius suerat discipulus, patriam ornauit linguam. Iohannis Wiclcui, & ipsius Berengarij in religione doctrinam sequebatur. Tractatus hæc fecit: Planctum proprium. Dialogum ad amicum. De quadam imperatrice. De arte moriendi. De cælesti Hierusalem. De quodam Ionatha. De regimine Principis.*

ᵃ Thomas Occleue of the office of the priuie Seale, sometime Chaucers scholler. The which Occleue for the loue he bare to his maister, caused his picture to bee truly drawne in his booke *De Regimine Principis*, dedicated to Henry the fift: the which I haue seene, and according to the which this in the beginning of this booke was done by M. Spede, who hath annexed thereto all such cotes of Armes, as any way concerne the Chaucers, as hee found them (trauailing for that purpose) at Ewelme and at Wickham.

Occleue in that booke where he setteth downe Chaucers picture, addeth these verses:

Although his life be queint, the resemblaunce
Of him that hath in me so fresh liuelines,
That to put other men in remembraunce
Of his person, I haue here the likenes
Doe make, to the end in soothfastnes,
That they that of him haue lost thought and mind,
By this printure may againe him find.

His Death.

Geffrey Chaucer departed out of this world the 25 day of October, in the yeare of our Lord 1400. after hee had liued about 72 yeares. Thus writeth Bale out of Leland: *Chaucerus ad canos deuenit, senisíque senectutem morbum esse: & dum causas suas, Londini curaret, &c.* Chaucer liued till he was an old man, and found old age to bee greeuous: and whilest he followed his causes at London, he died, and was buried at Westminster.

The old verses which were written on his graue at the first, were these:

*Galfridus Chaucer vates & fama poesis,
Maternæ hac sacra sum tumulatus humo.*

But since M. Nicholas Brigham did at his owne cost and charges erect a faire marble monument for him, with his picture, resembling that done by Occleue, and these verses:

*Qui fuit Anglorum vates ter maximus olim
    Gaufredus Chaucer conditur hoc tumulo:
Annum si quæras domini, si tempora vitæ
    Ecce notæ subsunt, quæ tibi cuncta notant.
        Anno Domini 1400. die mensis Octob. 25.*

About the ledge of which tombe were these verses, now clean worne out.

*Si rogites quis eram, forsan te fama docebit:
Quod si fama negat, mundi quia gloria transit,
Hæc monumenta lege.*

Now

Figure 4. Chaucer, *Workes* (London, 1602).

Even italic, perhaps the most meaningful and ideologically based of all west-ern typefaces,[16] does not always have a consistent meaning: the sign for a Chinese restaurant I saw recently, printed in italic characters, was purely a mannerism. And the italics now used in conjunction with most roman typef-onts mean only "this is a title" or "this is emphasized." Yet the scholarly mythology regarding these typefaces persists, particularly in the eighteenth and nineteenth centuries. Modern scholars repeat the banalities of their pre-decessors with a curious insistence, and it may well be that what I criticize as scholarly myths are indexes of legitimate traditions and actual typographical functions.

Continuity and Discreteness in Modern Bibliographical Scholarship: To Be Born in the Fifth Age of Word-Splitting Man

My analysis of the discreteness of type is doubtless an example of the kind of thinking and analysis I have in the past critiqued and will critique here as well. I have looked at printing history; I have imagined an "other," some-thing opposed to print—perhaps the Scribal. I have defined a boundary, in this case, relegating to the Scribal the implied evils of continuity. Since I will not be discussing the Scribal, and wish to say no more about it, I can hope that this will be excused. I am merely talking about early printing. Or, more precisely, I am merely seeming to talk about early printing. What I am really talking about is modern scholarship on printing, or what pretends to be modern scholarship about printing, Print, books, Books, and bibliography. I am projecting onto early printing history a phenomenon I confront in mod-ern bibliographical scholarship. I am trying to find something *there*—in fif-teenth-century type, in eighteenth-century title pages, in nineteenth-century illustrations—that may be analogous to what I find *here*. And what I find in modern scholarship is exactly what I find in the illusory opposition between print and whatever it is we decide is not print. Let's call it writing, or let's call it script. Scholarship has as its goal the discovery of continuities in the irritating singularities of the evidence: bits of evidence here, packets of evi-dence there, partial evidence here. These things do not exist "out there" in history, of course. It is scholarship that defines "what is evidence," examining the "out there" to define again, in more discrete packets, bits of evidence.

Over a century ago, what I am conventionally calling "evidence" might have been just as conventionally called "facts." And these things, or phenomena, or imagined events—these too were to be placed in a continuum by scholars. One of the most important of these nineteenth-century bibliographical statements (in the opinion of one of the most important bibliographers of the twentieth century) is Henry Bradshaw's dictum: "Arrange your facts rigorously and get them plainly before you, and let them speak for themselves, which they will always do."[17] But of course, what they speak is merely a repetition of their own unintelligible discreteness. It is only the scholar who hears a continuous statement.

It is that speech, its illusion of history, its implied continuities, that is the target of what I write in the chapters below. With a few rare exceptions, my critique is not intended as polemic, nor is it intended to reform any particular group of scholars or their fields. As long as other scholars continue to do what they do, I can continue to do what I do.

Fachleute, Specialists, Experts, and Other Persons of Interest

One of the most striking aspects of twentieth-century bibliography is the number of critical statements directed against an ill-defined group of characters known as "*Fachleute*," "Specialists," "Experts." The statements regarding them, even when deferential in form, are nearly always condescending or respectfully dismissive. Typography seems a particularly efficient trigger for such condescension. The dating of the *Astronomical Calendar* comes with its attendant astronomical *Fachleute*, whose testimony is sometimes invoked and sometimes simply dismissed. On the question of typefounding, we have reference to technicians such as Charles Enschedé, a typefounder, whose theories of typecasting and experiments were championed in the early twentieth century by Gottfried Zedler. But as we shall also see in Chapter 3, the testimony of such experts is so poorly understood that even prominent scholars are guilty of plagiarizing earlier paraphrases.[18] Paul Schwenke, the most important early twentieth-century scholar on the structure of the Gutenberg Bible, specifically characterizes himself as a *Nichtfachmann*:

> Ich verkenne nicht, dass sie einseitig ist und dass auch technische Untersuchung und Experiment ihr Recht fordern dürfen, aber ich habe mich als Nichtfachmann dieses Gebietes möglichst entschlagen, um so mehr, da vorläufig auch dort noch die Hypothese eine grosse Rolle spielt.[19]

[I do not deny that (historical-philological methods) constitute only one approach and that technical investigations also have a place here; but as a *Nichtfachmann*, I have stayed away from this area as much as possible, especially since hypotheses also play a large role there.]

This is a curious statement, since Schwenke is surely a specialist in most senses of the word; he may well be saying that only a specialist is able to separate fact and hypothesis in a given *Fach* (in this case, typefounding), a claim that leads to the somewhat paradoxical conclusion that these special fields are best avoided. Schwenke's cautionary tone here is rarely found in later rejections of such expertise. Henri-Jean Martin and Lucien Febvre characterize most of the discussion of late nineteenth-century bibliographical scholars as "puerile."[20] In the English of Elizabeth Eisenstein, bibliographical scholars are scorned as "specialists—custodians of rare books and other librarians, experts on typography or bibliography, literary scholars concerned with press variants"; none of these, according to Eisenstein, have anything of importance to contribute to the study of Print Culture.[21] If we were to take these statements seriously, we might note the exclusion of book dealers and owners here. Are they not professional enough for scorn? Do they not subscribe to such journals as *The Library*, *Gutenberg Jahrbuch*, *PBSA*? Are they not part of that odd community of bibliographers and scholars who in their notes and articles and promulgation of bibliographical minutiae make the task of the "grands narrateurs" of Book History, or "heroes of our time" as they are amusingly named by Nicholas Barker, so much more difficult?[22]

The Discreet Charm of the Discrete

In this study, I will be keeping these particularities in the foreground. I will not argue for an over-riding continuity between the problems faced by Gutenberg (is it Gutenberg?) and the problems faced by the illustrators involved in the production of Thomas Frognall Dibdin's *Bibliographical Tour*. The simple act of seeking such continuity (a fairly innocent and seemingly editorial decision) causes the kind of errors I am attempting to highlight and critique. Because we have no contemporary documents describing Gutenberg's production of type, we have no choice but to hypothesize a continuous development of typefounding through the seventeenth century, where such evidence finally begins to appear (see Chapter 1). Because we have no statements regarding the significance of the marginalia in certain early printed books, we are obliged to project the significances onto them we are accustomed to find in other books (see Chapter 5).[23]

The result of this, of course, is that book-copies begin to assume a greater role than books, and perhaps it is the entire notion that there is such a thing as a book, rather than a book-copy, that is at fault. A book-copy is a material thing, a singularity, with its own history, or rather its own discrete packets of evidence that constitute such a history. It is owned by an aristocrat; it is rebound; it is destroyed in a seventeenth-century fire; it is housed in the Huntington Library. A book, by contrast, is an abstraction: it is the illusory "being" consequent to what is a mere dream of printing—the production of identical copies of the same thing. It is the presumed realization of the printer's intention: the edition organizing as a singularity 1000 interchangeable copies. And it is an illusion forced on us by language. Ask visitors to the Huntington what they have seen in the display room and they will say, quite intelligently, that they have seen "*the* Gutenberg Bible," even though such a thing is un-see-able. They will also tell you, equally reasonably and intelligently, that they have seen "Chaucer's *Canterbury Tales*," that is, the thing itself, not a modern edition. In this case, they may be persuaded to qualify that as "*the* Ellesmere manuscript of Chaucer's *Canterbury Tales*," and in such a statement, they will accord with both their own and the Chaucerian's views on the matter. But ask them to correct their statements regarding the Gutenberg Bible (they have seen a copy, not the thing itself), and you will get nothing but quizzical stares. The myth of print culture, and the identities of its objects—these things are now as entrenched in popular culture as they are embedded in scholarly culture.

In my chapters below, I will attempt as much as possible to keep in view these discrete objects and events—the things we know as book-copies and the particular events of their various histories. And if my chapters succeed only in producing the same quizzical stares I have seen in Huntington visitors, that is good enough for me.

PART I

❧ ❧ ❧

Out of Sorts

❧

CHAPTER ONE

On the Continuity of Continuity:
Print Culture Mythology
and the Type of the Gutenberg Bible (B42)

Proponents of Print Culture have now for decades debated the nuances of this notion: its relation to Oral Culture, learning, individuality, technology, and the obligatory Rise of Humanism. Print culture is a given, and all that is left for scholars to do is mop up: when did print culture emerge? what is its technological essence? In 2003, I argued the reverse—not of one of these positions, but of all of them: the entire notion of print culture is constructed in bad faith, and acts not to reveal or uncover evidence but to create specious supporting evidence.[1]

My subject in this chapter is early type, how little we know about it, and how our ignorance challenges larger cultural narratives generated by modern studies in the History of the Book. Early typography was subjected to minute and detailed study by German, Dutch, and English scholars in the late nineteenth and early twentieth centuries (I discuss this further in Chapter 2 below). These scholars were what we now call "analytical bibliographers"— they looked at material books for evidence of early printing practices. The identification of a particular typefont could identify a particular printer; the nature of the impressions left by these typefaces could reveal the techniques used to manufacture them.[2] Yet in 1958 Henri-Jean Martin and Lucien Febvre, in one swat of Annales rhetoric, ruled all this once "unimpeachable"[3] evidence out of court: "We get no nearer to a solution [concerning early printing techniques] by looking at the books since no evidence of actual techniques used can be found by examining them."[4] This is an extraordinary statement, and even reading it today, I cannot help but look for a redeeming trace of irony that I realize is not there. Twenty years later, in her now seminal work on print culture, Elizabeth Eisenstein was equally cavalier, denying in her preface that any scholarship existed at all "on the subject"—the subject being her particular theory of print culture ("there was not even a small literature available for consultation").[5] Another extraordinary statement, and here I am not even tempted to look for irony.

The kindest thing one could say about either claim is that such an assertion was a devious way of defining as irrelevant mountains of material evidence readily available "for consultation" (the 10,000–15,000 incunables in the Bibliothèque Nationale and the British Library) and the equally imposing mountains of scholarly material that in fact had been written about such things, much of it inconveniently in German, and some of it even less conveniently in Dutch.[6] What do such statements imply about their own evidentiary basis?

The Myth of Continuity and the Early Fifteenth-Century Printing Press

A children's pop-up book from 1995 shows Gutenberg in his printing shop along with his familiar accouterments: the press, typecase, and so on.[7] (My Figure 5 I hope captures the spirit of this book, whose publishers will not allow it to be reproduced.) Nearly all these details come from descriptions of a seventeenth- or eighteenth-century printing house and the way things were done more than 200 years later. It is easy to deride the pop-up book, as some bibliographically inclined reviewers have done. But the assumptions embodied in this book have a strong pedigree in scholarship. I quote from some of the top experts and writers in this field:

Stephen Füssell (1999): "The technical essentials of Gutenberg remained unchanged for 350 years."

Maurice Audin (1972): "[from the fifteenth to the nineteenth century] l'atelier typographique n'a pas beaucoup varié."

Henri-Jean Martin (1987): "If Gutenberg had walked into the print shop of David Sechart of Angoulême as described in Balzac's *Illusions perdus* of 1820, he would have been at home in a few hours."

A variation appears even in R. B. McKerrow's classic *Introduction to*

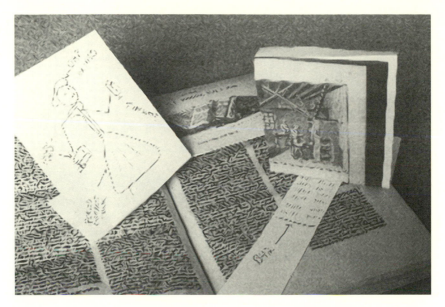

Figure 5. Gutenberg and his press.

Bibliography for Literary Students (1927): "After a comparatively short period of experiment, methods were evolved which remained extraordinarily constant for centuries so that we can say that in all essentials of book production there was little difference between the methods of 1500 and those of 1800."[8]

Yet there is very little evidence regarding the nature of fifteenth-century printing beyond the products themselves—those thousands of fifteenth-century books from whose examination Febvre and Martin claimed "nothing can be found." When those books present evidence that we can see, that evidence often shows the reverse of what these bibliographical scholars claim: not that early printers followed classical methods described in, say, Joseph Moxon's *Mechanick Exercises on the Whole Art of Printing* (1683) or in eighteenth-century encyclopedias, but rather that they did something else.

Here I will be considering typefounding. Although this is portrayed as a zealously guarded secret in early references, many modern scholars see it as the very essence of printing with movable type. The first visual description of typecasting is in 1568, in an often reprinted woodcut by Jost Ammon (*Book of Trades*; see Figure 8 below). The first detailed verbal account is by Joseph Moxon in 1683.[9] The woodcut was published more than a hundred years after the invention of printing; Moxon's manual was written more than a hundred years after that. Yet scholars seem to have reached a consensus: these and other later descriptions provide all the evidence we need. We don't have to look at early books for evidence of early typography; everything we need to know set out in great detail in the systematic and heavily illustrated manual by Pierre-Simon Fournier, *Manuel typographique* (1764) (a hundred years later than Moxon's account) or in the contemporary *Encyclopédie, ou dictionnaire raisonné des sciences, des arts et des métiers* (the source of my Figure 9 below). Martin, in 1987, goes even farther, and for details on fifteenth-century type, refers his readers to Philip Gaskell's 1972 *New Introduction to Bibliography*, whose descriptions are based entirely on eighteenth-century printing practices.[10] Google Image searches will pull up dozens of pictures of "Gutenberg's press" and "Gutenberg tools," most of them from Fournier or related eighteenth-century prints. These histories could be defended as teleological myths—they are simply imagined constructions of history with their goal the fully developed press of the eighteenth century. But they seem, rather, something less (or more): the fifteenth century does not lead to the eighteenth century through some Rise and Progress narrative; it simply *is* the eighteenth century.

The Gutenberg Bible (B42)

I begin with the typography of what is likely the most familiar early printed book: the Gutenberg Bible (known as B42). A series of studies by early twentieth-century scholars, chief among them Paul Schwenke, showed that this was produced some time between 1450 and 1455. The type used for B42 is contemporary with a second, somewhat larger type known as DK type. This was used to print a series of Donatus grammars, the variously dated *Astronomical Calendar*, and eventually the 36-line Bible (B36). I will be discussing problems associated with this second type in Chapter 2 below.[11]

Both typefonts are classified as texturas (squarish, gothic type, also known as Missal type or, in English, blackletter). They are, moreover, designed and typeset according to a characteristic set of conventions known as the "Gutenberg system." Figure 6 is a page from B42; Figure 7 shows a cropped image of line a7.[12] Note two things: the fence-post construction, shown more clearly in Figure 7, and the proliferation of typesorts: for each letter, different surroundings require different letterforms. Both features—the large number of ligatures and what is often characterized as the symmetry

of composition—are products of contemporary paleographical styles. Gottfried Zedler and others argued convincingly that some of the letterforms (*w*,
and upper-case *K*) show that the typefont is modeled more specifically on the
writing used for Missals.[13] In addition to ligatures, there are a series of alternate letterforms, constructed in imitation of (or perhaps more accurately "in
an allusion to") fifteenth-century scribal practice. Figure 6 shows two alternate forms of *r* in line 13a (in manuscript, the "round-*r*" is used in a number
of positions, following *p* or *b* or *o*; B42 uses it less frequently). Complicating
this are what German scholars called variously "Nebenformen" or "Anschluß-
formen"; the English term is "abutting forms." Certain letters in B42 or DK
type have "right extension," that is, the horizontal bars in these letters extend
to the right (*c*, *t*, *e*, *g*); see Figure 6, line 3 *propiciatorium*. In order to maintain
symmetrical or fence-post construction, every letter that follows these must
be modified; the slight spur on the upper left of the single vertical stroke (the
minim) must be shaved or the entire letter modified (see for example the *i*
following *p* in line 3). Under the conventions of modern printing, this would
entail more than doubling the size of the typecase and the number of letterforms, since an entire set of letters must be available with the features required by these abutting forms. This is particularly visible in the case of *i*.
Note the three different forms in the single word *sanctificationibus* (line 13b);
note further that the abutting form following *f* is not the same as the abutting
form following *t*. All these characteristics can also be found in the contemporary DK type (see Figures 3, 10, and 11).[14]

Schwenke claimed there were 290 different letterforms in the B42 typecase.[15] That figure is repeated by many scholars, even those who dismiss
Schwenke's work or who have never heard of him, as if its meaning were self-
evident. A number is a respectable, quantifiable thing, and there are plenty of
specialists or *Fachleute* who will compute these things for us. Yet the number is
based on the assumption of classical typecasting; it is tempting to say the true
figure may be higher; but the word *true* may have no meaning in this situation, depending as it does on a series of dubious assumptions.

The Gutenberg system of typesetting and the fence-post construction of
letters have some bearing on the techniques of early typecasting. To the modern scholar, accustomed to keyboards and imagined typecases where the combined number of characters, upper and lower case, is barely 100, the notion
of a 290-character typefont and this intricate system of abutting forms seems
extraordinary: not only did Gutenberg have to solve basic problems of typecasting, he was under even greater constraints to produce the so-called perfect

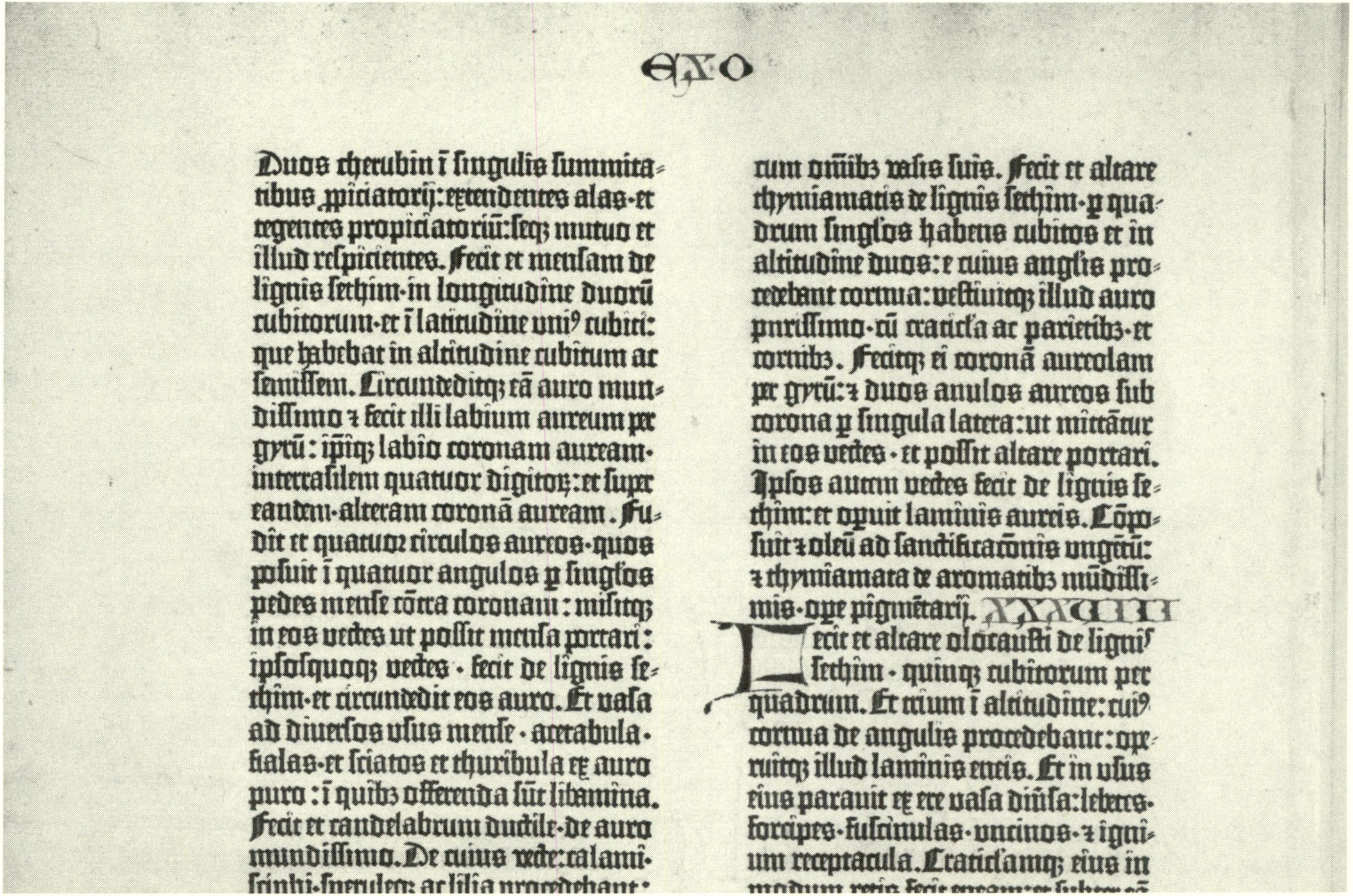

EXO

Duos cherubin ĩ singulis summita-
tibus ꝓpiciatorij: extendentes alas · et
tegentes propiciatoriũ: seq; mutuo et
illud respicientes. Fecit et mensam de
lignis sethim · in longitudine duorũ
cubitorum · et ĩ latitudine uni⁹ cubiti:
que habebat in altitudine cubitum ac
semissem. Circundeditq; eã auro mundissimo ⁊ fecit illi labium aureum per
gyrũ: ipsiq; labio coronam auream ·
interrasilem quatuor digitoꝝ: et super
eandem · alteram coronã auream. Fu-
dit et quatuor circulos aureos · quos
posuit ĩ quatuor angulos ꝑ singlos
pedes mense cõtra coronam: misitq;
in eos vectes ut possit mensa portari:
ipsosquoq; vectes · fecit de lignis sethim · et circundedit eos auro. Et vasa
ad diversos usus mense · acetabula ·
fialas · et sciatos et thuribula ex auro
puro: ĩ quibz offerenda sũt libamina.
Fecit et candelabrum ductile · de auro
mundissimo. De cuius vecte: calami ·
sciphi · spericlæq; ac lilia procedebant:

cum omnibz vasis suis. Fecit et altare
thymiamatis de lignis sethim · ꝑ quadrum singlos habens cubitos et in
altitudine duos: e cuius anglis procedebant cornua: vestivitq; illud auro
purissimo · cũ craticla ac parietibz · et
cornibz. Fecitq; ei coronã aureolam
per gyrũ: ⁊ duos anulos aureos sub
corona ꝑ singula latera: ut mittãtur
in eos vectes · et possit altare portari.
Ipsos autem vectes fecit de lignis sethim: et operuit laminis aureis. Cõpo-
suit ⁊ oleũ ad sanctificatõnis ungeñ:
⁊ thymiamata de aromatibz mũdissi-
mis · ope pigmẽtarij. XXXVIII
Fecit et altare olocausti de lignis
sethim · quinq; cubitorum per
quadrum. Et trium ĩ altitudine: cui⁹
cornua de angulis procedebant: ope-
ruitq; illud laminis ereis. Et in usus
eius paravit ex ere vasa diũsa: lebetes ·
forcipes · fuscinulas · uncinos · ⁊ igni-
um receptacula. Craticlamq; eius in
modum retis fecit ereeam ...

Figure 6. Gutenberg Bible. *From A Noble Fragment: Being a Leaf of the Gutenberg Bible* (New York: Wells, 1921). Courtesy of the William Andrews Clark Memorial Library, University of California, Los Angeles.

Figure 7. Line 7a cropped.

symmetry of the Gutenberg system of type. Gutenberg enthusiasts have been quick to point this out. But Gutenberg scholars should be more skeptical: the fence-post construction of type, whereby all minims are equidistant from each other, may not have made type manufacture more complex, since such a system might not have required the tools ordinarily used by later type-founders.

For an alphabet where every letter is unique, the most obvious method of typecasting involves an adjustable hand-mold, such as was used in the seventeenth and eighteenth centuries (see Figure 9 below). Early printers casting type to be set according to the Gutenberg system could get by with non-adjustable molds (if, that is, we concede that things comparable to mod-ern hand-molds were used at all): since typesorts had either one (*i*, *r*), two (*n*, *o*), or three (*m*) minims, and these were equally spaced, three fixed molds would do for ordinary letters, another fixed set for abutting forms. The fact that, say, *o* and *n* are almost indistinguishable does not make the problem of typecasting more difficult, it makes it easier. Why make things more compli-cated than they were already by inventing something close to what is pictured in the 1763 image from the *Encyclopédie* (Figure 9) or Fournier's 1764 *Manuel typographique*?

The 40-Line and 41-Line Settings of B42

As early as 1845, S. Leigh Sotheby noted that the Gutenberg Bible existed in variant states. Most copies show 42-line pages throughout, that is, 42 lines per page.[16] In a few copies, the first nine pages are in 40-line settings (leaves 1–5r), as are leaves 129–32 of volume 1. Page 10 in these copies (the last page of the first quire) has 41 lines. All other pages, even when they exist in multi-ple settings, show 42 lines per page. Schwenke, by examining the paper used in these sections and comparing multiple copies, found that the variant sec-tions in 40- or 41-line settings (leaves 1–5r and 129–32 of volume 1 of some copies) were set more or less simultaneously at the beginning of the printing project. At some later point (after these quires had been printed), the pro-jected edition expanded. Those earlier quires, including all pages set in 40 lines and the single page set in 41 lines, had to be reprinted, and they were all reprinted in the 42-line per page format.[17]

This analysis is consistent with what is now seen as a familiar case of an expanded edition, where extant copies show two variants of early quires and invariant later quires.[18] A printing project is begun with an imagined print run of, say, 500; after printing the first few quires, the printer decides the print run could be, say, 700. After all later quires are printed in 700 copies each, the printer must return to the early quires and reset and reprint 200 copies of each; all early quires will exist in two settings. The problem complicating the case of the Gutenberg Bible is that the early 40- and 41-line settings do not take up one line (or two lines) less vertical space than the 42-line settings: the vertical height of the various text blocks is roughly the same. In other words, the type used for these settings is not quite the same as that used in the 42-line settings. More precisely: what does the phrase *the same* mean in this context?[19]

In 1900, Schwenke claimed that this was the same type: the printer, having printed eight pages in 40-line settings, filed down each typesort individually, such that a newly set page of roughly the same size would contain 41 lines; he later (almost immediately) filed these sorts down again, such that a page set in this type would contain 42 lines.[20] This process would obviously have entailed enormous difficulties. By 1923, Schwenke had gone over all objections and alternative explanations; although he modified many of his earlier positions, he still maintained a version of the theory of the filing-down of type.[21] B42 type evolved during the process of printing, and certain identifiable letterforms make their appearance only later in the typesetting process; this is seen also in DK type and is characteristic of much early printing. But to change the measurement of an entire typecase is a more serious matter. Classical typefounding leaves no choice: you either file down one set of type, or you recast the whole typefont.[22]

How did printers do this? The short answer is, I don't know. Most modern scholars tell me that early printers cast movable type in a hand-mold, just as they did in the nineteenth century. So I will look there for answers.

The Adjustable Hand-Mold

In 1879, an English printer, Theodore De Vinne, entered the then standard discussions of the origin of printing and definitions of the "essence of the discovery." Presses, paper, ink, punches—all these things had existed prior to their use in printing. According to De Vinne, the essence of Gutenberg's discovery, and thus in modern terms the key to the development of print culture, was the adjustable hand-mold, a device for rapidly casting lettersorts required for printing books with movable type in the roman alphabet.[23] Gutenberg's alphabet requires typesorts of different width: *m* has three fence posts or minims; *n* and *a* have two; *i* has one. Furthermore, the minims of letters that require following abutting forms are not centered on the type-body. An adjustable mold or set of molds would be necessary. De Vinne does not go into the problem in detail, but he clearly thought that the key figure was not the typecutter (typecutters themselves had become the Great Heroes of printing in some histories—Griffo for Aldine italics, and later designers such as Garamond), but rather the translation of their designs and punches into usable pieces of type.[24]

De Vinne's statement became within decades the canonical view of the matter, although some early twentieth-century scholars of Gutenberg, most notably Gottfried Zedler, denied it, or argued for more complex histories.[25] In the technology of the hand-mold, presumably, is that "fascinating" nexus of technology and intellectual history described by Stephan Füssell quoted above. Through the hand-mold, technological continuity between the modern period and the fifteenth century is now established, and just happens to support all our ideological presuppositions about early modern education and the rise of humanism. All the late twentieth-century studies cited in my text above mention the adjustable hand-mold—something carefully depicted in the children's pop-up book as well—and all cite the Jost Ammon woodcut of 1568.[26] Albert Kapr goes so far as to criticize the 1568 woodcut as inaccurate, not because it does not conform to evidence of fifteenth-century printing practices, but because it does not conform to the discussion in Moxon (1683) and the eighteenth-century Encyclopedists.[27]

Paul Needham

In 2000, a wrench (a well-used one) was thrown into the works. Paul Needham had studied the typography of B42 and early printing for decades, and was outspoken in his allegiance to the methods of analytical bibliography developed by Schwenke and Karl Dziatzko in Germany and Henry Bradshaw in England. In 1982, he proposed a theory of the printing of the *Catholicon* (a book that may have been a late product of Gutenberg's press), first redating the three apparent issues of the book on the basis of paper evidence, and, in a series of remarkably funny and savagely polemical articles, on readings of its colophon. His proposal for the type was a radical one, more radical in

le accessories of his art about him. We see
melting the metal, the bellows, the tongs and
harcoal. That the man is founding types is
nly from the bowl of cast types on the floor
, but
with
Here
e dif-
type-
tands
; the
Am-
lown.
1683,
oulds
forty
vided
ring,
atrix
; the
n has
wire
in a
box,

Type-Casting as Practised in 1564.
[From Jost Amman.]

e used as a protection to the hand. How the
ed in the box, how the matrix was attached
ow the cast types were dislodged from the

Figure 8. Jost Ammon, *Book of Trades* (1568). Reprinted in Theodore De Vinne, *The Invention of Printing* (1876; 2nd ed. New York, 1878), 62. Courtesy of the University of Southern California, on behalf of USC Libraries.

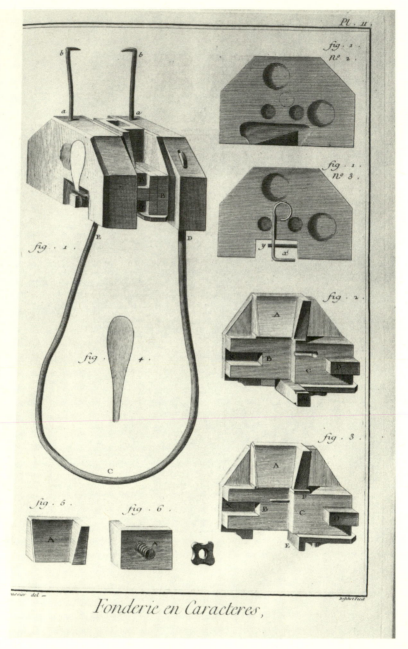

Pl. II.

Fonderie en Caracteres,

Figure 9. Hand-mold. From *Encyclopédie, Recueil de Planches*, vol. 2, pt. 1 (Paris, 1763), Pl. 2. Courtesy of the University of Southern California, on behalf of USC Libraries.

1982 than it might have seemed a century earlier. By examining multiple copies of the *Catholicon* (in defiance of the Febvre-Martin claim that nothing could be learned from them), he found that variants between copies always moved in two-line units. His tentative proposal: the text was constructed from basic typesetting units of two-line slugs (much like the slugs used in modern linotype); these slugs were preserved, and a new impression taken from them a decade after the first edition.[28]

In his work of 2000, a no less polemical Needham enlisted the services of a computer technician to examine B42 and DK type.[29] What they noticed was that those letterforms, canonically numbering 290 for B42, were really many more. Some of their findings are easily seen without the computer model (see Figures 3 and 6), and can be seen in both B42 and DK type: the variants of the letter *i* are cast as one sort, but there is no stable relation between the forms of the shank and the forms of the dot. The dots show one set of variants, the shanks show another, and the two sets of variants do not correspond.

I do not want to paraphrase what Needham claims, since those who risk that do so at their peril. But most tentatively: these letters are not cast according to traditional procedures of typefounding, just as the *Catholicon* was not set according to traditional procedures of typesetting. Thus, what print historians have for over a century described as the "essence" of the invention, the adjustable hand-mold, disappears from early printing history. And with that, more than two hundred years of continuity (from 1683 to 1450) disappear as well. We are back to square 1, or maybe square 2. We know all about texts; we know a lot about paper; we know something about ink; we know very little about type, or at least, what passed as type for the earliest printers.

If such findings were confined to B42 or if, say, one of the radical and conflicting histories of Gottfried Zedler regarding the production of early Dutch type were accepted, we could view these results as indicating the inevitable halting preliminaries to the development of the modern process of typefounding. If the hand-mold was not in use for the earliest type, perhaps its invention can be related to specific developments in later type (for example, the smaller type used by Gutenberg in the Indulgences of 1454–1455). But the oddities or what I call the recalcitrances of B42 type are not unique. When we examine other early type and typesetting methods, we find similarities, or (as a theory of continuity would require that they be called) anomalies.

In books printed by Johannes Koelhoff of Cologne, the same variance of type height as found in B42 is also seen. What the British Museum Catalogue calls 88G (a gothic type measuring 88mm per twenty lines) becomes, midway through a book, 92G; that is, the same number of lines of type occupies greater space, 92 mm instead of 88 mm.[30] This could be described or explained by leading, that is, the insertion of metal or even paper strips between typeset lines. But that explanation was also proposed for the 40- and 41-line pages of the Gutenberg Bible, and specifically and convincingly rejected by Schwenke. Why would it be accepted for Koelhoff's books? If variation in type measurement in early printed books were due to strips of leading, why is there not even more apparent variety in fifteenth-century type than there is? Through a manipulation of leading, printers could produce a text block of any size they wished.

What is striking about type height in fifteenth-century type is not its variance but rather its singularity and stability. So consistent is type height that a 20-line measurement has become a central component in the identification of early types—it is one of only two features of early type now listed in standard bibliographical catalogues: "140G" in an incunable catalogue refers to the "gothic type measuring 140mm for 20 lines," that is, the type used in B42. If printers routinely used leading, this feature of type identification would be nearly useless.[31]

Examples of similar anomalies appear wherever one looks hard enough for them. It is a matter of bibliographical doctrine that fifteenth-century printers set books by the page, rather than by the forme. They did not follow the standard method described in all seventeenth- and eighteenth-century printing manuals; these manuals describe the printing process as based on the unit of a full sheet of paper—two pages for folio books, four for quartos, eight for octavos. The earliest Cologne printer, Ulrich Zell, is even more eccentric by modern bibliographical standards, printing by the page, from half-sheets, including blank leaves, and combining as one edition what appear to the bibliographer as two separate editions.[32] Even Italian printers produce books in curious ways: there is no accounting for the practices used in the 1475 Terence (Venice, attributed to Adam of Amergau), a book whose quires exist in two and sometimes three separate settings, and whose individual copies seem put together with no regard to these often incompatible settings of text.[33]

Conclusion

I have been obliquely dealing with the myth of continuity throughout this chapter. Ordinarily, the notion of continuity operates somewhat differently.

Fernand Braudel's variant, "la longue durée," is a means of organizing seemingly disparate historical details into larger, more stable patterns. Continuities, consistencies, *mentalités*—these remain even though details change, and it is the obligation of the scholar to find out what those larger stabilities are.[34]

Note that in the case I have been describing here, the myth of continuity operates in a manner completely opposed to this. Instead of organizing details, it creates evidence and detail that is not there. We have not discovered a *mentalité* linking, say, a fifteenth- and a seventeenth-century print shop; we have, rather, transferred material and textual evidence from the seventeenth century and even the eighteenth century to the fifteenth century. The hand-mold is only one example. Perhaps that is why Febvre and Martin can say the books provide no evidence, or why others dismiss the turn-of-the-century scholarship that detailed such, evidence.

German scholars with their often disparaging remarks about "Specialists" (Kapr, 12) and *"Fachleute"* (Ruppel, 11) have somewhat surprisingly joined this chorus. Füssell justifies the study of early printing as revealing the "fascinating" nexus between technology and such grander cultural things as education and humanism (7). But this implies first, that we know something about the rise of humanism (whatever that is); second, that we know something about the techniques of early book production (which we might not); and third, that we can coordinate our sometimes grand abstractions with the pedestrian material from early printing history.[35] Somewhere in all this there ought to be a place for those tens of thousands of material books; and the more we study them, the more inconvenient and recalcitrant they reveal themselves to be.

CHAPTER TWO

Gottfried Zedler and the Twentieth-
Century History of DK Type

Zedler claims that he can arrange the existing Donatus fragments in
chronological order on the basis of the occurrence or absence of
secondary letter forms which he painstakingly investigated and
noted in his monographs. But his views in this respect can no longer
be considered as authoritative, since Dr. Wehmer's discoveries have
knocked the keystone out of his whole chronological system.[1]

DK type is the second of three types associated with early Mainz printing
and Gutenberg. It is a large textura measuring 164mm/20 lines, slightly larger
than B42 type. It is designed and set according to the same conventions as
B42 type, with fence-post construction and multiple abutting forms, and its
history is parallel to or linked to the history of B42 type. The conventional
name DK refers to the early texts found printed in this type: Donatus grammars and so-called "Kalender" and ephemera, often known as "kleine
Drucke"; these include the *Astronomical Calendar* (= *AK*),[2] *Türkenkalender*,
and the mnemonic calendar *Cisianus*. It also appears in a single line in one
of the two indulgences from 1454/1455 (the other uses B42 type for the same
passage). All these texts are roughly contemporary with the Gutenberg Bible.
The last appearances of this type are in the 36-line Bible (once thought to be
earlier than B42), and in later books from the 1460s printed in Bamberg by
Pfister. Altogether, there are some 150 examples of this type, most of them
fragments.[3]

Constructing a basic history of this type is difficult. Most fragments are printed on vellum, which precludes the possibility of using paper evidence either for determination of an edition or for external dating of a fragment (two of the Kalender are on paper, but neither has been securely dated on that basis). Only a few have evidence of dating: Pope Calixtus's *Bulla Turcorum* is issued in 1456, which permits dating both the German *Türkenbulle* (*TB*) and the Latin version; the 31-line Indulgence has a printed date of 1455; and a printed date of 1454 appears in the text of the *Türkenkalender*. These fragments are not easily accessible, particularly in the United States. And much of the standard scholarship is based on early twentieth-century reproductions, many of which are, by modern standards, mediocre (for an example, see Figure 3).[4] Even what constitutes an edition is not clear. The *Gesamtkatalog der Wiegendrucke* (GW) classifies Donatus fragments formally, according to the inferred number of lines printed per page, but there is no certainty that such formal differences represent historical editions or printing projects.[5] The more recent Incunabula Short-Title Catalogue (ISTC) accepts the distinctions of GW.

The history of DK type in the twentieth century would finally turn on one document—the so-called *Astronomical Calendar*, a broadsheet discovered in 1902 by Gottfried Zedler. The astronomical references in this broadsheet were for planetary positions of the year 1448, and on this basis Zedler dated the printing to 1447. Zedler's date provided, at least for a few decades, what seemed to be secure external evidence of date (the earliest recorded date for examples of this type) and thus a place to stand for dating the other examples of DK type. Most histories of DK type and of Gutenberg written in the first half of the twentieth century were based on this date. In 1948, the dating of this document was disputed by Carl Wehmer, and, as we shall see later, the presumed secure foundation for dating the earliest examples of DK type disappeared.[6] The *Astronomical Calendar* became the "Planetary Table," and was redated to the mid 1450s. Yet what should have led to a discrediting of one type of evidence (the dating of texts by external means) led to a discrediting of an opposed type of evidence (the analysis of the internal evidence provided by the type impressions). Among the results are the despairing and disparaging comments on material bibliographical evidence already cited in Chapter 1 (the dismissal of the examination of physical books by Febvre and Martin) and a growing skepticism of both kinds of evidence as seen in the quotation by Otto Fuhrmann at the head of this chapter.

Analytical Bibliography: Methods and Assumptions

But we must not forget that the question of the invention of printing (palaeotypography) and bibliography in general has hitherto very
seldom been a field on which we could hope to encounter brilliant
talents. (J. H. Hessels, *Haarlem Legend*)[7]

Die ältere Literatur vor Hessels enthält so viel Phantastisches und so
wenig tatsächliche Angaben und Beobachtungen, dass nur ausnahm-
sweise Veranlassung war sie anzuführen. (Schwenke, *DK Type*, 6)

[Scholarship before Hessels contains so much of the fantastic and so
little factual material and observations that only exceptionally is it
cited.]

The key word in Hessels's 1871 characterization of bibliography is "hitherto." Hessels is acknowledging what was felt to be a radical change in the
nature of bibliography and in particular the study of incunabula. This new
kind of bibliography was associated with work of William Blades and Henry
Bradshaw in England, J. W. Holtrop and M. F. A. G. Campbell in the
Netherlands, and in Germany Karl Dziatzko and following him Paul Schwenke. These scholars defined and promoted a new kind of evidence, based
on typographical and structural features of the books themselves, which I
refer to here as internal evidence. These books (copies, say, of B42) had not
been easily accessible and were not easily accessible even in 1880; without
them, it was difficult to coordinate "histories of printing" with "descriptions
of products of early printing"; Dziatzko, in 1880, was one of the first serious
scholars to be in a position to compare physically copies of B42 (Gutenberg
Bible) and B36 (the Bible printed in DK type), and thus was the first to be
in a position to answer even the apparently simple question of priority: B36
was set up from B42.[8]

The most important internal evidence was (or seemed at the time to be)
typography; to Bradshaw, the history of early printing was analogous to the
work of contemporary naturalists; books could be classified and arranged on
the basis of their type.[9] The 1902–1903 issues of VGG, containing Zedler's
Das älteste Gutenbergtype and Schwenke's *Die Donat- und Kalender Type*, were
concerned almost exclusively with typography and became the basis of all
twentieth-century scholarship on DK type. These two monographs provided

descriptions and photographic reproductions of the key monuments in this history organized in the chronology implied by variant typeforms seen in these examples.

Compare two examples of DK type, or rather, as an example of what most Gutenberg scholars saw, reproductions of Zedler's own reproductions: the Paris fragment of the 27-line Donatus (D27Paris) (above, Figure 3) and the variously dated *Astronomical Calendar* (Figures 10 and 11; Burger's 1904 color reproduction is shown here in black and white). Even in these facsimiles of facsimiles, the features that impressed themselves on early bibliographers are readily apparent: in the Paris Donatus, the type "dances" on the line (this is particularly apparent in line 2); in the *Astronomical Calendar*, as in the 36-line Bible, the lines are straight (they are also straight in the Gutenberg Bible). Other features seem obvious, but less quantifiable: the "sharpness" of the ligature *de* in *AK* ("Februarius," line 1) vs. what is seen in lines 14 and 15 of the Donatus. These features are matters of "Druck" (presswork). Also distinguishable are matters of "Satz" (composition): the use of round *r* (instead of standard *r*) (*AK*, "vor" in line 1) follows scribal practice and would be described by Zedler and Schwenke as "correct" (round *r* is generally used after letters with right-hand bowls such as *o*, *b*, and *p*); cf. the regular *r* misused in line 1 of the Donatus, and many other opportunities to use it in the first ten lines. Zedler and Schwenke cited (not always systematically) many other features distinguishing the two apparent states of this type, some involving the use and even existence of particular typesorts, others involving general features of printing. Among these were typesorts for abbreviations, "eckige *a*," "bad or left-leaning initial *s*," punctuation, right justification, proper use of abutting forms (see further, Appendix 1 below).

On the basis of these features, Schwenke defined what are still considered the three groups or "Stuff" or "Zustände" of the type represented by the following texts and fragments: (1) the Paris fragment of the 27-line Donatus (D27Paris); (2) various calendars and the Donatus fragments from Oxford and Bodley; (3) B36 and "Pfister-drucke." Theoretically, any example of DK type could be placed within this imagined continuum based on the typesorts or letterforms and the use of the particular typesetting conventions implied by these typesorts.[10]

There are several methodological problems in dating fragments by internal means. Typesetting conventions implied by the type are only expressed through the typesetting conventions of particular compositors, and these could develop in opposite ways. *Satz* (the setting conventions implied by the

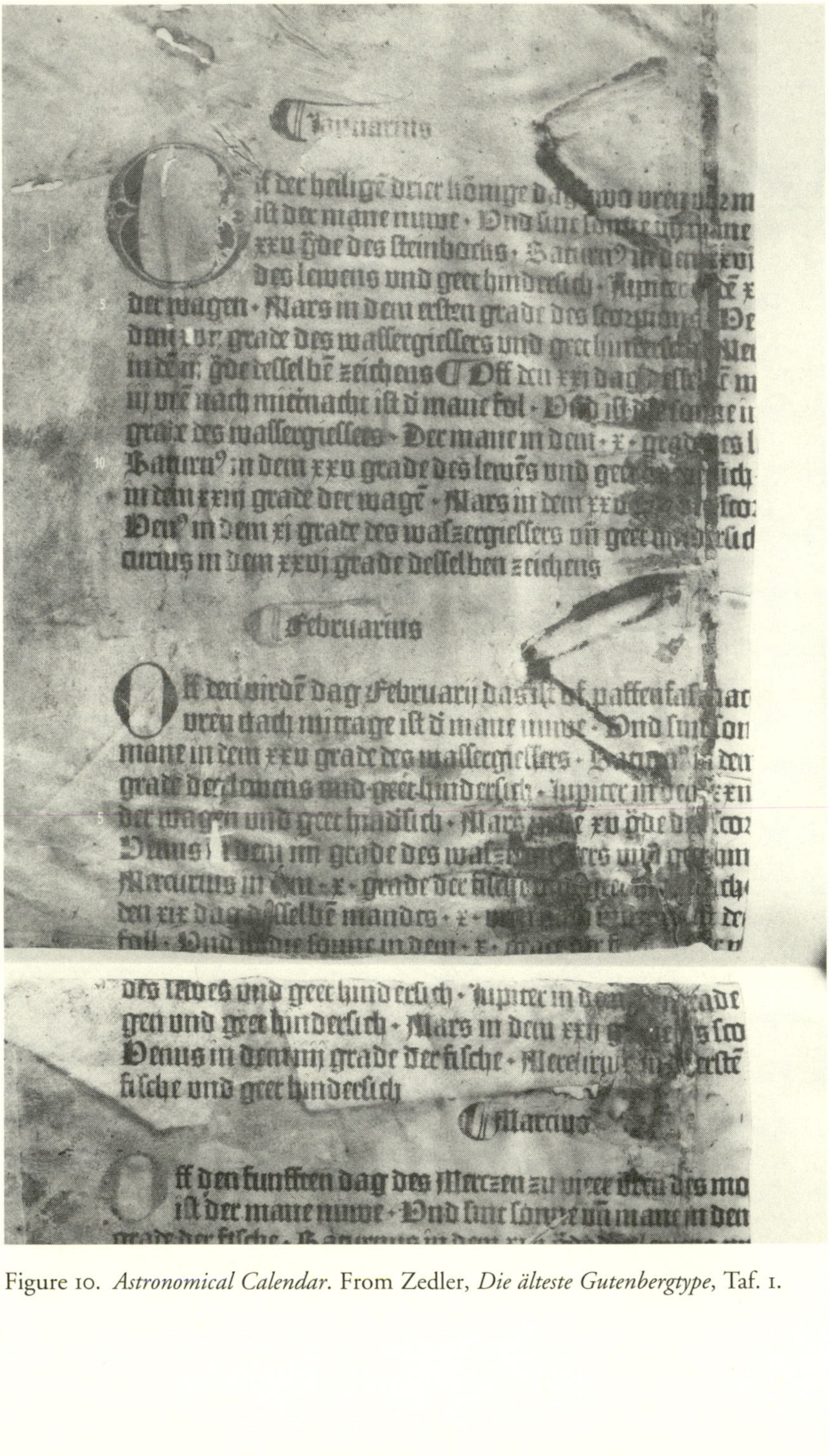

Figure 10. *Astronomical Calendar.* From Zedler, *Die älteste Gutenbergtype,* Taf. 1.

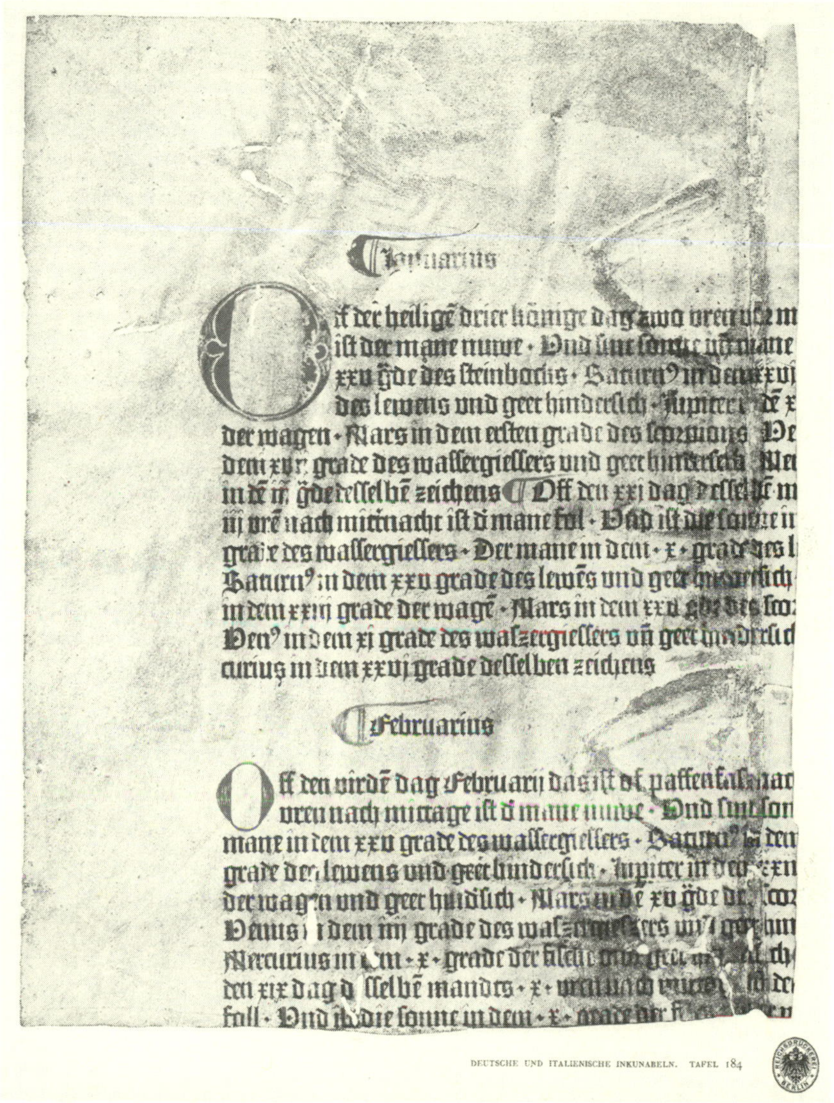

Figure 11. *Astronomical Calendar.* From Konrad Burger, *Monumenta Germaniae et Italiae typographica* (Berlin, 1904), Pl. 184. Courtesy of the Henry E. Huntington Library, San Marino, California.

typeface) thus blurs into *Setzung* (the actual practices of a compositor, also implied by extant examples). Both Zedler and Schwenke noted that individual fragments and the texts they contained are not comparable: each text is the product of a unique typesetting situation. Some fragments are proofsheets (what are called the *Reindruck* and *Probedruck* of the *Astronomical Calendar* differ considerably). Some are in German, others in Latin. Examples of DK type are often fragmentary: the apparent absence of a particular letterform (round-*r*, for example) means nothing if there is no opportunity in a fragment to use it. Furthermore, what a compositor sets is based on both textual and material context: Donatus texts uniquely require considerable numbers of particular typesorts; a single page might contain dozens of grammatical forms of the word "ferre," and in such a case, the typesetter might be forced to use an unconventional form of *r* simply because typesorts of the proper forms were all used up.[11] When a compositor nears the end of a page, setting conventions might be modified due to problems of casting off copy (for example, abbreviations might be used to compress text to conform to a required page break). Finally, much of what seems to be the most important evidence is impressionistic, for example, the apparent "sharpness" of the type.

The historical model contains much that is self-contradictory. It assumes an improvement in the typeface and typesetting, but this is coupled with a material deterioration in particular typesorts and a corresponding deterioration in the typesetters' awareness of the original conventions regarding that typeface (they no longer understood the "Gutenberg system" of typesetting). Because of these opposing forces, one toward perfection (*Vollkommenheit*) the other toward deterioration (*Abnutzung*), the same detail can be described variously: an indistinct type impression could be "primitive" and "unsharp" (and thus early) or "worn down" (and thus late). The reasoning always involves a degree of circularity: how one describes a detail depends in part on the state to which a fragment is assigned. And neither Schwenke nor Zedler claimed that a date or state could be assigned to an example of this type on a purely mechanical basis.[12]

This history of DK type also depends on an assumption questioned in chapter 1 above—that identifiable type, or typefonts, behave like modern typefonts. That is, they are produced by some discrete method; the sorts deteriorate through repeated use, and they are replaced by some method of casting comparable to modern typecasting. Only if type behaves as a modern type is imagined to behave do these histories work.

Gottfried Zedler I: The Coster Legend
and the History of Typecasting

> [Zedler's] lifelong habit of constructing far-reaching hypotheses on
> slight and shaky evidence, and then treating his results as adaman-
> tine truth, could serve as a fascinating case study in the annals of
> scholars' diseases. Life would be simpler and more pleasant if the
> corpus of Zedler's writings could be swept aside. (Paul Needham)[13]

Gottfried Zedler was the most prolific and enthusiastic scholar of these
problems in the early twentieth century, and his works are still basic to any
discussion of DK type.[14] Zedler was a proponent of the "Coster hypothesis,"
or "Coster legend" as it is now known, the theory that attributed the invention of printing to the Dutch. All of the raw evidence Zedler provided, including the earliest systematic facsimiles of DK type, was to some extent
described in the service of the larger hypothesis of the Dutch origins of printing. The appearance of type impressions was presumably evidence. But this
evidence was to Zedler bound up with speculation on its origins—both as a
product of typecasting procedures, and even more tentatively as a product of
particular national methods of typecasting. To get to Zedler's raw data of
analytical bibliography, scholars must first get through this.

The Coster Legend

The basis for this hypothesis comes from two texts: the Cologne Chronicle
of 1499, and the sixteenth-century *Batavia* by Hadrianus Junius. I quote these
here in Hessels' translation:[15]

> This highly valuable art was discovered first of all in Germany, at
> Mentz on the Rhine. And it is a great honour to the German nation
> that such ingenious men are found among them. And it took place
> about the year of our Lord 1440, and from this time until the year
> 1450, the art, and what is connected with it, was being investigated.
> And in the year of our Lord 1450 it was a golden year (jubilee), and
> they began to print, and the first book they printed was the Bible,
> in Latin; it was printed in a large letter, resembling the letter with
> which at present missals are printed. Although the art (as has been
> said) was discovered at Mentz, in the manner as it is now generally
> used, yet the first prefiguration (*die erste vurbyldung*) was found in

Holland, in the Donatuses, which were printed there before that
time. . . . One named Omnibonus, wrote in a preface . . . that a
Walloon from France, named Nicol. Jenson discovered first of all
this masterly art; but that is untrue, for there are those still alive,
who testify that books were printed at Venice before Nic. Jenson
came there and began to cut and make letters. But the first inventor
of printing was a citizen of Mentz, born at Strasburg, and named
Junker Johan Gutenberg. . . . The origin and progress of the art was
told me verbally by the honorable master Ulrich Zell, still printer at
Cologne, anno 1499, by whom the said art came to Cologne. (*Cologne Chronicle*, trans. Hessels, 8)

In the year 1440 a certain Laurens Janszoon Coster lived at Harlem,
a man who 128 years afterwards, by the mouth of Hadrianus Junius,
reclaims the honour of having invented the art of printing. . . . He
began to cut letters in the bark of a beech. He printed these letters
reversed on paper, and thus made, out of amusement, some lines,
which were to serve as copies to his grandchildren . . . Junius has
seen a specimen of this printing, a book in the Dutch language, of
an unknown author, entitled "speculum nostrae salutis." . . . Afterwards Coster changed his letters to leaden ones and these again to
tin. (*Batavia*, 568, trans. Hessels, 59)

Dziatzko's skepticism concerning such legends and the discussions they generated led him to develop methods for analyzing material book-copies (the
two copies of B42 and B36). Zedler, by contrast, was committed to the narrative in these legends; he gave them the apparent backing of modern bibliographical method by speculating on methods of typecasting, and only
subsequently applying Dziatzko's principles of analytical bibliography.

Typecasting Methods

The argument in favor of the early dating of Dutch printing depended on
evidence that could match the word "vurbyldung" (prefiguration) in the
Chronicle description quoted above. Zedler found this evidence in what is
now known as Dutch prototypography: early fragments of Donatus and the
Speculum humanitatis salvationis printed in a combination of movable type
and woodblocks, works now assigned to the 1460s but dated much earlier by
Zedler.[16] The Dutch letterforms differ noticeably from those used in Mainz,

and to explain this, Zedler hypothesized differing typecasting techniques, based on the technical work and speculation of modern typefounders, "specialists" such as Charles Enschedé. Zedler assigned to Gutenberg the invention of the hand-mold in accordance with a growing consensus since De Vinne (see Chapter 1 above), but separated that from the "origin of printing" discussion. The invention of printing was to be found in alternate printing techniques, such as sand-casting, used in early Dutch printing.

There are many problems with Zedler's argument. The "Fachleute" to whom Zedler appealed were far from disinterested (the Enschedés had a long history in discussions of the origins of printing). Furthermore, the logic of Zedler's argument is not sound. By comparing examples of Dutch prototypography with B42 type and DK type, Zedler concluded that Dutch type was more primitive and thus earlier. But the notion "primitive," whether applied to the appearance of the type or to the method of casting it, does not necessarily mean "early." If I were to cast type today, and if by some miracle I were to do it successfully enough to print with it, the results would be far more primitive in appearance than any of the surviving fragments from the mid-fifteenth century. The case can also be argued in reverse: because DK type and B42 type are so well formed, then there must be earlier, unrecorded Mainz type: in other words, the history of Mainz type must go back earlier than any of the recorded examples.

According to Zedler, the evidence for determining typecasting methods is found in the type impressions ("Buchstabenbilder") seen in books. Yet to analyze these one must also know the presumed endpoint of these techniques: modern methods of typecasting ("die Praxis des heutigen Shriftguesses," 23). Zedler thus constructed a history of early printing according to three methods of typecasting, assigned to Dutch printers, Gutenberg, and Peter Schoeffer. For Dutch prototypography, Zedler hypothesized a method of sand-casting, supporting his hypothesis concerning the unique features of this type, the "Verbindungslinien" or "Verbindungstrich," thin lines joining parts of a letter or abbreviation marks and type body (*Die sogenannte Gutenbergbibel*, 23; *Die älteste Gutenbergtype*, 33–34).[17] To Schoeffer, Zedler assigned a method of casting with copper matrices that was essentially the same as the method of typecasting in seventeenth-century manuals. For Gutenberg (of B42), he hypothesized what could be characterized as a transitional method, one involving lead matrices as opposed to Schoeffer's copper ones (*Die sogenannte Gutenbergbibel*, 13).[18]

But Zedler was not consistent in describing Gutenberg's methods and there are in his histories three or sometimes four stages in the development of modern typecasting:

(1) prototypography (sand-casting) (Dutch process described in *Das älteste Gutenberg-type*, 35);
(2) *Abklatsch*-method (two-part casting "in zwei tempi" with lead matrices);
(3) single-casting (*Von Coster zu Gutenberg*, 170) "in einem Tempo in Blei zu giessen" (Gutenberg cast each letter in a sandform, used this as a punch, and through this obtained a lead matrix);[19]
(4) copper matrixes (classic typecasting method, used by Peter Schoeffer).

The most obscure of these methods is what Zedler in 1902 called the "Abklatsch-method," based on Charles Enschedé's technical manual of 1901, *Technisch Onderzoek*. Enschedé was from a family of typefounders and thus one of the *Fachleute* variously cited and condemned by printing historians. Zedler based his theories on Enschedé's typefounding experiments, but he paradoxically conceded (or claimed) that Enschedé's book was full of errors.[20] This method was a presumed transitional form of typecasting and involved a separate casting of the type letter and the shank. I will attempt here to translate and summarize what Zedler says, but this will not be easy, as all the problems with Zedler's writings seem concentrated in this single passage.

Enschedé (in Zedler's description) assumed that the punch (patrix) was cut in bronze (in Zedler's view, these were cast in sand). From this patrix, a lead matrix was formed, either by casting lead over the patrix, or by pressing the punch into cold lead. "The second method is simpler." To form the patrix, Gutenberg used a 2mm bronze plate, from which a "Letterchen" was cut, without a stem. This was pressed into lead, assuring the depth of each letter would be the same. Each letter thus was cast in two steps (Zedler's "in zwei Tempi"): first, the small letter on the plate, then the plate laid under a "Giessform" such that a stem can be cast with it:

Das Letterchen mit dem Plättchen erhielt man nicht dadurch, dass man das Schriftmetall in die Matrize goss, sondern umgekehrt dadurch, dass man letztere in das geschmolzene Schriftmetall abklatschte. (Zedler, *Die älteste Gutenbergtype*, 23 paraphrasing Enschedé)

I think what Zedler means by "Letterchen" is the "bronze letter" without a typebody, thus "You don't obtain a letter from the plate by casting metal in a matrix, but rather the reverse; you (stereotype) the matrix in the hot type-metal."

This process depends on casting lead in lead, whereby the type-metal hardens as it hits the cooler matrix. Enschedé claimed (according to Zedler) that this method would work with large type sizes (B42 type and DK type), but not with smaller letters (the type used in the text portions of the 1454/1455 Indulgences). Therefore, the development of modern typecasting methods would conveniently be associated with the development of smaller type (DK > B42 > Indulgence type).

I struggled mightily with this passage. But then I recalled that the same question had been taken up by Hessels in his excellent article in the 1911 *Encyclopedia Britannica*, conveniently available on-line. Perhaps the English version would be easier for me than Zedler's paraphrase.

Hessels refers directly to Enschedé's 1901 *Technisch Onderzoek*, 15ff. (the page reference does not appear in Zedler and is incorrect; the relevant passage begins on page 28). I summarize Hessels here. Punches were made of brass, from which one could make lead matrices, either by pouring lead over the patrix or by pressing the patrix into lead. After the matrix was made, the letter was cast by the *Abklatsch*-method. The letter was cast "in two tempos," first on a small plate, then placed underneath a casting form to fix it to a shank: "The letter on the plate was made not by pouring the metal into the matrix, but by beating the matrix into the molten metal."

I still struggle. With my minimal Dutch, I can confirm (more or less) that Hessels is providing a fair translation, but Hessels's English is hardly clearer to me than Zedler's German, and the reason for this is that Hessels is providing not a paraphrase or summary of Enschedé but rather an English version of Zedler's paraphrase, a word for word translation of Zedler's text. The minor changes Hessels introduces often make things even more obscure; as an example, what Zedler means by "Letterchen" is the bronze letter cut from the plate, and what Hessels means by "letter" in the exact same sentence is the final cast letter.[21]

Because I cannot read Dutch with anything resembling fluency, I am limited to poring over the versions in Zedler and Hessels and trying to coordinate them with Enschedé's 1901 manual. Most of the phrasing in both comes from Enschedé; that is, they are translating, not paraphrasing. But no passage from Enschedé will account for such phrases as "Enschedé möchte

. . . glauben" in Zedler and the corresponding "Enschedé thinks . . ." in Hessels.

I can only conclude from this that at least one of these scholars (Hessels or Zedler) does not fully understand the process described in Enschedé, even though both are fluent in Dutch.[22] And very likely neither of them does.

Gottfried Zedler II: The Sogennant *Astronomical Calendar*

Zedler built on the methods of late nineteenth-century bibliographers such as Dziatzko, but was less interested in the niceties of analytical bibliography than in "how it was" or at least in speculating how it was. Whereas Schwenke began with the printed evidence and worked toward an account of it, Zedler began with historical hypotheses and used those as a framework in which to classify the evidence. This tendency in Zedler led to the prominence he gave to the recently discovered *Astronomical Calendar,* the crucial document in the early twentieth-century history of DK type.

What is now called the *Astronomical Calendar* exists in two fragments, one, the Wiesbaden fragment, discovered by Zedler and published in 1902 (Figure 10, from Zedler's reproduction) and the second, a proofsheet published in 1948 by Wehmer.[23] The type-state of the *Calendar* is much the same as that of *Türkenkalender,* securely dated 1454, and other "kleine Drucke" such as the *Cisianus, Türkenbulle,* and indulgences—all examples of Schwenke's second "Zustand" of DK type (works dated in the mid-1450s). But the date Zedler assigned to the *Astronomical Calendar* (1447) was seven to ten years earlier than the dates assigned to these other examples.

Zedler's argument involved two major assumptions: (1) that the Paris 27-line Donatus was older than the newly discovered *Astronomical Calendar* based on analytical or internal evidence; (2) that the *Calendar* was an "astronomical calendar," which could thus be dated by external evidence. The date for the planetary positions described in the fragment was established by astronomers as 1448, placing the date for printing as 1447, and this in turn provided a "certain foundation" for dating the Paris 27-line Donatus, which, on the basis of its type-state, seemed more primitive. Zedler's description of this fragment is full of the language of certainty: "der Fund eines unzweifelhaften Gutenbergdruckes, der in das Jahr 1447 gesetzt werden muss" [the discovery of a print unquestionably by Gutenberg, that must be dated 1447]; "ist auch jetzt durch den neu entdeckten Druck für die Beurteilung des

Donat eine sichere Grundlage gewonnen" [through the newly discovered print, a certain foundation has been won for the dating of the Donatus] (*Die älteste Gutenbergtype*, 1). The analytical evidence had already established the 27-line Donatus as earlier than other examples of DK type due to the "blurriness" of type impressions and uncertain lineation. The *Astronomical Calendar* showed the antithesis of this type-state, and Schwenke's first two states of DK type were defined on the basis of these two fragments: DK type meant that type whose earliest form was that of the Paris 27-line Donatus, and whose later form was that of the *Astronomical Calendar* (see Figures 3 and 10).

Without the erroneous date assigned to the *Astronomical Calendar*, the history of DK type could have been built coherently around a few securely dated examples such as the *Türkenkalender* of 1454. These show the type in its perfected state, and are roughly contemporary with the date assigned to the Gutenberg Bible. The 36-line Bible (B36) and securely dated prints of Pfister could thus be later products of recasting. Fragments such as the 27-line Donatus from Paris would thus provide a primitive version, and the history of DK type could be seen as a three-step development and refinement taking place over ten to fifteen years. The dating of the *Astronomical Calendar* to 1447, however, required that the perfected form of the type found there appear eight to ten years earlier than other, securely dated examples of the same type-state. More primitive examples of this type (D27 Paris, the more recently discovered *Weltgericht*, and the Donatus fragments from Berlin), once vaguely dated as early 1450s, now had to be dated 1445 or earlier. Another result was the reconsideration of the notions of "deterioration" and "perfection"; if the *Astronomical Calendar* could not be dated as roughly contemporary with other examples of what appeared to be the same type-state (that found in various other calendars and "kleine Drucke"), a more complex history would have to be constructed: perhaps involving a return to a more primitive state of type in the mid-1450s after the apparent perfection of the type in 1447, or an unexplained "deterioration" of the type;[24] minimally, this history required accepting the paradox that texts in the same type-state could be separated by as much as ten years.[25]

Zedler conflated many types of argument and evidence in this new history:

Nach dem Vorhergehenden kann es nicht zweifelhaft sein, dass der Kalender für das Jahr 1448 bestimmt war. Naturgemäss muss er

daher schon 1447 gedruckt worden sein. Wir haben es also mit
einem Druck zu tun, der sieben Jahre früher als die bisher bekannten
ältesten fest datierbaren Drucke ist. Eine astronomische Ephemeride
wie diese kann nur für das Jahr gedruckt worden sein, für das sie
berechnet war. (*Die älteste Gutenbergtype*, 7)

[Considering all this, there can be no doubt that the calendar was
intended for the year 1448. Naturally, it would have to have been
printed by 1447. We thus have an example that was printed seven
years earlier than the oldest securely dated example of DK type (*Türkenkalender*). An astronomical work like this can only have been
printed for the year for which its reckonings were intended.]

This passage contains scientific arguments (concerning the planetary positions represented in the *Calendar*), analytical arguments (concerning the development of type), and, less obviously, literary and purely speculative
arguments (concerning the nature of the text and the appropriate date for
such a text to be printed). These arguments are so intertwined in Zedler's
discussion, and even in these four sentences, that Zedler's conclusions were
accepted, illogically, as purely scientific.

In 1948, Carl Wehmer destroyed the foundation of Zedler's argument.
The so-called *Astronomical Calendar* was not an astronomical calendar, but
rather an astrological chart. It was designed for casting horoscopes, and there
was no essential relation between the year of its printing and the year appropriate to the planetary positions used (1448). With this change in definition,
the *Calendar* (or "Planeten Tafel" as it would be become known) could be
redated on analytical grounds; that is, it could be positioned formally in the
history of the development of DK type based on the internal evidence of the
type impressions. It was thus redated to 1457, contemporary with other DK
fragments that showed roughly the same state of type.

This could have made histories of DK type somewhat easier to construct;
but certain features of the then conventional history seemed impervious to
change. The accepted history prior to this redating can be seen in Ruppel's
Johannes Gutenberg: Sein Leben und sein Werk (1939), whose sober and clear
chronology of the type includes a misdated *Astronomical Calendar*.

An dieser Type können wir die Arbeitendes Erfinders um ihre technische und künstlerische Vollendung beinahe von Druck zu Druck

beobachten. Wenigstens 12 Jahre lang wurde ständig an der Verbes-
serung dieser Type gearbeitet, bis sie ihre Vollendung in der 36zeili-
gen Bibeltype erhielt. (Ruppel, *Gutenberg*, 118)

[In this type, we can observe Gutenberg's work on the technical and
artistic perfection of this type almost from print to print. He worked
at least twelve full years on the improvement of this type, until it
obtained its perfection in the 36-line Bible.]

If it were not for the inconvenient 1447 date accepted by most scholars in the
1930s for the *Astronomical Calendar*, this statement would be logical; one
could follow the improvement or perfection of the type through several securely dated works: *TK* 1454, *TB* 1455, and finally the late examples from
Bamberg.[26] But the dating of the *Astronomical Calendar* to 1447 means that
this twelve-year improvement from the most primitive form to the perfected
form ("etwa 1445" for D27Paris to "etwa 1455/57" for B36) is roughly a two-
year improvement (the perfected form is also seen in *AK*, here dated 1447);
Ruppel attributes this strange chronology to an improved casting instrument,
followed by a virtual stagnation.[27] Later improvement must apparently be
due to presswork alone, not "continuous recasting."[28]

Ruppel's chapter headings, clear and straightforward as they are, obscure
the problem posed by the then accepted date of the *Astronomical Calendar*.
These headings are largely formal: 1. *Weltgericht* (etwa 1445); 2. *Die Donate*
(122ff.); 3. *Die Kalender* (3a. *AK* für das Jahr 1448) . . . ; 4. *Türkenbulle* (1455/
56); 5. *Die DK 31-line Ablassbrief* 1454/55; 6. *B36* (etwa 1457/58). They appear
to form a chronology because the earliest Donatus is by this scheme to be
dated "either in 1445 or 1446" (p. 123). But of course, many of the Donatuses
are later than this, and the various calendars described in section 3 also span
nearly the entire range of development.

It is to Ruppel's credit that he did not attempt to distort the internal
evidence to accord with his chronology, and he conceded the sometimes
"ragged" presswork of examples dated by this scheme later than the *Astronomical Calendar*.[29] Nonetheless, the most readily apparent indications of
date, including line integrity, right justification, sharpness of type, are now
at odds with the history.

Following Wehmer's work in 1948, the standard chronologies set forth
in Ruppel's monograph and in DeRicci's *Catalogue raisonné* had to be revised. The *Astronomical Calendar* was dated close to other works showing the

same type-state. The apparent clash between internal and external evidence
could have been eliminated in this process, or should have been eliminated.
But many details from earlier histories had been so well integrated into the
history of DK type that they remained, particularly the early dates assigned to
the Paris Donatus. Eliminating the *Astronomical Calendar* from consideration
meant there was no reason to date the earliest Donatuses earlier than the
early 1450s (a few years before *TK* or B42). Albert Kapr, however, in 1988
dated these early Donatuses even earlier than they had been dated by Zedler:
to Strasbourg as early as 1440. Kapr appears to take full account of Wehmer,
but seems to ignore the implications.

> [The redating of AK to 1457] provides absolutely no justification,
> though, for advancing the early dating of the 27-line Donatuses or
> the *Sibylenweissagung*.
>   It is quite right to place the items printed in the DK-type in a
> sequence determined by the state of the type material, but at the
> same time external factors, such as political or social considerations,
> need to be taken into account in dating any piece of printing.[30]

That is, there is no reason to change Ruppel's dating of these texts to "around
1445."

Kapr claims to accept the internal evidence entirely: the 27-line Donatus
from Paris and the *Weltgericht* (= *Sibyllenbuch*) are to be dated earlier than
all other examples on the basis of the type-state. Yet when the *Astronomical
Calendar* was postdated by a decade (to 1457), Kapr antedated the early Donatuses to the early 1440s, as if the elimination of the *terminus ante quem* (the
date before which the Paris Donatus had to be printed) were actually the
elimination of a *terminus post quem* (a date after which the Paris Donatus had
to be printed). Instead of taking two years to improve the state of DK type
from the Paris Donatus to the perfected state found in the *Astronomical Calendar* (the time required in Zedler's and Ruppel's histories), in Kapr's history,
it now takes almost fifteen years for the improvement from the early Donatus
to that same state of type (now represented in the more securely dated *Türkenkalender*).

One might justify this by appealing to Zedler's own prejudice in favor
of Dutch origins of printing: perhaps the only thing that prevented Zedler
from dating the Paris Donatus even earlier than he did was his desire to keep

the origins of printing safely in the hands of the Dutch. But it is hardly justifiable to correct one of Zedler's errors by invoking another one.

Conclusion

Zedler's claim to have established a "scientific place to stand" led straight back to the unscientific, arbitrary, and ideological arguments of the chroniclers so dismissed by Dziatzko, Schwenke, and often by Zedler himself. Neither science nor type analysis provided a firm basis for answering the question of who was responsible for the printing of various texts, and conflicting, speculative narratives continued. More perniciously, Zedler's presumed scientific errors led to a general skepticism regarding all evidence he assembled. Fuhrmann claimed to believe that Wehmer's refutation of the hypothesized date of the *Astronomical Calendar* was a refutation of the entire system of chronology based on type analysis. But the inaccurate dating of this text not only did not depend on type analysis, it went against all the evidence of type analysis. This kind of blanket skepticism, or the similar dismissal of all findings of the Gutenberg Gesellschaft voiced by Charles Mortet in 1922, did nothing to advance scholarship on early type;[31] rather it returned the state of the question to what it was when Dziatzko addressed that issue in 1880.

The publications of the Gutenberg Gesellschaft marked a shift in the kinds of evidence that would be the basis of discussion. Equally important, those publications began to make that evidence accessible to readers in the form of photographic reproductions. Zedler's presentation of this evidence and his discussion of it had little to do with what are now considered his faulty conclusions, and in fact challenged his own dating of *Astronomical Calendar* to 1447.[32] Zedler's error (or what we now consider to be an error) did not challenge the validity of the methodology promoted by Dziatzko and Schwenke, nor did he use this new external evidence (as he might usefully have done) to test the validity of these methodologies. It simply made the already tortuous explanations of the history of a typeface even more mysterious.

Appendix 1: Arrays of Letterforms

The analytical history of DK type established by Zedler and Schwenke was based on differences of letterforms and setting conventions. Zedler in Table

XIII of *Die älteste Gutenbergtype* published a table of letterforms seen in individual texts (D27Paris, *AK, TK, Cisianus, LaxK,* D27London, and B36). Portions of Zedler's Table are often reprinted, despite the fact that it is full of
errors and does not deal with many of the key features that distinguish these
types. Zedler's table is a visual depiction of the typesorts presumably available
in the DK typecase. The table is similar to that found in Blades's *Life and
Typography of William Caxton* of 1861. By the turn of the century, such tables
were a conventional means of describing particular typecases, and Zedler's
own analytical table of B42 is the basis of the familiar assertion that Gutenberg's typecase contained 290 typeforms (see Chapter 1 above).

   Zedler's Table XIII is unreliable: looking over an example like *Türkenbulle*, I find typesorts not listed in this table for that text (most important,
the so-called "eckige *a*"). Furthermore, the type variants shown are not keyed
to Zedler's discussion: which of the capital *F*s is the "small ugly form"? (I
know the answer, but it was not immediately apparent from the table); the
various *i*-sorts described and distinguished clearly in Zedler's discussion (dot
with the bowl opening to the left, dot with the bowl opening to the right)
are easily found in Zedler's reproductions of the relevant texts, but they cannot be clearly seen in the typeform Table. A "left-leaning *d*" occurs throughout the history of DK type, but I am not entirely sure where it appears in
Zedler's table, nor do I see that Zedler considered the problems of this particular typesort.[33] Finally, even if the table were accurate (which it is not), there
is no note on the relative frequency of each typeform, nor is there any indication how any one of them is used. Is the typeform depicted in the table the
principal form of that letter? or does that form appear infrequently? or only
once? If such tables are to show the evolution of the type, which appears to
be their function, some guidance must be given. Zedler's table, thus, provides
neither a systematic history nor even the evidence for one, although it is often
cited as if it did. The scientific impression a reader might get from this visual
of typeforms is an illusion.

Schwenke's Analysis in Die Donat- und Kalender-Type

In his 1903 *Die Donat- und Kalender-Type,* Schwenke lists in a much more
systematic fashion than Zedler each of the key texts in the history of DK type
and describes in a consistent manner the key features of the type associated
with these texts. Schwenke describes the texts in the chronological order
accepted in 1902: D27Paris, *AK, Abl* (1454), *TK* (1455), *AdlK* (1457*), Cisianus,*

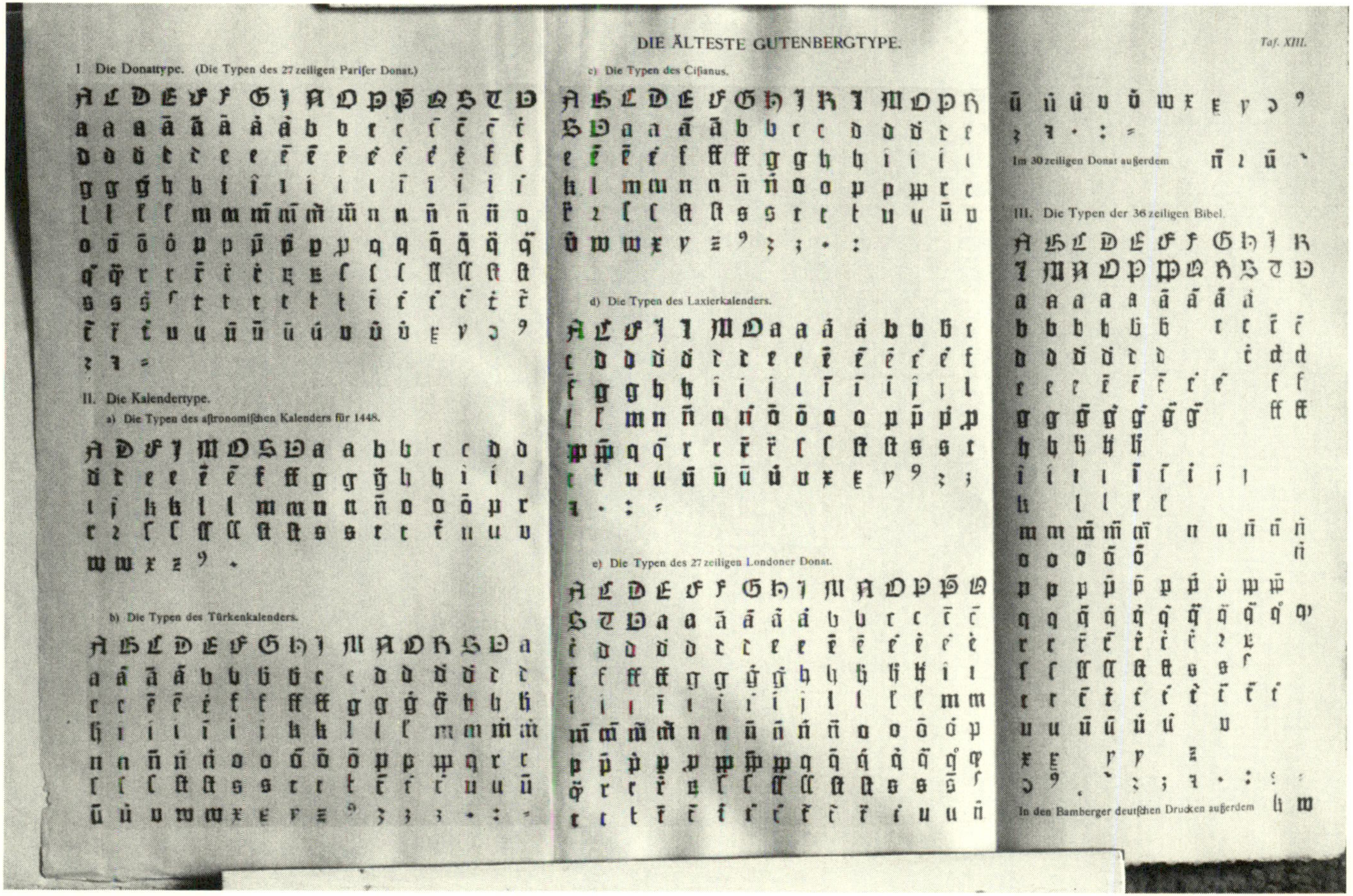

Figure 12. Table of DK type; Zedler, *Die älteste Gutenbergtype*, Taf. XIII.

D27London, D27Munich, D27Oxford/Bamberg, D30Oxford/London, D28. In his discussion of each of these eleven groups, Schwenke defines a number of distinctive features:"eckige *a*" (a distinctive, two-storied *a*); round-*r* after letters with right-hand bowls at *n*-height (*b*, *p*, *o*, etc.); high *t* (used in -*tt* or -*ct*); *d* filed to form a ligature with following vowel; variant abbreviations for -*que*; distinctive lettersorts (e.g., variant abbreviations involving *p*); variant forms of s^1, particularly a left-leaning form; *i*-forms; distinctive punctuation; general "Verbindungsregeln" (the use of principal and abutting forms); the distinction *v/u*; word division; right justification; lineation; sharpness of type; general form and layout. The appearance of some of these features allows certain fragments to be classified together: for example, the Oxford and London fragments of the 30-line Donatus are confirmed by type evidence to be of the same edition; the 28-line Donatus shows "all characteristics of B36"; for the 27-line Donatus fragments of Oxford and Bamberg, the "Erhaltungs-zustand" of the typecase and indifferent use of abbreviations for *z* are decisive for late dating.

Because of Schwenke's consistent description of these features, it would seem a simple, albeit time-consuming matter to arrange these in a table, comparable to the detailed tables Schwenke constructed for the paper evidence of the Gutenberg Bible in his 1900 *Untersuchungen*. Yet Schwenke never constructed such a table, or at least never published one. And when I attempted to do so, reducing Schwenke's notes to categories such as the sixteen listed above, sometimes adding categories and table columns for particular typesorts, always taking Schwenke's analysis at face value, my results were ambiguous. Certain features support particular groupings of texts: *TK* and *AdlK* share a high *t*, a bad casting of *e*, a left-leaning form of *s*. Other features suggest a clear and rational historical development through all examples: the badly cast *e*, the punctuation mark consisting of four points, conventions for right justification. But no feature or combination of features provides a decisive distinction between type-states, nor an unambiguous chronology, whether that chronology involves the *Astronomical Calendar* as misdated in the early twentieth century or as dated today. Even presumably foundational features of this type, such as the difference between "sharp" and "blurred," are insecure; and Schwenke himself questions whether the description "blurred"[34] applies to the 27-line Donatus of Paris, once considered the earliest example of DK type on that very basis. Detailed microhistories, some of which apply to individual typesorts,[35] are unstable; they do not coalesce in any quantifiable way to form a coherent history of this type.

To place an example within this history requires reference not to a verbal description, but rather to the facsimiles Zedler and Schwenke provide. The facts, in Bradshaw's terms, do not speak as they should.

Appendix 2: The Two-Color Initials

The *Astronomical Calendar* has a series of two- and four-line initials, in alternating colors, red and blue.[36] In 1902, Zedler described these very cursorily as the "product of a rubricator," who worked according to ordinary conventions of rubrication. Schwenke, citing Zedler's p. 12, described them as follows:

> Für den Rubrikator ist am Anfang des Januar ein Quadrat von 4,
> bei den übrigen Monaten eins von 2, in der Mittel des Monats eins
> von 1 Kegelhöhe ausgespart, das letzte nur zur Setzung des C-Zeich-
> ens, wogegen an dieser Stelle der Punkt fehlt. (Schwenke, *DK-Type*).

> [Unused space is left blank . . . A quadrant of four lines is left for
> the rubricator at the beginning of January, a two-line space for other
> months, and within each month a one-line space for the setting of
> paragraph marks where there is no punctuation.]

By the late 1930s, this standard description had changed. Zedler by 1937 had predictably reversed his earlier opinion, now claiming that anyone who looked at the initials could see that they are printed.[37] In 1939, Ruppel describes these initials as follows:

> Zum ersten Male finden wir hier auch eingedruckte Initialen, so ein
> abwechselnd rot und blau gedrucktes *O*, dessen Typenkörper of-
> fenbar in Holz geschnittet war. (Ruppel, *Gutenberg*, 220).

> [For the first time, we find here printed initials, thus an *O* printed
> in alternating red and blue, the type body of which is clearly cut in
> wood.]

Ruppel does not note any controversy about this: the initials are obviously printed from wooden blocks. On page 165, this assumption has a consequence; it proves for Ruppel that Gutenberg was involved in the 1457 Psalter of Fust and Schoeffer, noted for its large, two-color initials.[38] The *Astronomical Calendar*, for Ruppel dated in the late 1440s, is an early precedent for these initials, and thus Ruppel credits Gutenberg for their conception (166).

In fact (rather, in post-1948 fact), Zedler, Schwenke, and Ruppel are wrong. The *Astronomical Calendar* should be dated not as early as 1447, but closer to 1457 (the date of the Fust and Schoeffer Psalter). Thus the initials in the *Astronomical Calendar* are not a precedent for those in the Psalter; they are contemporary with them. And when the date for the *Calendar* changed, so too did the consensus on whether these initials were painted or printed. The present consensus follows Wehmer's note 7 (p. 13) of his 1948 *Probedruck*, the monograph responsible for the redating of the *Calendar*.[39] "That the initials are painted by hand is perfectly established according to the examination of the originals by Rudolf Juchhoff." The matter seems (as so often in this history) closed; and Wehmer, somewhat uncharacteristically, neither critiques Juchhoff's argument, nor details what that argument or the evidence is.[40]

The article by Juchhoff is "Wandlungen des Gutenbergbildes," *Zentrallblatt für Bibliothekswesen* 57 (1940): 202–14. Juchhoff here not only expresses skepticism regarding Zedler's dating of the *Astronomical Calendar* but, more important, notes the radical consequences of this early date, which effectively overturns all histories of this type based on analytic evidence and the development of typeforms.

Juchhoff had not examined the *Calendar* initials before his article went to press. In the body of the article, Juchhoff notes only that the nature of the two-color initials is important, whether they are printed (as Zedler eventually supposed) or painted by a rubricator (as Hupp claimed). In a note added while the article was at press, Juchhoff says that he has now had the chance to inspect the original. The initial appears "to the impartial eye . . . as the typical work of a rubricator," as claimed by Zedler in 1903 and, following him, Schwenke. "Aber auch eine genaue Untersuchung ergibt eindeutig, dass die Initialen eingemalt sind" [Moreover, a serious investigation reveals unambiguously that the initials are painted.] This leads to Wehmer's more strongly worded paraphrase quoted above: that the initials are painted is "established unambiguously" ("einwandfrei festgestellt").

There is little basis on which to critique Juchhoff's conclusions; no one will examine these initials except in Burger's color reproduction (reproduced in black-and-white here, Figure 11).[41] But Juchhoff does not detail the features that led him to his conclusion: absence of "squash" at the edges of the initials? color? nature of the ink?

The early reproductions of the now destroyed Wiesbaden fragment seem to me ambiguous. The first reproduction by Zedler in 1902 is barely clearer in the original than in my own Figure 10 here. There are four initials, the first in two colors, red and blue, the next three in alternating red and blue. If these were printed, they were certainly cut on woodblocks (not cast). The right-leaning orientation of the second *O* strongly suggests a misaligned print. Burger's color reproduction shows the two-color initial more clearly (Figure 11). The initial shows the same fine (white) line between colored areas that are seen in the Psalter initials or those of the 1460 *Catholicon*. This would be difficult for a rubricator to maintain freehand, and could be seen as an obvious product of a woodcut (or cast) initial in two parts. I'm not sure why a "disinterested" eye would not conclude (even erroneously) that such an initial is printed. Most important, the "disinterested" eye after Wehmer's 1948 *Probedruck* would not be the same as one in 1940. If the initials could be examined today, they would be examined under the assumption that the *Astronomical Calendar* and the Mainz Psalter are contemporary (ca. 1457); the well-informed eye might well see something other than what Juchhoff saw in 1940, when the *Calendar* was securely dated ten years prior to the Psalter initials.

For Zedler in 1902, the most important conclusion was the 1447 date, and a two-color printed initial of the type associated with Fust and Schoeffer's Psalter of 1457 would have spoken strongly against this. Thus, these initials were handdrawn by the rubricator, pure and simple. Zedler's facsimiles were not clear enough to provide much evidence either way. Schwenke, looking only at Zedler's black-and-white plate and description, and accepting with some reluctance the 1447 date, would have had no basis on which to object to Zedler's views, and simply repeated them.

By 1939, however, Zedler's dating of the *Astronomical Calendar* was so conventional and so long accepted that conflicting evidence posed no threat to it. Thus Ruppel, looking at the same evidence, saw the initials (now thought to be printed) not as a challenge to the accepted date, but rather as confirmation of something greater: Gutenberg, the subject of his Life and Works biography, could now be seen as the intellectual force behind the Psalter of 1457, since he had developed the idea of these initials some ten years earlier "when Schoeffer himself was hardly more than 20 years old" (Ruppel, *Gutenberg*, 165). Evidence seemingly contrary to the accepted narrative (the similarity of the initials of the misdated *Astronomical Calendar* to those of the Mainz Psalter) was not seen as conflicting with the narrative, but rather as a platform for constructing an even more elaborate narrative.

I don't doubt Juchhoff's good faith examination, nor am I in a position to doubt his conclusions. But for many scholars other than Juchhoff, the nature of this evidence (an obvious "fact") seems to have been determined by the larger narrative which it served.

※

CHAPTER THREE

The Voodoo Economics of Space: From Gothic to Roman

Renouard asserts that the return to Gothic character was forced upon the printers of Italy by the demands of the reading public for inexpensive books. There certainly was a large economy in space, and therefore in cost, secured by the use of Gothic type.

Sardini [*Esame*] proves how great that saving is. He calculates that the Mamotrectus of Jenson (1479), if printed in the equivalent Roman character, would occupy double and four per cent. more space than it does in Gothic.[1]

Horatio Brown's comments from his *The Venetian Printing Press* of 1891, quoted above, were an effort to explain what to bibliographers for over a century had seemed a basic paradox concerning the history of Venetian printing in the fifteenth century—the printing of books in gothic type by supposed humanist printers. To nineteenth-century bibliographers, Venetian printing was enmeshed in the ideology of the Rise of Humanism, and many details of its typographical history were read to support that. For example, fifteenth-century Italian printing culminates in the books of Aldus Manutius and thus has as an endpoint the production of presumably inexpensive editions of the classics; these texts were printed in italic or roman type rather than gothic type; Nicholas Jenson created one of the most important roman typefaces of the period, one that would centuries later receive the important endorsement of William Morris. Printing history thus shows the replacement of so-called "Mainz" characters (textura, blackletter, gothic) with modern roman or italic typefaces.

A problem or paradox embedded in this largely ideological history is that Jenson also produced books in gothic type. The earliest systematic bibliographies (most important, Michel Maittaire in his *Annales typographici* of 1719) revealed something even more inconvenient.[2] Jenson does not replace his gothic fonts with roman fonts, nor does he increase the number of books printed in roman type, as the myth of the rise of humanism seems to require. The reverse appears to be true: Jenson prints more books in gothic during his later years. For eighteenth- and nineteenth-century bibliographers, the most basic bibliographical facts of Jenson's printing career thus seemed at odds with the bibliographical myth (or hope) that the rise of printing could be associated with the rise of humanism.

The real or mythical rise of humanism is still a standard cliché of many popular printing histories (see, for example, the comments of Lucien Febvre and Henri-Jean Martin cited in the conclusion to this chapter). Why is the paradox that so troubled eighteenth- and nineteenth-century bibliographers no longer threatening to modern bibliographical versions of the same myth? This chapter focuses on the comments of Giacomo Sardini, *Esame sui principj della tipografia ovvero storia critica di Nicolao Jenson* (1796); this life-and-works biography of Jenson seems to be the sole basis for the comments by Brown.[3]

Giacomo Sardini and the Defense of Jenson's Gothic

Jenson's roman type has been the subject of praise since the earliest systematic bibliographies in the eighteenth century; it was used as a model by William Morris and still used as a standard in Daniel Updike's classic *Printing Types*, the only type deserving of a full fold-out page.[4] Because of its presumed excellence, and because of the obvious replacement of gothic type by roman type in Western European history, historical bibliographers were hard pressed to explain Jenson's design and use of gothic type. Why did he bother producing such a retrograde typeface?

Sardini's *Esame* is the first book-length study of Jenson, and the first serious attempt to answer this question.[5] Sardini provides a biography, a full bibliography and chronology of Jenson's press, a discussion of the paper used by Jenson, and most important, of his type. In his discussions of type, Sardini is responding to two questions raised by eighteenth-century bibliographers: (1) was Jenson responsible for introducing gothic type to Italy? and (2) why did he continue to use it?

Maittaire had addressed these issues in 1719; his words suggest that he is responding to what was then a familiar question:

> Subit interim, cur Nicolaus Jenson characteres, cum Romanos habe- ret tam peculiari venustate praecellentes, Gothicos aliquando ma- luerit, in Bibliorum potissimum, Theologorum ac Juridicorum editionibus. Quod sic ab eo factum non arbitror, quasi litteras hu- maniores pluris quam Theologiam aut Jurisprudentiam aestimaret, et typis illas formosissimis, has non nisi deformioribus dignas judica- ret: sed id potius consuetudini tribuendum est, quae hujusmodi typos, lectu utcunque difficiles & visu deformes, Theologiae, Jurisp- rudentiae ac Philosophiae, jure tanquam proprio, ac distinguendi magis quam infamandi causa, assignavit. Gothicus character ante Nicolai adventum Venetiis ignorabatur; quo cum socio Johanne Co- loniensi usus est. (*Annales*, 7)

> [Why did Jenson use gothic type, when he had romans distinguished by a peculiar beauty? He occasionally preferred it particularly in his editions of the Bible, theology or jurisprudence. I don't believe he did this because he considered his "humane letters" more valuable than theology or law, and those books more worthy of beautiful types, whereas these only of ugly type. But rather it is to be attrib- uted to the custom, which assigned those types to Theology, Law and Philosophy, even though difficult to read and deformed to the sight, as if by proper right, for purposes of distinguishing them rather than shaming them. Gothic type was unknown in Venice before the arrival of Jenson, although used by his associate John of Cologne.]

Jenson's decisions regarding gothic are described using the language of the lawbooks he printed in that typeface, and the typesorts (*characteres*) as having travelled the same path from Mainz to Venice as Jenson himself did. "[Type- faces] had traveled far from the rude and exiled 'typeface' of the ancient Mainz, never to return to the black crassness of the Gothics (*in atram Gothic-*

orum crassitudinem)." According to Maittaire, the reason Jenson prints in gothic is simply "custom."

The first step in Sardini's defense of Jenson is to deny Jenson's responsibility for introducing roman type to Italy (vol. 2, chap. 6: "Non fu la Stamperia Jensoniana che introducesse in Italia il carattere Gotico," 54ff.).[6] Sardini criticizes what he calls the somewhat obscure defense of Jenson by Franciscus Laire, who claimed that Jenson was only following the use of gothic type by Ulrich Zell of Cologne.[7] To Laire, Jenson's use of gothic amounted to a desecration of his press:

> Sed dolendum est tantum virum praela sua, suamque famam deinde foedasse adhibito charactere Gothico, qui, durante uno quasi saeculo, non sine magna Typographicae artis injuria per universam fere Europam grassatus est.

> [It is to be regretted that such a man besmirched his press by bringing in the gothic character, which, for about a century, not without great injury to the typographical art, roamed over nearly all Europe.]

Sardini follows Laire in attributing to others the "opprobrious introduction" of gothic and the consequent "funestral depravation" it represented (55–56). Gothic type was introduced into Italy not by Jenson but by Ulrich Han, in books printed in "rotondo" (semi-gothic) with gothic headings in textura, or "Mainz style."[8]

The most important part of Sardini's defense for our purposes is in chapter 7: "Rationi a favore de i caratteri Gotici del nostro Nicolae" [Reasons supporting the gothic type of our Nicolas]. This defense no longer involves the bibliographical and historical argument used in chapter 6, but rather a rationalization and reimagining of the problems Jenson faced; it includes what Sardini describes as an "exacting experiment." Since gothic is a "depraved custom, inimicable to the Muses," one that introduced a "fatal idiom" among writers, Sardini reasons that Jenson must have had sound reasons for using it; if this typeface merits the opprobrium it has received, a feeling that all bibliographers share, Jenson and his associates must have been mightily deceived.[9]

The case for gothic imagined by Sardini is based on economies of space. To print in gothic takes up less room than to print in roman.

Nulladimeno francamenta si dirà, che alcuni de'caratteri gotici di
questo tempo superano per la finezza dell'artificio ogni più bel carattere rotondo . . . S'abbia in ciò specialmente riguardo alla piccolezza
delle lettere, alla spessezza delle medesime, che per cagion poi delle
stesse abbreviature non poco accorciano la materia, onde si viene a
ristringere in un piccolo tomo ciò che, prevalendosi del carattere
rotondo, richierderebbe un volume assai maggiore.

[Nonetheless, some of the characters are superior to roman in terms
of the "finesse of the artifice." Each has minute and distinct parts,
and many abbreviations. If you have special regard for the smallness
of the letter, and the thickness of them, which because of the abbreviations themselves shorten the material not a little, thus it becomes
possible to compress in a small volume that which, in roman character, would require a much greater one.]

I know of no bibliographers who have flat-out denied this notion and many
who have referred to it vaguely enough to suggest that it is considered common knowledge. But is this true?

To Sardini, the economy of gothic type can be proven by experiment,
the details of which are too tedious for him to enumerate.

Crederemmo d'abusare della compiacenza dei nostri Lettori, si ri-
portassemo estesamente con tutte le avvertenze, che somministra
l'arte un calcolo diligentissimo da noi fatto sopra alcune pagine del
libro jensoniano intitolato *Mamotrectus*, conteggiando quanto spazio
avrebbe occupato, se ora si volesse stampare in un carattere tondo,
che corrispondesse nella stessa grandezza d'occhio alle di lui lettere
gotiche. Facendo il confronto coi caratteri, che si fondono nella
stamperia Granducal di Firenze troviamo, che il Silvio, le di cui
madri vennero già d'Olanda, ha la misura richiesta, preso insieme
l'occhio e la spalla, e che prorterebbe presso a poco il doppio del
volume che bastò allora al nostro Editore. Ma la sola misura d'occhio
della lettera è pero d'un atomo minore nel carattere di Firenze, e
meglio corrisponderebbe quello del nostro Mamotrecto al Silvio di
Parma della officina Bodoniana, il quale circa un quattro per cento
di maggio agio vorrebbe nella carta, in confronto di quella che oc-
cupa l'indicato carattere fiorentino.[10]

[We think we would abuse the patience of our Readers, if we reported extensively on a most diligent calculation done by us over a few pages of a Jenson book entitled *Mammotrectus*, concerning how much space it would have occupied if he had wished to print it in a roman character that corresponded in its own *grandezza d'occio* (letter height) to the gothic letter. Making the comparison with characters that are cast in the Granducal press of Florence, we found that Silvio type, whose matrices once came from Holland, has the closest measure, both in height [*occio*] and in the shoulder [*spalla*], and that this would take double the volume our edition would require. But the letter height alone is perhaps a bit smaller in the Florence character, and the type of our *Mammotrectus* would better correspond to the Silvio of the Bodoni Press, which would take 4 percent more in the page than would the Florentine character.]

Occhio is a technical term, and refers to "letter height"—the height of a letter impressed on a page. *Spalla* is the "shoulder" of the actual typesort, its width or its height; the difference between the size of the letter and the size of the typesort seems to be the point Sardini is making at the end of this passage. For twentieth-century incunabulists, type-body height (that is, the height of the typesort, not the size of the letter on that sort) would translate into a 20-line measurement indicating how much vertical space twenty lines occupy. The measurement of the *Mammotrectus* is 72mm.[11]

A Less Exact Experiment

Sardini compares the Jenson gothic to the Silvio in two contemporary presses. Silvio is a roman typefont in late eighteenth-century Italy (see below), and since I had no chance of actually typesetting a book in this type, I decided to begin by repeating Sardini's experiments as best I could, using the modern, readily available fonts on my Mac.

I performed an idiotically simple test, adjusting the screen size on my computer until I produced a font with the correct a 20-line measurement of 72 mm, the same size used in Jenson's *Mammotrectus* (again, following the standard twentieth-century convention of measuring early types by height of typesort). I then transcribed a column of Jenson's book, expanding all abbreviations. The Jenson is in two columns. The text block is 139 x 89 mm (this does not include running head or signature). The width of each column is 41 mm. (The margins from the headings and signature marks are 55, 41, 10, and 14.) I thus set the column width at something roughly the column width in Jenson (41 mm). I counted the number of lines required to produce a column of the Jenson text.

With the Courier font adjusted on my screen at 72 mm/20 lines, I was close to Sardini's suggested figure. It took 62 lines to produce Jenson's 38 lines (the first few lines of the Jenson text are shorter due to a space left for a large initial; I did not take these differences into account). This is not double the space required by Jenson's gothic, but close. Word of course does not normally hyphenate unless set to do so; so I went through the lines performing some very, very amateurish typesetting, which consisted only of breaking words at convenient places. With very minor adjustments, I compressed Jenson's text into 56 lines (maybe a 10 percent gain). To set Jenson's *Mammotrectus* in a comparable Courier thus would require at least 50 percent more space.

But I generally print my own papers in Times New Roman, a somewhat more compressed font. So I hit "Select all" and changed the font, still keeping the basic 20-line measurement of 72 mm. I performed the same minor typesetting as I did with Courier; it took 39 lines to type the text printed by Jenson in 38 lines. In other words, I could set Jenson's *Mammotrectus* in a roman font with the identical 20-line measurement, expand all abbreviations (adding 15 percent to the text), and still come within a few percentage points of the space used in 1479 to print the text in gothic type. To set Jenson's *Mammotrectus* in Times New Roman requires no more space than to set it in Jenson's gothic.

These experiments are of course not exact, and hardly what could legitimately be called "a most diligent calculation." But they must be of the same intellectual order as those conducted by Sardini in 1798: I used what was for me the most readily available tool; I took the most readily available font; I transcribed the text; and that was that. Anyone can easily reproduce this experiment.

My conclusion is simple: gothic type is not more economical than roman type. Period. Those who claim otherwise are mistaken; either they are citing the wrong authorities, or perhaps they have performed a different kind of experiment.

Silvio Type

Sardini does not explain how he obtained his figures. Sardini was the "principal collaborator" for the director of the Tipografia Bonsignori of Lucca and could well have had the text physically set in a comparable roman typefont.[12] Or he might have calculated the space required through one of the methods outlined below. Or miscalculated it.

Sardini names Silvio type as the roman type comparable in size to Jenson's gothic. Silvio is both a roman typeface and a standard type size in late eighteenth-century Italy. In the Bodoni type-specimen catalogues of 1771, *Fregi e majuscole incise e fuse di Giambatista Bodoni* (Parma, 1771), it is one of six standard sizes of roman type; in the 1818 catalogue *Manuale tipografico del cavaliere Giambattista Bodoni* (Parma, 1818), it is one of more than a dozen. In the 1771 catalogue, Silvio type measures 102 mm for 20 lines; in the 1818 catalogue, the same type seems to measure about 104 mm for 20 lines. These are clearly much larger than the gothic of Jenson's *Mammotrectus*, which has a 20-line measurement of 72 mm. Perhaps Sardini means that the type face (*occhio*) is the same size, although it is hardly more than a tautology to say that a text set in a larger type body (regardless of face size) takes up more space than the same text set in a smaller one. If he had the Jenson text set in this larger type, this says nothing about the relative economy of gothic and roman.

Let us imagine how Sardini might have calculated the space required for typesetting without having the text set physically. Let us forget for a moment the discrepancies in 20-line measurements and consider the problem in terms of number of lines required to print the text. Measuring the Silvio type horizontally shows that each sort requires very roughly two millimeters of column width. In the 1771 catalogue, all lines typeset in Silvio are 46 mm in width, and Silvio has, in the printed lines, between 20 and 23 sorts (excluding spaces); in 1818, types are set in lines of 78 mm. Measuring these at 46 mm gives the same figures for all varieties of Silvio, 19–23 sorts for 46 mm of column width. Translating this into a meaningful relation to the Jenson type is not particularly difficult, although the results are hardly exact. In Jenson's *Mammotrectus*, the number of characters per 41 mm line (including spaces this time) ranges from 24 to 35 and the average is 30. Silvio would get about 20 sorts per 41mm line. Thus, on the face of it, Jenson's 72G gets 50 percent more letters per line than does the eighteenth-century Silvio.

This is getting close to Sardini's figure. If we further assume that all abbreviations are to be expanded if the text is set in roman, we can get even closer. Again, checking through the Jenson transcription, I find an average of 4.6 characters omitted due to abbreviations in each line. We must add that to the space required to set the text in Silvio. If Jenson's 72G requires X lines, then Silvio requires X multiplied by (1.5 x 1.15), that is "15 percent more than one-and-a-half-times" the number of lines required in Jenson. By this, I get the following: set in Bodoni's Silvio, with all abbreviations expanded, the *Mammotrectus* would take up 1.725 times as many lines as it does in Jenson, although the precision of the figure is of course illusory: "1.725" means only "more than half again as many."

I suppose this is close to Sardini's "double." One way to expand further the space required for the roman type would be to "un-type-set" it. That is, one could invoke a set of word-break restrictions that would apply to roman but not to gothic type. A few adjustments to the column width could, I think, produce a text requiring double the number of lines as those in Jenson. I can now imagine a process of reasoning that would produce Sardini's figures of "double," but the calculations are very rough. In addition, to produce my imagined (or even a real) "roman-*Mammotrectus*-requiring-double-the-space-as-a-gothic-one" in any of the variant procedures described above requires a basic violation of typographical norms: texts set in roman in the fifteenth century are not generally set as narrow, double-column texts. A conventional single-column block would reduce the space required to print the text, both by eliminating the white space column between the printed columns and by decreasing the number and difficulties of word breaks on which Sardini's larger figure must depend. Sardini's real or imagined "roman *Mammotrectus*," taking double the space of the real gothic one (or "double plus four percent"), would have looked like few other books of the time.

The above paragraphs represent one possible way of obtaining Sardini's figures using the eighteenth-century Silvio type he invokes. But any calculation based on Sardini's explicit assumption that the Jenson gothic is comparable to the Bodoni Silvio is seriously in error. These typefaces are not comparable. So wedded was Sardini to the notion of economy that he did not notice a fundamental mistake in his "most diligent calculation," whether that involved the physical setting of type or the counting of typesorts. Silvio is not at all "close in height and width" to the gothic type used in the *Mammotrectus*. It is much larger. Sardini had used as the basis for his calculations the wrong typefont.

Jenson has several gothic types. *BMC* now lists three.[13] Sardini speaks of two, both used in the *Decretals* of 1476 (*Esame* 3:43), one for text and one for notes. He measures them by how many lines are required per page: "il carattere gotico più grande pel testo, ed il più piccolo per le note, del quale entrano linee 68 per pagina, e 60 del maggiore" [the gothic character used for the text is larger; a smaller version is used in the notes, which uses 68 lines per page; the larger has 60 lines per page]. The smaller of these two types is the one used in the *Mammotrectus*. It is described by *BMC* as having a 20-line measurement of 74 mm. (In all my measurements on the Huntington Library copy of *Mammotrectus*, I came up with a 20-line measurement of 72 mm for this type.)[14] What Sardini calls Jenson's larger gothic has a 20-line measurement of 104 mm (*BMC*'s 104G). That is nearly exactly the 20-line measurement of the Silvio typefont in the Officina Bodoni. The coincidence is too great: Sardini somehow chose the wrong gothic font with which to conduct his experiments. Sardini should have noticed this, but it is understandable that his later readers might not. Since the word "Silvio" is not a standard term in typographical histories or in typographical manuals of the following century, there would be no particular reason for a French or English commentator to question what Sardini says: to them, even if they had the *Mammotrectus* in front of them, there would be no reason to doubt Sardini's assertion that the Italian "Silvio" was close in size to the small gothic type Jenson used in the *Mammotrectus*.

Mammotrectus is a small book, and Sardini was impressed by that, as his discussion in his chapter shows. Looking at the page (Figure 13) certainly suggests that a large amount of text was compressed onto a very small page. Why wouldn't he accept the "diligent calculations" that provided mathematical support for this observation? Gothic takes up less space than roman? Perhaps even "double plus four percent"?[15]

All these methods, my own and my own imagining of Sardini's method, are very rough ways to proceed, and the results one gets will depend to some extent on the results one wants. I found myself torn between two opposing biases as I was checking and reimagining Sardini's calculations. On the one hand, I wanted to show that the choice between roman and gothic is not one of economy, and I am likely to have made decisions affecting this experiment accordingly. For example, when I began my amateurish typesetting of the text, I started with Courier, and switched to a font I knew from experience to be more compressed; this supported the conclusion that roman and gothic were comparable. On the other hand, I also wanted to reconstruct Sardini's thinking on this; and to come up with his "double" figure, I doubtless ad-

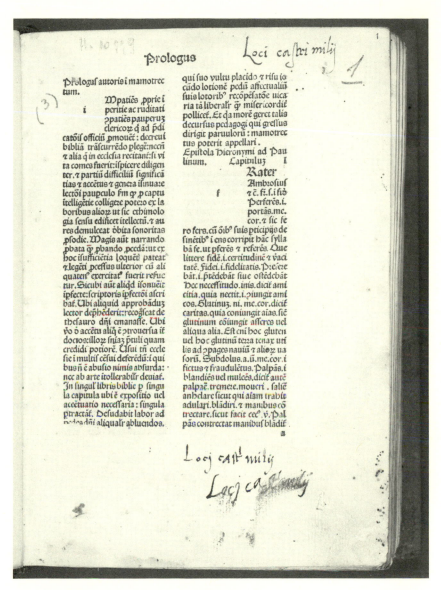

Figure 13. *Mammotrectus super Bibliam* (Venice: Jenson, 1479) Goff M239. Courtesy of the Henry E. Huntington Library, San Marino, California.

justed my measurements, my imagined typesetting conventions, and even my
representation of the basic problem.

None of this has the status of exact science or diligent calculation, contrary to what Sardini says. And it could not have been an exact science to
Jenson, who had the advantage over both of us by virtue of having the typecases in front of him. If Jenson had been concerned with economy of space,
he could have very easily found out which typeface, gothic or roman, would
accomplish that. I don't know how much gothic might save, perhaps between
0 and 20 percent.[16] Would such a saving have been worthwhile? particularly
if it violated his imagined preference for roman? A single glance at the *Mammotrectus* in Figure 13 shows that far more space than that could have been
saved simply by adjusting the very ample margins.

It is thus absolutely incorrect to state that Jenson chose gothic over
roman for reasons of economy of space.

The Persistence of Error

Sardini's experiments, whatever they were, worked because he wanted them
to work. Before he began mentally or materially typesetting the *Mammotrectus*, he "knew" he had found the reason for Jenson's choice of gothic (something earlier scholars had not discovered). So he chose the Bodoni roman
font that would prove it, one that was comparable not to the Jenson font in
question, but to a much larger Jenson font. He had no reason to check these
results, nor to discover his error, since the result was the one he wanted,
perhaps an even better result than he had imagined. And there was no reason
for anyone else to check these results, since they accorded with and provided
scientific support for the myth of humanism's relation to typefaces.

Maittaire and Laire both criticized Jenson and excused him: Maittaire
reasonably enough on the basis of the desires of Jenson's readers, Laire by
claiming that printers other than Jenson could be tarred with the accusation
of introducing gothic to Italy. Sardini's Jenson is different: he is not simply
acquiescing to public taste, but rather serving the economic interests of his
readers by providing cheaper texts (just as Aldus, according to a standard
typographical myth also at variance with facts, would do a few decades
later).[17]

Sardini's argument (or versions of it) became an accepted tenet regarding
gothic and roman type. Brown, in 1891, cites Aug. Ant. Renouard in support

of this theory of economy, without giving a page or source reference. I assume he is referring to Renouard's *Annales de l'imprimerie des Alde, ou Histoire des trois Manuce et de leurs éditions* (3rd. ed. Paris: Renouard, 1834). Renouard's general notions are expressed on p. 378, at the beginning of his "Vie d'Alde ancien":

> Les imprimeurs ses confrères, soit de Venise, soit des autres villes, entraînés par le goût du siècle, ou sacrifiant à diverses convenances, sourtout d'intérêt, n'imprimoient presque que des ouvrages de scolastique, des livres mystiques ou de jurisprudence, et fort peu de bons ouvrages de littérature ou d'ancienne philosophie. Il étoit réservé d'Alde de changer la direction des idées, de donner une impulsion nouvelle à l'Imprimerie, qui dès-lors reproduisit dans toute l'Europe beaucoup mois de ce fatras scolastique.

> [His contemporary printers, whether at Venice or other cities, constrained by the taste of the era or sacrificing to diverse conveniences, especially of material interest, printed almost nothing but scholastic works, mystical books or lawbooks, and very few good works of literature or of ancient philosophy. It was reserved to Aldus to change the direction of these ideas, and to give a new impulse to printing, which until then reproduced in all of Europe little more than scholastic nonsense.]

Aldus's contemporaries compromised themselves; the only reason to print works of scholasticism, law, and "mysticism" was economic; Aldus changed the entire direction of European printing by reducing the amount of this "scholastic fatrasie." Renouard cross-references his own page 283 here, and I believe this is the path followed by Brown. This page is in the bibliographical section and contains the entry for Andreas Torresano's 1482 *Compilatio decretalium Gregorii IX*:

> Ce sont donc les lecteurs, les acheteurs de livres qui ont en quelque sorte contraint les Imprimeurs d'abandonner presque complètement leurs belles lettres romaines et d'employer le gothique, afin d'entasser dans des noires pages une plus grande quantité de matière.

> [These are then the readers, the buyers of books who had in some manner constrained printers to abandon almost completely their

beautiful roman typefaces and to use gothic, in order to squeeze into
their black pages a greater quantity of matter.]

The same notion is expressed. The Aldus family is portrayed as held back
and "constrained" by their customers; they use gothic only to fill their black
pages with more material (a variant of Maittaire's "in atram Gothicum crassi-
tudinum"). This is a casual note for which no reference or support is given.
If the assertion were a serious one, the logic would be strained. Pages set in
gothic are "black" not because "more matter" is included in them (as Renouard states here), but rather because more ink is required to print a gothic
letter than a roman one.

It is this ideology, sanctioned now by the undefined but detailed experiments of Sardini and the authority of Renouard, that reaches Brown, who
does no more than recycle these sources. Again, all the details are reasonable:
gothic type is a bad thing; yet it is familiar to readers less sophisticated than
Jenson or Torresano; it has a black crassness; there are economic considerations—economies of price, economies of space. Humanism is on the rise.
What were Jenson and Torresano to do?

The mythology shared by Sardini, Renouard, and Brown involves many
clichés regarding Renaissance humanism. In this mythology, Jenson could
circumvent one cultural virtue (the superiority of roman type to gothic) by
privileging another (scientific calculations of cost). Even aesthetics contri-
butes to this: Jenson's gothic type must be beautiful or readers would be
turned away before appreciating its economic virtues (Sardini, *Esame*, 2:56).
But this myth is fantastic. What Jenson did was the more pedestrian act of
printing a book in the visual genre of that book. Why would his buyers have
wanted a text in roman type that they were used to reading in gothic?

Conclusion

In 1991, Martin Lowry examined the reputation of Jenson from an historical
point of view. Lowry claims he began expecting "to evaluate the reputation
of a cult-figure." His view of this reputation changed: "gradually, I came to
understand that my real task was to explain why a cult existed when there
was no figure behind it."[18]

What Lowry meant by "no figure" was that there was no historical figure, Jenson's own life being little documented by anything other than com-

ments in his will. The Jenson of cult, however, was never this historical figure; the cult-figure Jenson is the Jenson represented by books, or, as Lowry argues, by "books said to be by Jenson." More narrowly, the cult depended on the typography of Jenson.[19] Because Lowry's focus was on the historical figure of Jenson, the aspects divorced from that (abstractions of aesthetics, for example) necessarily seemed mythic. Given Lowry's purposes, it was enough to cite this narrative, without subjecting any of it to critique.

In sharp contrast to Lowry's examination of the mythology surrounding Jenson are the comments by Febvre and Martin in 1956, where the Rise of Humanism mythology is very much alive. I quote the often reprinted and increasingly popular English version:

> Thus when printing first appeared certain small groups, lovers of belles lettres (let us not say humanists), appreciated and knew how to read the new script, but of course the vast majority at that time were faithful to the traditional gothic. . . .
> The distinctive story of roman was a triumph of the humanist spirit, the story of a victory which deserves telling. (*Coming of the Book*, 8, 30)[20]

I have critiqued elsewhere Febvre and Martin's careless and superficial understanding of typefaces. Here it is enough to note the ruling ideas in their notion of typefaces. Their ironic qualifications of the term "humanist" do less to put the term into question than to relieve Febvre and Martin of the inconvenient task of justifying it. Febvre and Martin derided earlier bibliographical scholarship, the "hoary old arguments" concerning the origins of printing (9); and although they praise "historians and specialists" such as Ludwig Hain, Konrad Haebler, and Robert Proctor, they dismiss entirely "problems of attribution" or questions of "the paternity of printing and its improvement" (45). Since Hain and Proctor (and even Haebler in his 5-volume *Typenrepertorium*) were entirely concerned with such "problems of attribution," it is difficult to construct in any coherent fashion what Febvre and Martin imagine they mean here. Without the lists of books in such enumerative bibliographies, especially those organized by town or printer (for example, Panzer's 1793 *Annales typographici*, cited with enthusiasm by Sardini, or Robert Proctor's British Library catalogue),[21] the paradoxes that troubled earlier bibliographers disappear. Without them, there is no inconvenient evidence to contradict bibliographical mythology, and even the heroic and miscalculated diligences of Sardini are no longer needed.

CHAPTER FOUR

҈

The Typographical Gothic: A Cautionary Note on the Title Page to Percy's *Reliques of Ancient English Poetry*

With Svetlana Djananova

In Chapter 3, I dealt with a persistent myth concerning gothic type and the way the bibliographical evidence seems to be subordinate to particular bibliographical myths. The following chapter considers the term used to describe this type, and how the mythology surrounding that term influences what should be a straightforward history of classes of type.

The "rise of the Gothic" in the late eighteenth century is a truism that would seem to require less in the way of support than mere corroboration. While we may not know precisely what "the gothic" or "the Gothic" is, any more than we might know precisely what we mean by "the sublime," we also know that the lack of precision in such terms is not the same as their invalidation. Furthermore, we know that our use of this term is not entirely arbitrary, since we find that word used in the texts of the late eighteenth century we consider central to literary study: Richard Hurd's *Letters on Chivalry and Romance* (1762) and Thomas Warton's *History of English Literature* (1777–81).

The definitions of "the gothic" or "the Gothic" are various and it is not the purpose here to offer a new one, nor to critique those that already exist. Rather, we will consider how material bibliographical evidence is deployed in support of these terms, and whether it is possible, or advisable, to raise to the level of a text's meaning those bibliographical and material features of the book (its format, layout, and typography) that until the late twentieth century were generally considered extratextual.[1]

Our example is a canonical one: Thomas Percy's *Reliques of Ancient English Poetry*, 3 vols. (London, 1765). Obviously, this book must be central to discussions of the gothic in England, but how to define the centrality of this book, and how to define the book itself, is not entirely obvious. Are we simply to say that whatever features this book possesses came to be (or were) gothic? Or can we say that the features that are clearly not gothic in any meaningful way must be seen as in dialectic with those that are (or must be)? There is not any clear way of articulating this question, and it is part of our contention that the way the question is asked will determine to a large extent any conclusions that could be drawn.

Percy's *Reliques* went through numerous printings in the eighteenth century; copies were and still are readily available.[2] The first edition is a small, three-volume octavo; it is in format and in its frontispiece identical to the second edition of 1767 (the second edition is essentially a resetting). Although the text and its various problems have been much discussed in scholarship, the late twentieth century brought a new aspect of the book into discussion: since the book's *texts* are central to discussion, so potentially is what might be called its bibliographical form (typography, layout, and design). A seemingly casual remark by Nick Groom and its more elaborate rebuttal by Christine Baatz pose the central problem we look at here. To Groom, the book's typography is Gothic, pure and simple: "Percy's title pages were Gothic in their very profusion of typefaces and rambling lines." Christine Baatz, looking in large part at the collection of title pages published by Nicolas Barker, notes that the Percy title page also contains features that are describable as "classical"; therefore, "In the *Reliques* a sophisticated typographical programme is used to achieve a twofold aim: first, to claim 'classical' quality for the texts presented . . . second, to stress the texts' different, indigenous, 'Gothic' nature."[3]

The implied dispute between Groom and Baatz concerns only the extent to which the gothic exists and how it is used in Percy's title page, the facing frontispiece, and the typography of the text pages; they do not consider the more fundamental question of whether the gothic can be found or should be sought in these features, nor what it means to assume that such a thing as the gothic is there at all (see Figures 14 and 15). As long as the material (and typographical) nature of this book is deployed within some *grand récit* of

Figure 14. Thomas Percy, *Reliques of Early English Poetry* (London, 1765), frontispiece. Courtesy of the Henry E. Huntington Library, San Marino, California.

RELIQUES

OF

ANCIENT ENGLISH POETRY:

CONSISTING OF

Old Heroic BALLADS, SONGS, and other
PIECES of our earlier POETS,

(Chiefly of the LYRIC kind.)

Together with some few of later Date.

VOLUME THE FIRST.

DURAT OPUS VATUM

LONDON:
Printed for J. DODSLEY in Pall-Mall.
M DCC LXV.

Figure 15. Percy, *Reliques*, title page. Courtesy of the Henry E. Huntington Library,
San Marino, California.

literary history (for example, "the rise of the Gothic"), these claims seem reasonable. Percy's *Reliques* (as a literary textual entity) is certainly a legitimate part of this narrative (something we do not deny); therefore, it must be part of this narrative bibliographically (that is, in its material and typographical aspect). But if the material and typographical aspects of any book provide evidence for a literary-historical narrative, they must be described not simply in the context of that literary-historical narrative (something that begs the question); rather they must be described in contexts independent of that narrative: for example, the history of title pages, type, format, etc. What, in these contexts, is so gothic about this undoubtedly gothic book? Or what, minimally, are the specific features of this book that distinguish it from those specific features of other books that are conventionally non-gothic?

Title Pages

We begin with Macpherson's *Fingal*, in its first edition of 1762, a work included in many eighteenth-century discussions of the gothic.[4] This selection is to some extent mischievous. Macpherson, on the title page, uses terms that might be properly classified as "classical": "an ancient epic poem" (Figure 16). Furthermore, it is a book that has been seen as in dialectic with Percy's *Reliques*, Macpherson's "Celtic" vying with Percy's "gothic" in a mythological search for poetic origins.[5] Its large quarto format also distinguishes it from the octavo and duodecimo books we will describe later, although how we describe such a format depends in part on the conclusions we want.[6]

The engraving is designed by Samuel Wale, the same artist who designed the frontispiece in Percy's *Reliques*.[7] This engraving shows a Homerically blind bard in flowing classical robes (he also has what must be intended as Homer's haircut and beard). He is sitting under a tree at what might be a tomb, gesticulating wildly; his harp seems to be hanging on the tree, or perhaps it is merely hovering allegorically. The landscape is wild and uncultivated (perhaps sublime?): there are steep rocky crags and a blasted tree in the background; some tufts of grass and a brook in the foreground. Clouds cover the sky; a storm may be brewing (depending on the darkness of the engraving, something as much related to printing state as to artistic intent). A brooding female figure in *contraposto* (a muse?) stands to the right of the bard; to his left, figures descend on clouds (the forefathers?). A Latin motto

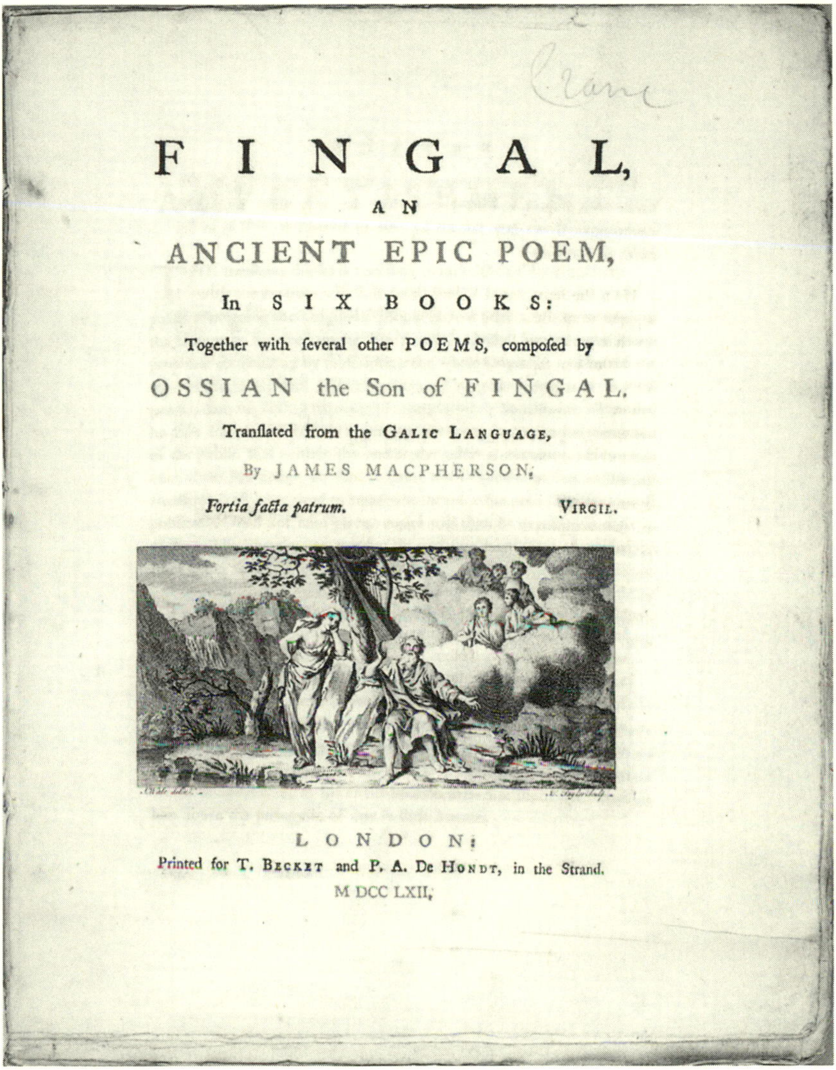

F I N G A L,

AN

ANCIENT EPIC POEM,

In SIX BOOKS:

Together with several other POEMS, composed by

OSSIAN the Son of FINGAL.

Tranflated from the GALIC LANGUAGE,

By JAMES MACPHERSON.

Fortia facta patrum.   VIRGIL.

LONDON:

Printed for T. BECKET and P. A. De HONDT, in the Strand.

M DCC LXII.

Figure 16. James Macpherson, *Fingal* (London, 1762), title page. Courtesy of the Henry E. Huntington Library, San Marino, California.

from Virgil appears above the picture (*fortia facta patrum*—"the brave deeds
of the fathers"—referring to heroes depicted in the clouds?).

Many elements in this engraving are familiar from classical iconography:
the muse, the classical robes, and so on. If we were forced to describe its
gothic elements, we might refer to such details as the "darkness visible" on
the borders, the wind-blown tree, the sublime cliffs, the gesticulating bard.[8]
But without the specific program of the artist, it is difficult to say which of
these are in and of themselves gothic. We know what this engraving means,
and we know how to classify and interpret specific elements in it, because we
are given direction in the words printed on the same page.

The frontispiece in Percy is also by Wale, and many of the same elements
occur (Figure 14). We have a classical motto (*non omnis moriar*, from Horace,
Carmina, 3, 30). Macpherson's bard is in the wilderness, while Percy's seems
more rooted in the medieval world. There is a gothic spire in the background,
a knight in armor in the foreground; the characters, as well as the bard himself? are dressed in pseudo-medieval (actually Tudor?) costumes.[9] The sky
again is peopled here by *putti* of some kind (signifying whatever it is *putti*
signify). The bard's harp is similar to that in *Fingal*. The vignette in the
facing title page has many of these elements: the gothic arch, the harp (seemingly identical to the one Wale designed for *Fingal*), the blasted tree, and a
Latin motto, *durat opus vatum*.

These engravings contain specific motifs that doubtless are associated
with gothic, and there are certain iconographic features (the gothic spire in
Percy, and some of the costuming in Percy) that could even distinguish
"gothic" from "Celtic." These are what might be called emblematic or lexico-
graphic elements of the iconography (that is, a gothic spire cannot refer to a
druidic monument). But to what extent can the gothic be signified beyond
such specific motifs? Does it extend to matters of style and typography? Or
are the definitions that would include such elements as necessarily gothic too
broad and voracious to be of much use?

Let us look at a contemporary frontispiece, this one from a tradition that
opposes whatever it is we call gothic and doubtless whatever variant of that
we see in Macpherson as well: the 1747 edition of Pope's "Essay on Man"
(Figure 17). This page is referred to specifically by Baatz (although not reproduced) and is discussed as an example of the classical as incorporated in
Reliques (Baatz, 111). But the actual details are not as securely classical as
might be supposed: the ruins, the blasted tree, the solitary bard-like figure,
the Latin mottos, light, dark, the fragments of broken architecture with their

ironic Latin mottos showing the transience of physical monuments (*Roma aeterna*), a skull, a cobweb. Again, there are certain lexical elements of the iconography here (Roman classical ruins as opposed to medieval gothic ones). But all the remaining elements would be quite at home in any context assumed to be gothic (for example, in a collection of poems described as gothic). In fact, even the ruined classical architecture could easily be defined as suggestive of some gothic attack on the classical.

The above considerations deal with iconographic matters, and suggest that even the most seemingly secure elements of the gothic or the classical are context dependent. As we move further away from what might be called lexical features (words and specific iconographic details), the importance of these contexts is even greater; and when we are dealing with typographical and bibliographical elements, these contexts are themselves much more difficult to define. A particular book may have an identifiable format, layout, and typography; but we cannot classify or interpret such things in and of themselves. Note that the language of Groom and Baatz identifying presumably gothic features of the type and format of these books is very abstract: "profusion of typefaces" (Groom, *Making of Percy's Reliques*, 202); "flamboyant Medieval exoticism" (Groom, "Formation of Percy's *Reliques*," 33); "flowery, even cluttered . . .," "rambling lines," "intriguing tension [between] title and subtitle" (Baatz, 111). Baatz even concedes that the argument distinguishing classical from gothic is no more than one of "general impression": here, describing specifically the relation of the Pope and Percy title pages: "while the minutiae of the style introduced by Pope and Tonson are successfully applied [in Percy], the general impression of the title-page is nevertheless not one of 'classical simplicity'" (111).

Such general impressions are not necessarily invalid, but they do depend on contexts. And how we identify and classify the stylistic features we find in the title pages shown here depends not on the title page alone, but rather on what group of title pages we choose as a comparison and how we arrange them. Should we choose only contemporary works? Do we arrange them in chronological succession? Or is any such selection arbitrary and its coherence a specious one, since eighteenth-century readers might well have placed their new books (a new copy of Percy's *Reliques*) in whatever context happened to be on their shelves (an indifferent assortment of variously bound seventeenth- and eighteenth-century books)?

Barker's article, the basis of Baatz's discussion, reproduces dozens of title pages from the period. Anyone looking at these can easily classify them,

Figure 17. Alexander Pope, *Essay on Man* (London, 1744), frontispiece. Courtesy of the Henry E. Huntington Library, San Marino, California.

recovering the unstated categories that seem to be used by Barker himself: relative date, country, and very occasionally a broad genre (a Bible or a legal text might look different from a literary one). Yet when it comes to content, there is almost no information of any kind on these pages beyond the specific words printed on them. We know what these texts are about, or like, by virtue of what is said specifically in their titles and subtitles.

Other selections yield similar results. Figures 18–20 show the title pages of the following: *Wit and Mirth or Pills to Purge Melancholy, being a Collection of the Best Merry Ballads and Songs, Old and New . . .* 5th ed. (London, 1719); *A Collection of Old Ballads . . .* (London, 1723); *The Tea-Table Miscellany: or, a Collection of Choice Songs, Scots and English . . .* 11th ed. (London, 1750). These are roughly the same genre, and all texts (although not these particular editions) are cited specifically by Percy.[10] We might describe any of the images in this series with the words used by Groom and Baatz: the profusion of typefaces, the rambling lines. But of course, these typefaces and line structures have nothing to do with the accidental content of these books. They are simply typical of title pages of their time, and one can date these pages because they have all the features associated with such dates: the loss of the double rule, the increase in the size of margins, etc. These are the same features noted by Barker and by Baatz, with reference to Barker. And the series here could easily be inserted in Barker's own chronological series.[11] When one goes beyond the eighteenth century, employing hindsight unavailable to eighteenth-century readers or printers, the same principles apply. Scott's ballad collection, *Minstrelsy of the Scottish Border* (1802 and later editions) is modeled on Percy's *Reliques*, but again, its title page (Figure 21) reveals itself typographically as a product of its date, not its genre.

Imagining the appropriate context in which to judge the specifics of any particular title page and frontispiece is not easy. We have suggested several series here—books cited by Groom in this context, books cited by Barker. But others can be easily imagined: all the eighteenth-century English books on our personal bookshelves, many in late editions (Macpherson, the *Tatler*, the *Spectator*, Milton, Chaucer, Sterne, Dryden); the title pages presented in such standard collections as *Printing and the Mind of Man*, *Art of the Printed Book, 1455–1955* or Johnson's *One Hundred Title Pages*.[12] These contexts yield the same results: the title pages and frontispieces sketch out the standard developments in English and European typography. Their appearance is unrelated to content. For the meaning of these features, we might turn to iconographic details (for example, a lone bard); but even here, the meaning of this

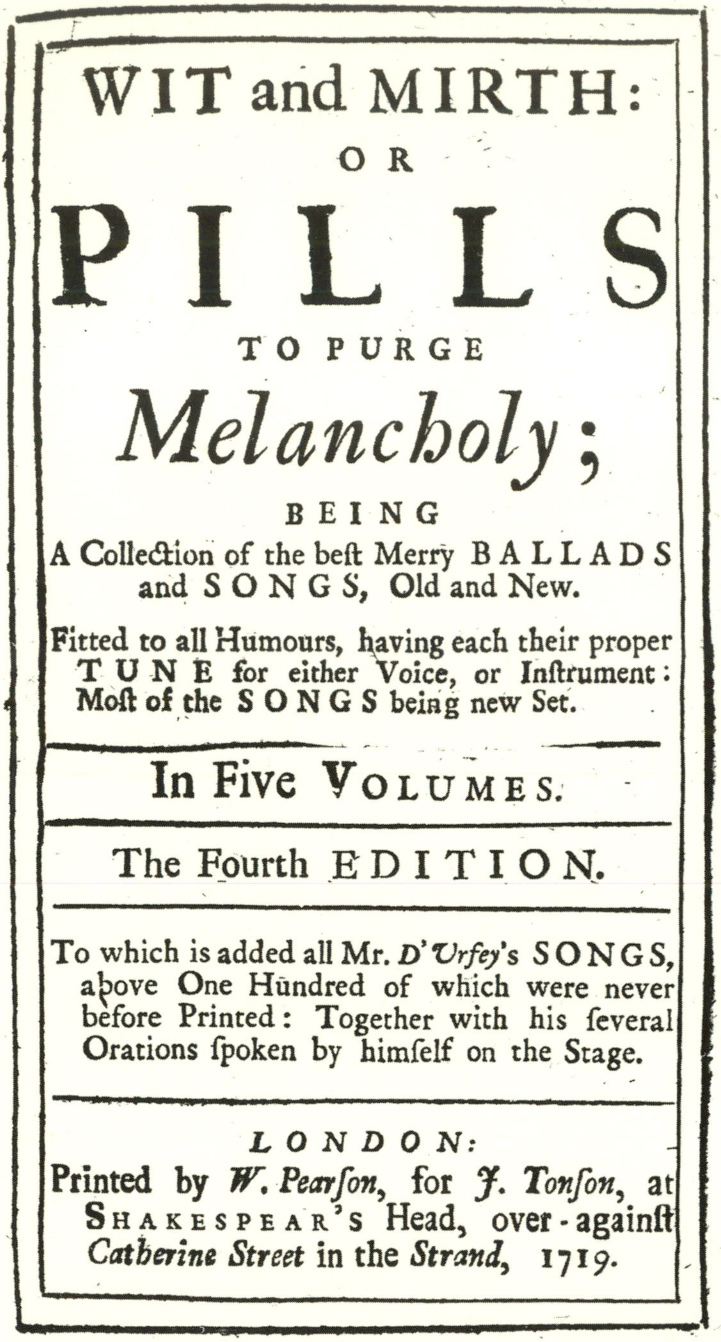

WIT and MIRTH:

OR

PILLS

TO PURGE

Melancholy;

BEING

A Collection of the best Merry B A L L A D S
and S O N G S, Old and New.

Fitted to all Humours, having each their proper
T U N E for either Voice, or Instrument:
Most of the S O N G S being new Set.

In Five VOLUMES.

The Fourth EDITION.

To which is added all Mr. *D'Urfey*'s S O N G S,
above One Hundred of which were never
before Printed: Together with his several
Orations spoken by himself on the Stage.

L O N D O N:

Printed by *W. Pearson*, for *J. Tonson*, at
S HAKESPEAR'S Head, over-against
Catherine Street in the *Strand*, 1719.

Figure 18. *Wit and Mirth* (London, 1719), title page. Courtesy of the William
Andrews Clark Memorial Library, University of California, Los Angeles.

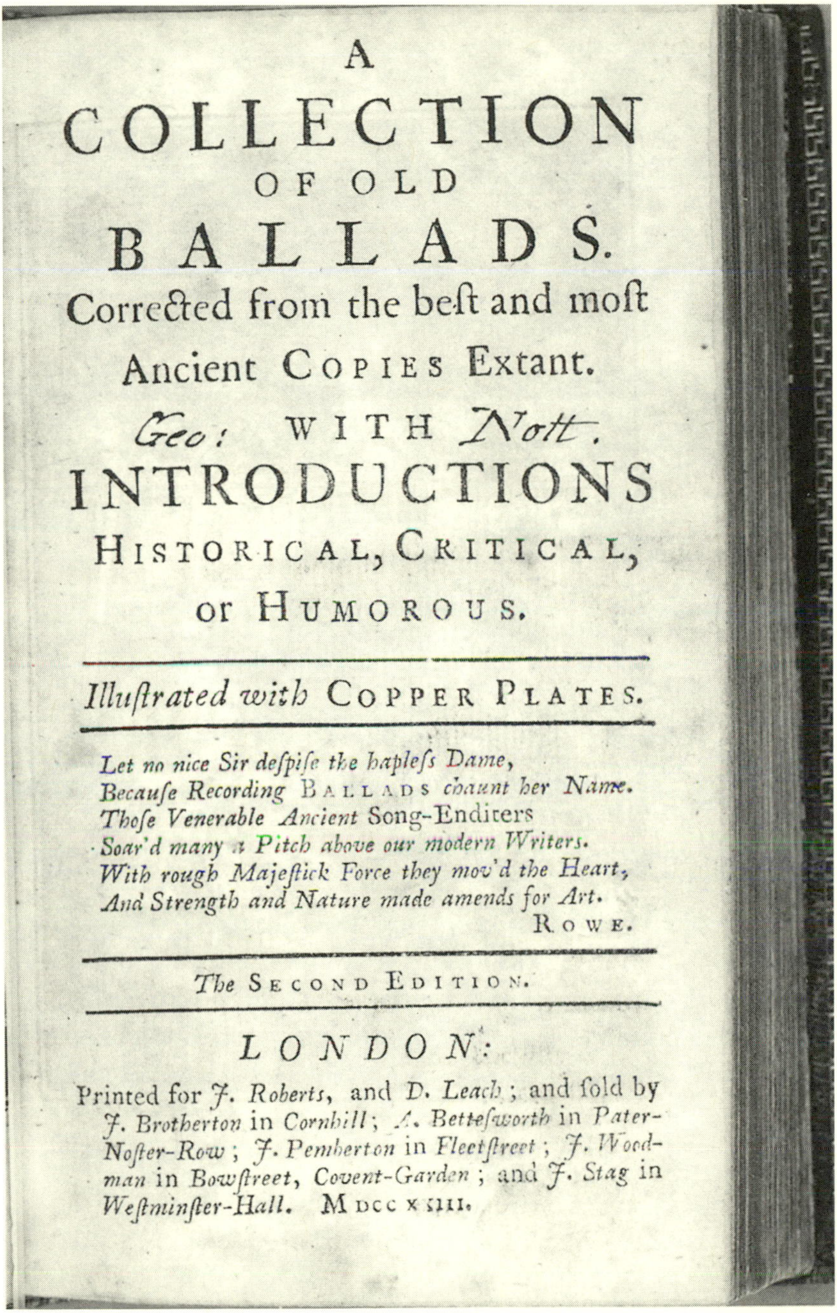

A COLLECTION
OF OLD
BALLADS.

Corrected from the beſt and moſt
Ancient COPIES Extant.

Geo: WITH *Nott.*

INTRODUCTIONS
HISTORICAL, CRITICAL,
or HUMOROUS.

Illuſtrated with COPPER PLATES.

Let no nice Sir deſpiſe the hapleſs Dame,
Becauſe Recording BALLADS *chaunt her Name.*
Thoſe Venerable Ancient Song-Enditers
Soar'd many a Pitch above our modern Writers.
With rough Majeſtick Force they mov'd the Heart,
And Strength and Nature made amends for Art.
R O W E.

The SECOND EDITION.

LONDON:

Printed for *J. Roberts,* and *D. Leach* ; and ſold by
J. Brotherton in *Cornhill* ; *A. Betteſworth* in *Pater-*
Noſter-Row ; *J. Pemberton* in *Fleetſtreet* ; *J. Wood-*
man in *Bowſtreet, Covent-Garden* ; and *J. Stag* in
Weſtminſter-Hall. M DCC XXIII.

Figure 19. *A Collection of Old Ballads* (London, 1723), title page. Courtesy of the Henry E. Huntington Library, San Marino, California.

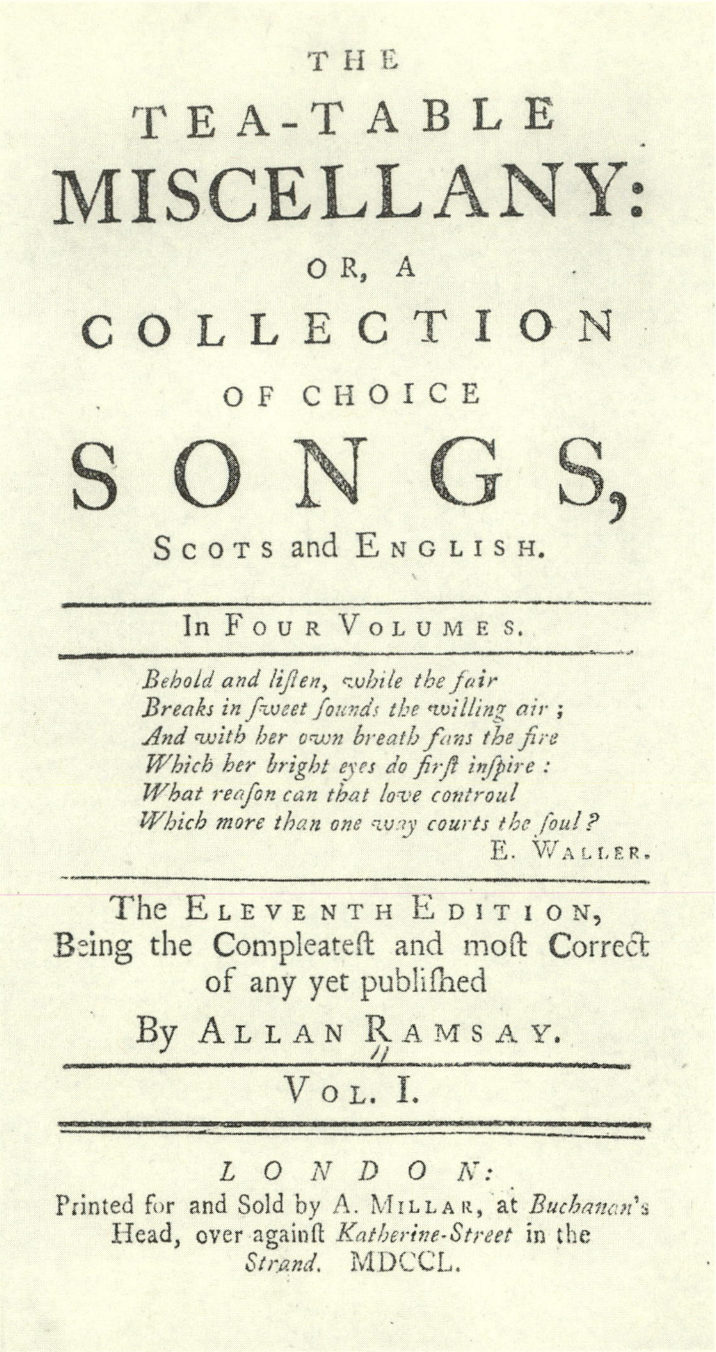

THE

TEA-TABLE

MISCELLANY:

OR, A

COLLECTION

OF CHOICE

SONGS,

SCOTS and ENGLISH.

In FOUR VOLUMES.

Behold and listen, while the fair
Breaks in sweet sounds the willing air ;
And with her own breath fans the fire
Which her bright eyes do first inspire :
What reason can that love controul
Which more than one way courts the soul?
E. WALLER.

The ELEVENTH EDITION,
Being the Compleatest and most Correct
of any yet published

By ALLAN RAMSAY.

VOL. I.

LONDON:
Printed for and Sold by A. MILLAR, at *Buchanan's*
Head, over against *Katherine-Street* in the
Strand. MDCCL.

Figure 20. *The Tea-Table Miscellany* (London, 1750), title page. Courtesy of the
William Andrews Clark Memorial Library, University of California, Los Angeles.

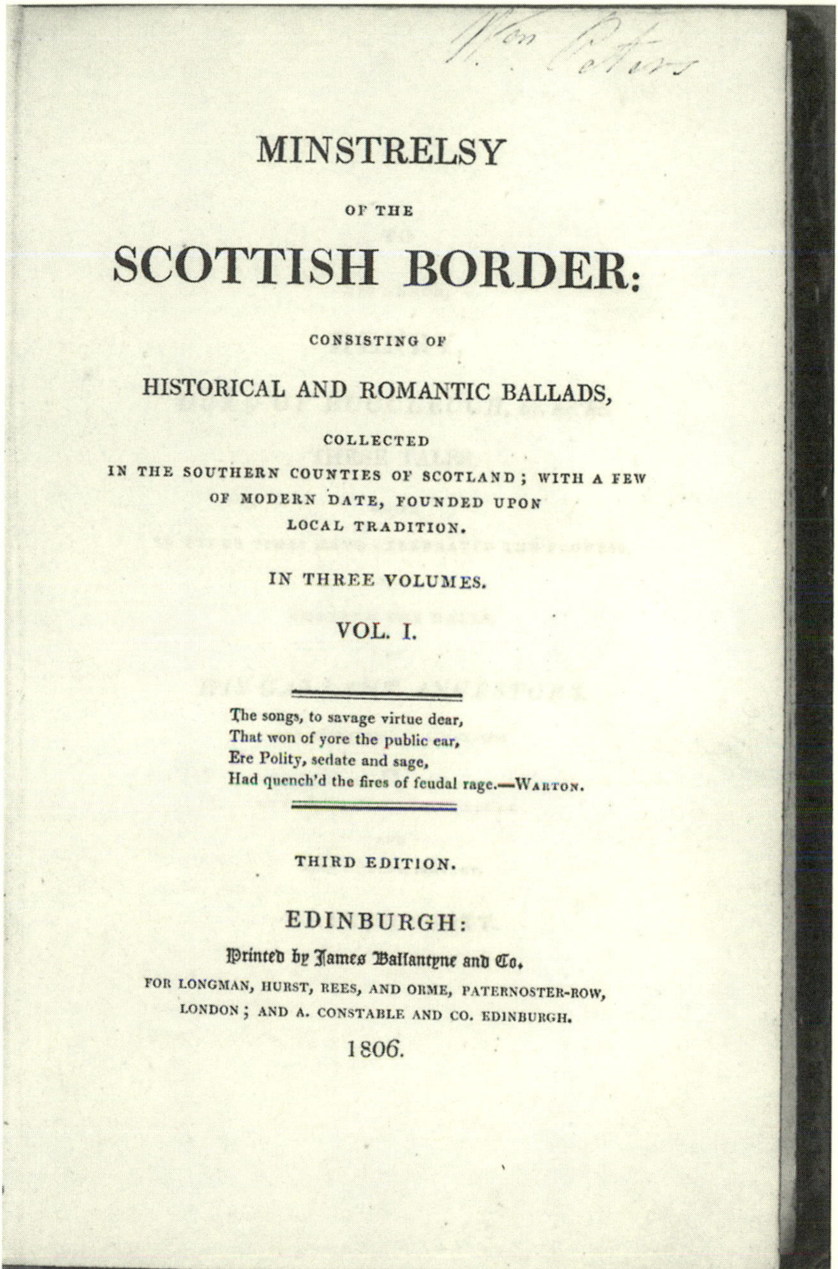

MINSTRELSY

OF THE

SCOTTISH BORDER:

CONSISTING OF

HISTORICAL AND ROMANTIC BALLADS,

COLLECTED

IN THE SOUTHERN COUNTIES OF SCOTLAND; WITH A FEW
OF MODERN DATE, FOUNDED UPON
LOCAL TRADITION.

IN THREE VOLUMES.

VOL. I.

The songs, to savage virtue dear,
That won of yore the public ear,
Ere Polity, sedate and sage,
Had quench'd the fires of feudal rage.—WARTON.

THIRD EDITION.

EDINBURGH:
Printed by James Ballantyne and Co.
FOR LONGMAN, HURST, REES, AND ORME, PATERNOSTER-ROW,
LONDON; AND A. CONSTABLE AND CO. EDINBURGH.

1806.

Figure 21. Walter Scott, *Minstrelsy of the Scottish Border* (3rd ed., Edinburgh, 1806) title page. Courtesy of the Henry E. Huntington Library, San Marino, California.

image is determined not by a visual detail (the robes) but by the words on the page itself.

A final mischievous example that is found in many of the contexts we considered is the 1762 edition of Horace printed by Baskerville (1762 edition in octavo; 1770 edition in large quarto) (Figure 22). This title page is often reproduced, for example, in Barker's collection and in Johnson's *One Hundred Title Pages*. The vignette is by Wale, the same engraver who designed the vignette in *Fingal* and the frontispiece in *Reliques*. The motto, *monumentum aere perennius*, is from the same Horace ode that provides the motto for the *Reliques* frontispiece (*Odes* 3, 30). This page was much admired by William Shenstone and discussed extensively in his correspondence with Percy—correspondence which is in turn the basis of much of the discussion by Groom.[13] The page is simpler in appearance than the title page of *Reliques*, and the type (at least to us) is recognizably that of Baskerville. But we would be hard pressed to find more classicism here than that. Why are the small capitals in Percy a "profusion of typefaces," but the italics and small capitals of Baskerville something else? As for the simplicity of the title page, is that a matter of meaning? genre? or simple convenience? No one needs to be told on a title page what an edition of Horace contains. But until Percy's *Reliques* became as well known as these Latin classics, potential readers would need some explanatory subtitle, just as they would for something entitled *Pills to Cure Melancholy* (ballad collection? or medicinal manual?).

When we look at Percy's title page in such contexts as this, neither its "Gothicism" nor its "classicism" is very secure. One can find such elements and their implied opposition only by a *petitio principii*. That is, *since* the opposition gothic/classical is fundamental to the late eighteenth century, *therefore* it finds an example here.[14]

Typographical Elements

A final element of these pages is the typography itself, and there are certainly major changes in eighteenth-century typography that could be mapped onto other cultural changes—the decline in the use of blackletter fonts, the creation of what is now called "new style" typeface. But do these changes in eighteenth-century typographical styles and conventions and even the contemporary language used to describe that (the *grand récit* of typography) support that other *grand récit* of literature (the rise of the gothic)?

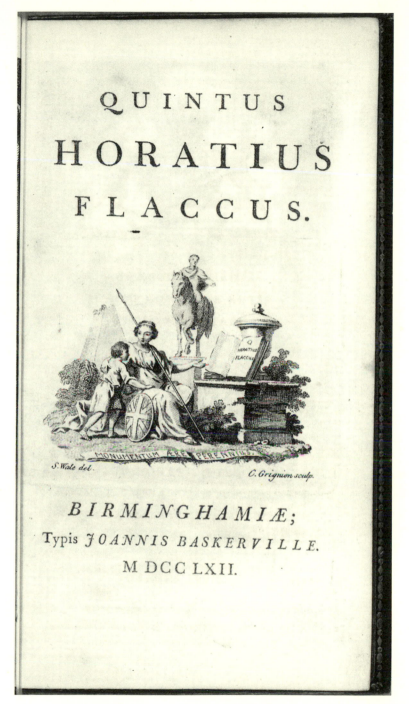

Figure 22. Horace (Birmingham: Baskerville, 1762), title page. Courtesy of the Henry E. Huntington Library, San Marino, California.

One of the fundamental categories or classes of type is known as "gothic," and by this, many scholars mean that type commonly called in English "blackletter." It seems reasonable, given this terminology, that Baatz invokes this feature of Percy's title page in this context. If a book or title page is to have gothic (or non-gothic) elements manifested in its typeface, surely the presence or absence of what is commonly called "gothic type" is significant (Baatz, 115). Barker himself cites in passing Young's *Night Thoughts* in its editions of 1743 and 1760 where a single line of blackletter is used in the title, and the presence of that typeface may be significant.[15] But is the absence of blackletter equally significant?

There is no question that the opposition between blackletter and roman was real, was perceived to be significant, and was subject to rules of decorum familiar in much eighteenth-century aesthetics. And in the seventeenth century, some printers followed a clear convention of printing medieval English in blackletter, as opposed to modern English, which was printed in roman (see the 1602 Chaucer shown in my Introduction, Figure 4).[16] But for eighteenth-century printers, these common distinctions do not apply in ordinary texts. The opposition blackletter/roman, which functioned coherently for a seventeenth-century English reader, had become obsolete, and blackletter was confined to legal texts, some religious texts, and antiquarian documents.[17] In ordinary eighteenth-century English printing, roman is not "non-Gothic" as it had been a century earlier; it is simply the "zero degree of typography" and in and of itself of no significance.[18] Even the word *gothic* (the word that makes typography seem to modern scholars particularly relevant to this discussion) meant something else to eighteenth-century printers, not "blackletter," but rather the font used to print the single text written in the language known as "Gothick." The word used for what we call "gothic" was "English."[19] So if, say, an imaginary Richard Hurd had demanded of his printer a suitably "gothic" type to support his notions of the rise of what he called "the gothic," what he would have gotten was not blackletter but the strange type used only to print the fourth-century translation of the Bible by Wulfilas.

The opposition blackletter/roman is not a universal in book history, nor does it function the same way in the fields of book production and book reception. The choice of a typefont differs from the choice of a word or a text. Writers can choose any word they want, and are not even confined to what might be called their own cultural lexicon. But until very recently they could not utter that text or word in any font they wanted. The printer utters that text in the fonts that printer has available—fonts which reflect oppositions that may well only exist in the particular typecases owned by that printer, and will be interpreted in the context of other typecases owned by other printers. Complicating this situation even further is the gap between the system of typefonts imagined by a printer and the more haphazard system of typefonts in the libraries or reading experience of individual readers. These readers might indifferently place that new book and its typography in the context of old books and their typography, or simply, an obsolete book and its typography in the context of more cutting edge aesthetics.

The change from blackletter to roman is not the only *grand récit* of English typographical history that spans this period. From a typographical standpoint, an equally important change in eighteenth-century English typography is in the transition from what is called Old Style to Modern face. This is one of the most fundamental changes in the development of English roman type and the basis for most histories of typography in the period. That most readers reading this sentence are not entirely certain of what we refer to is one index of the problem we are pointing out. When one compares, say, the type in the title page of *Wit and Mirth* (1719) with that of Scott's *Minstrelsy* (1806), one notices the more radical difference between wide and narrow lines, the changed appearance of serifs (Figures 18 and 21). Although most readers do not immediately perceive the details, they distinguish a seventeenth-century English book from a nineteenth-century one on the basis of such features, and it is easy to see how fonts such as Baskerville's are, in retrospect, "transitional" (see Figure. 22). Typographically, the change is fundamental, and permitted the self-conscious use of historical types ("old style types") in the later nineteenth century (the most obvious example is William Morris). Yet in an eighteenth-century printing context, there was never a functioning opposition of old style/modern face analogous to that of gothic/classical or to any other cultural opposition. Printers were aware of the changing style of type but simply replaced old fonts with new ones. That change in typography makes dating their books relatively easy and could be used as a basis for organizing chronologically all of those reproduced here; but it operates independently of specific aesthetic genres. Only in the late nineteenth century would it be possible for a printer to deploy this opposition in accord with the *grand récit* of the "rise of the gothic."[20]

Conclusion

When describing specific bibliographical features of books of this period (typography, layout, design, etc.) there are several histories at work: the history of engraving, the history of typography, even the history of ballad collecting. Such histories can be usefully described in terms of particular developmental narratives of typography or bibliography: the change from blackletter to roman and italic; the change from old style to new style typeface; the change from folio to octavo. But these histories also develop independently of each other. Typographical changes concern typographers; and changes in the nature of published ballads concern readers of those ballads; changes in engraving styles concern engravers. A critical or historical term such as "gothic" is not problematic simply because it is vague or ambiguous. Rather, it is problematic because our very invocation of such a term creates bodies of evidence ("gothic features of title pages") that constitute illusory supporting microhistories.

Interlude

At the Typographical Altar:
Interlude for Randall McLeod

Among the always interesting and amusing articles by Randall McLeod are
two based on George Herbert's seventeenth-century "The Altar" and "Easter
Wings"; to English literary historians, these are the *loci classici* of the shape
poem.[1] I assume that what drew Prof. McLeod to these poems was the difficulty they posed to the editorial enterprise; what draws me to them here is a
similar difficulty they pose to what I have called the typographical enterprise.
Modern textual criticism, which McLeod spent most of his early career un-
dermining, is based (theoretically) on literals; these might be letters, typographical elements, or even speech sounds. Changes and variations in these
letters through the history and accidents of transmission of any text are what
modern textual critics record and, through a wide range of theories and methods, evaluate.

How, I imagine Prof. McLeod thinking, would these same textual critics
deal with the tradition of the visual image? not just images generally (which
are transmitted I assume by the same imagined processes and missteps that
apply to textual transmission), but those images that are transformations (or
representations?) of originary typographical constructions?

In printed editions, Herbert's "The Altar" and "Easter Wings" appear
in two basic forms. (1) The words of the poem are typeset in such a way as
to form a shape similar to the object described in the poem. That is how these
poems are represented in most modern editions; the typographical layout, in
this case, refers directly to the meaning of the poem and even conveys that
meaning. You can look in any modern anthology and find an example. (2)

The object described in the poem (wings, an altar) is represented by an engraved image within which the words of the poem are engraved; this is the way these poems are presented in various eighteenth-century editions. Such engraved images may be considered legitimate products (or elaborations?) of the shapes implied in the two earliest manuscripts for Herbert's poems. Or they may be accidents or mistakes of transmission.

If Prof. McLeod was ever thinking what (for my own convenience) I imagine him to have been thinking, the richness of the evidence seems to have distracted him from this enterprise. Instead of exposing a particular problem in textual-critical theory, these poems and their histories presented him with a morass of error, murky affinities, and of course many examples of readerly interventions of the kind that enjoyed an especial currency at the moment of his writing these essays.

"Easter Wings": FIAT fLUX

What we know as "Easter Wings" is in modern editions one poem, represented visually as a familiar typographical shape that is easier to recognize than to describe. Prof. McLeod's analysis of the poem in "FIAT fLUX"[2] is less an analysis of anything Herbert wrote or initiated than a record of reception in which McLeod allows editors to speak (or misspeak) for themselves. Following the introductory (or is it the central?) portion of the essay, McLeod constructs what he calls an "Easter Wings Gallery," a section that constitutes the bulk of the essay (86–125). Included in this Gallery are summaries and quotations from eighteen editions of the poem from the 1836 Pickering edition through late twentieth-century editions, including anthologized versions from the late 1980s. I have read this article and the Gallery entries several times, and I am still not certain of the principle of order in the Gallery: I believe it is a formal one based on an analysis of the types of errors found in these editions. It is thus less an historical record of the reception of the poem than a catalogue of possible editorial errors: type facsimiles of modern editions masquerading as type facsimiles of (no more authoritative) early ones, mistranscriptions, disordered stanzas, uncritical definitions of the basic unit of concern (one poem or two); effacement of basic elements of the poem; ignorance. More precisely (or less so):

Well, if mutation of messages is the way of this world, how are we to react to Herbert's editors? Does their inexhaustible fertility issue in sublime adaptation or merely befuddled degeneration?

Nothing is easier than to mock the editorial tradition. . . . A stroll through the Easter Wings Gallery shows appropriation drifting inappropriately according to fashion; this drift forestalls literary criticism's approach to a science. This is not to say that editing is not a highly intellectual practice, for it is. But its intellect is self-absorbed; it is virtually cut off from the objects it needs to contemplate. ("FIAT fLUX," 148)

I think the grammatical ambiguity in the final phrase of this paragraph is deliberate (objects required for an act of contemplation? objects that the intellect must contemplate?). But I am not certain of that. It is difficult to summarize "FIAT fLUX" (as I am sure its author intended it to be), and as the article is not my central focus, I won't misrepresent it by attempting to do so.

"The Altar"

My primary focus is on McLeod's companion article: "Enter Reader" in *The Editorial Gaze: Mediating Texts in Literature and the Arts* (1988).[3] The title of the collection alone gives an idea of its direction, or at least the direction that the editors of this volume, Paul Eggert and Margaret Sankey, expect or imagine. Historical editors are to be accused of oppressing, subjugating, and modifying their object texts (through the mechanism of "The Gaze"). But even as they are critiqued for such practices, they will be the subject of praise: editors have power, and thus can be critiqued in the same manner as anyone else who holds power in the world of politics, art, or psychology.

McLeod's "Enter Reader" can be located within this duplicitous world of editorial concerns, or so it is located by the editors of this volume.

[McLeod's article] demonstrates how editors have misunderstood the nexus between page layout and meaning in editions of George Herbert's poems. His essay counsels reading the evidence rather than editing and then reading it. Editing, then, for McLeod is a process

which provokes misreading. Paradoxically, these very misreadings
may point to the hidden dynamic and potentiality of Herbert's text.
(Eggert and Sankey, "Introduction," x–xi)

In other words, by following invalid codes set up by the editor of a literary
text, we come to a truth that is transcendent of the half-truths held by those
who naively follow valid codes of that editor.

Let us look at what McLeod does here, as well as what he might or
would have done, circumstances having been other than what they were. The
article seems to be structured like his earlier article "FIAT fLUX." That article traced the history of Herbert's "Easter Wings" by beginning with the two
early manuscript authorities for the poem (the Jones and Tanner manuscripts), reading through changes in the first 150 years of printed editions,
and then cataloging the versions of the poem found in editions of the last 150
years. The second article, "Enter Reader," focusing on "The Altar," has no
concluding catalogue of errors: there is no gallery of nineteenth-and twentieth-century editorial misreadings of the poem.

We are now only half-way through this essay. To end it, I'd have
liked to sketch the bewildering textual variety in the entrance to The
Temple in the first editions of the next century—and on through to
the fetching destabilizations of our own day. ("Enter Reader," 41)

"To sketch the bewildering textual variety . . ."—this must mean to create a
Gallery on the model of the earlier article. But the article has to end, and this
"half-way" mark is actually on the next to last page of text: "There is room
here merely to excerpt . . ."; "all these disorientations even before we have
begun reading *inside* the poems—that task I've left to you" (41). What
McLeod has left to us is not entirely clear. I had originally assumed I was
invited to construct a Gallery of misreadings for myself, that is, to rewrite
this essay on the model of his earlier essay. Yet Prof. McLeod challenges me
to quote this directive and claims not to have issued it or even to see it.[4] I
must be misreading him, or perhaps I am simply too influenced by him.

Whether the unprinted Gallery is unconstructed or simply unpublished,
the article is not something other than it appears (a version of the earlier
article); it is, rather, what it is. Stripped of this potential Gallery (the heart of
the earlier article "FIAT fLUX"), "Enter Reader" becomes a surprisingly
traditional, albeit complex, article focusing on a very particular textual ques-

tion only peripherally related to "The Altar" and shape poems in general; it
provides also a traditional textual-critical answer.

Most English undergraduates and nonspecialist English teachers know
"The Altar" as a single, autonomous poem. It is actually the second of a
clearly related pair of shape poems constructed by Herbert. With the exception of some recent anthologists, editors usually edit these together: the first
poem, preceding what is now known as "The Altar," is the two-stanza (or
two-poem?) work now known as "Superliminare." It begins either "Thou
whom the former precepts . . ." or "Avoid profaneness . . . ," depending on
which of the two stanzas is considered the first. The main arguments of
"Enter Reader" concern this poem.

The two earliest manuscripts and the earliest printed edition agree on
the order "Thou whom . . ." followed by "Avoid profaneness . . ."; they
differ, however, in many textual details, including the question of what the
title is and whether this is one poem or two.[5] In later editions, "Superliminare" is consistently presented as a single two-stanza poem, but the two stanzas are (or appear to be) in the order "Avoid profaneness . . ." "Thou whom
. . ." These differences lead to the same type of questions as those addressed
in the introductory sections of "FIAT fLUX" on the stanzas of "Easter
Wings": how many poems? what is the order of the sections within them?
what is the source of this particular textual error or textual variant?

As in his discussion of "Easter Wings," McLeod shows here that such
seemingly straight-forward textual-critical questions cannot be answered or
even addressed solely with reference to literal matters or to typographical
ones (the normal province of textual criticism). Both the source of the stanza
ordering and the source of the textual error (if we consider it an error) lie in
the visual format of the book; in the case of "Superliminare," differences in
what we consider the order of stanzas are the result of the transformation of
the poem from a typographical construction to an engraving.

There is a deceptively simple explanation for the alternate forms of "Superliminare." The 1633 edition prints the stanzas in the order found in most
modern editions: "Thou whom . . ." followed (after a horizontal rule) by
"Avoid Profaneness . . ." This is also the order in which these stanzas? qua-
trains? poems? are represented in the two early manuscripts. The printed
editions beginning in 1633 add ornaments and other visual elements: rules
around "The Altar" (rules which McLeod shows are reused in later editions),
surrounding ornaments for "Superliminare." The visual form finally over-
comes the typeset words, and with the 1674 edition both poems appear as

engravings, now facing each other on a single page opening. The order of the stanzas in "Superliminare" is at that point destabilized or in McLeod's word "unstuck."

The reasons and evidence for this are presented in great detail by McLeod, although the reader trying to follow his argument might stumble on (or upon) the fact that the illustrations of various editions are not all labeled on the pages where they appear (this was no doubt a technical oversight at press, since they are clearly identified in McLeod's text). As a result, you cannot read or understand the various engravings from early books on their own terms; you must read them through McLeod's argument. In each of the late seventeenth- and early eighteenth-century engravings, the writing used to depict the two stanzas is not uniform. In the earliest engraved version,[6] the two stanzas seem intended to represent a step in some way: the lower stanza is depicted as if on the facing plane of the step; the upper stanza as if spread out on the horizontal surface. They seem to be numbered "1" for the lower stanza, and "2" for the upper stanza. In later versions, the writing of the two individual stanzas is also opposed, perhaps still representing a step, but in different ways. In the 1703 edition (see Figure 23), the writing of the top stanza is smaller; since I will be talking about perspective in a later chapter, I will describe it as farther away and foreshortened. There is no numbering, but we can still imagine reading the lower stanza (the nearer one) first, the upper stanza second. If a copyist were to ignore the visual frame and the appearance of the writing, and follow only the convention of reading from top to bottom, the stanzas might well be printed in reverse order: "Avoid profaneness . . ." "Thou whom . . ." And that is how they are represented in later typographical editions.

Since "Enter Reader," unlike "FIAT fLUX," does not follow this textual-critical argument with a Gallery of Errors, the essay becomes both utterly convincing and completely textual-critical: those later editions that reproduce the second order of stanzas (if they do) are not interesting or amusing or examples of readerly freedom; they are simply wrong.[7] I don't believe McLeod wants his article to be reduced to such a textual-critical banality; but without the Gallery, it is hard to read (or misread) it any other way.

Reading "The Altar"

McLeod's ideal reader might be inspired to follow the method of "FIAT fLUX" and examine all modern Herbert editions; a less conscientious reader

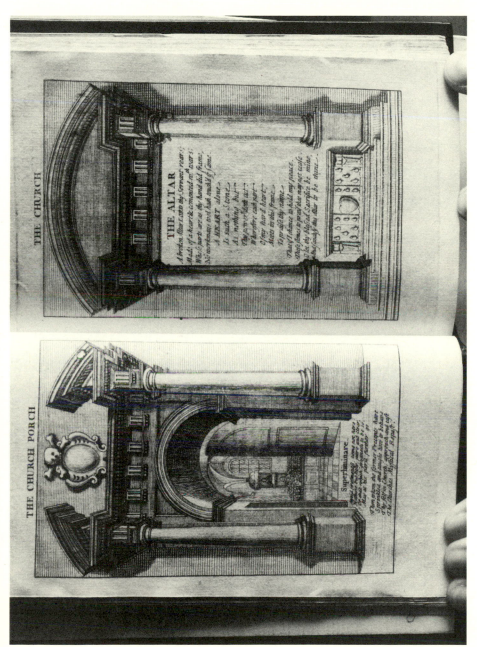

Figure 23. George Herbert, *The Temple* (London, 1703).

might be satisfied with picking up an edition at random. I am looking at the
1703 edition; it is not an important edition from the standpoint of textual
criticism or editorial history, but it is of some importance to me since I found
it on my bookshelf. It is obviously copied from the earlier (tenth?) edition,
or so I conclude by comparing it to the reproductions in McLeod's article.
Any of these late seventeenth- or early eighteenth-century versions of the
poem could be seen as the visual culmination of a process begun with the
earliest manuscripts. In both manuscripts, "The Altar" is written out in the
shape familiar to any reader of this poem, a shape maintained in the typography of the 1633 edition, and one still visible in the engraved text in the 1703
version. In the 1634 edition, the obvious shape of the poem is reinforced with
surrounding rules, rules which reappear in 1635 and 1638 (see "Enter Reader,"
20–21). In 1674, the once decorative visual elements take over: the typographical altar becomes an engraved altar.

For the engravings in my 1703 book, two things strike me, perhaps because of the context of the present study. The first is the implied (but seemingly incorrect) perspective. The second is the representation of particular
hands (roman capitals, italics).

A number of perspective lines seem to intersect on a vanishing point on
the word "Altar" in the last line (those from the base of the columns and the
outer edges of the top cornices). Other pairs intersect higher on an implied
central vertical axis (those from the inner edges of the cornices). The image,
with its implied vanishing points, thus reproduces in very trite and banal
ways an equally trite and banal image of the systems of perspective imagined
to apply to classical art (see below, Chapter 7). Copied from earlier engravings are the steps leading to the altar. Yet instead of drawing the reader in,
here they are in absolutely flat perspective. An infinite viewing distance is
implied, with no vanishing point. In the facing engraving for "Superliminare," a reader (reading as McLeod suggests) might still be "drawn into" the
Church through the steps. The comparable steps in the 1703 "The Altar"
engraving, however, do nothing of the kind; if the reader is at all susceptible
to rules of perspective, the incorrect perspective here keeps that reader at bay.

The engraved poem (or the representation of written words) does not
imitate the way this poem appears or would appear in manuscript; it represents, rather, the typography of an imagined printed version. It imitates a
family of typefaces (classical italics), complete with curlicue at line end. This
is likely a remnant of early Italian writing conventions, but eighteenth-
century readers, less familiar with Italian manuscripts than of course we are,

know it as a remnant of early Italian typographical conventions. That is, it alludes to early sixteenth-century print versions of italics.

The creation of the image and the transformation of the poem into pseudo-type transform the nature of the poem. What could be called its iconicity has become superfluous. The engraved words do not represent an altar even though the now traditional shape of the altar is maintained; they rather allude to the typographical construction of an altar. And the shape poem is no longer a shape poem at all; it is, rather, a "shaped" poem, one that is within a form of the poem that calls it into being, but no longer directly invokes it.

The Typographical Altar

In McLeod's reading, "Superliminare" (if there is a poem with that title and if it can be said to have a being embodied in its various editions) exploits the possibilities of engraving: an originary act of writing looks forward to a fully visual engraved image that can elicit spatial readings. McLeod's imagined readers are then further encouraged to exploit the critical possibilities provided by these real and imagined editions. But in my reading, all seems constrained by the institution of typography, the topic of my own study and thus of the book I am looking at. This is the institution foreseen in the manuscript representation of the poem, with its carefully ruled lines and borders, the form of the engraved letters themselves transforming them into ersatz typesorts, and the recasting and misreading of the visual display as a new text, one that except in the most deliberately perverse readings is both editorial and erroneous.

McLeod, or my version of him, wanted two things: (1) a postmodern reading of Herbert (or the phenomenon of Herbert), whereby the multifarious nature of anything we could call a text is both part of our own reading experience and part of anything we could attribute to or call "Herbert"; (2) a similar reading of his own work, whereby readers would complete the unwritten work according (perhaps?) to the model set forth in "FIAT fLUX."

Yet neither enterprise is fully realized. Those who, say, mistranscribe the order of stanzas of "Superliminare" are wrong. They are no less so because readers in the late twentieth century claim to be able to read texts any way they want, or construct whatever texts they want from the chaos of, say, an electronic archive or a multitextual edition of Shakespeare. As for McLeod's readers, they do what they want, not what he wants.

Or perhaps I can read his article as something altogether different and even more convenient. McLeod here moves beyond his notion of the villain-editor (there is no reference to "un-editing" here). McLeod's target is not editing at all, but classical typography, and his subject becomes not what he imagines, but what I need it to be here. Herbert's "The Altar" advances from manuscript to letterpress type to engraving in a logical progression. It is the transformation of this visual edition back into the domain of typography in our own editions that produces not the classically "incorrect" edition, but more villainously, the post-post-modern "unreaderly" one.

[After long negotiations (see notes 2–6) Prof. McLeod and I determined that he would intervene at some point in this chapter. This led to the resolution expressed in the following e-mail:

Dansk,

How about, from the first places you mention "FIAT *f*LUX" or "Enter Reader", a series of little dots rising from inside the body of your page to a marginal CLOVD (i.e., balloon), in which those graphic forms of the titles would appear? A most serene intervention.

These could be provided on a plastic sheet, to be laid over your printed page, so that all could be photographed to provide the final image.

The noodle references were obliquely to the eatery you mentioned.

Cheers,

R

18 Jan. 2010

These plans proved unfeasible.]

PART II

❧ ❧ ❧

Images and Texts

❦

Fists and Filiations in Early Chaucer Folios, 1532–1602

The preceding chapters of this study have considered typography as a matter of typesorts and letterforms. The following chapters deal with extratextual aspects of typography. Here, I consider a once obscure aspect of sixteenth-century typography, one brought into prominence by William Sherman's *Used Books*.[1] That is what Sherman calls the "manicule," that is, the pointing hand found in the margin of many manuscripts and in manuscript notations in early printed books. These marginalia seem to mark *sententiae* of some kind—something the readers of these books found worth noting. In the following chapter, I will look at the printed version or transformation of these hands, fists, or manicules. What did the printers have in mind in reproducing these marks so common in late medieval manuscripts? Sherman's introductory disclaimer is worth repeating:

> Anyone who turns to marginalia with high hopes of easy answers
> quickly discovers that the evidence they contain turns out to be (if
> not always thin, scattered, and ambiguous) peculiarly difficult to
> locate, decipher, and interpret. (xiii)

There are no easy answers to understanding what a reader's particular annotations may mean, nor are there obvious guidelines on how they should be interpreted. For printing, we have an even more complex situation: we are not dealing with the idiosyncracies of a reader, but the idiosyncracies of those who produced the material basis for that text; we don't know whether they typeset what they intended, or whether what they intended to typeset had any relation to the content of the annotated text. Yet these actions, whatever their source, are not left as mere personal quirks; they are legitimized by virtue of being reproduced throughout the print-run, and often, as we shall see here, throughout subsequent reeditings.

The subject matter here is the series of Chaucer folios produced during the sixteenth century. The first section of the chapter focuses on the matter of filiation: how to determine the copytext of each successive edition, and in particular, the extratextual elements that bear on these questions—their page layout, line composition, and so on. The prominence of these elements in determining the relations between versions of the same text is of course contrary to some of the accepted tenets of classical and postclassical textual criticism. The second section focuses on the mysterious marginalia typeset in the texts of the *House of Fame* and the consequences of the transmission of those marginalia. Examination of these extratextual elements first provides evidence for printer's copy used in the various editions (a question often obscured by editorial concentration on textual matters), and second, illustrates a process of rationalization whereby printers reinterpreted details of their tradition that they understood no better than we do.

Filiations

William Thynne's 1532, double-column folio edition of Chaucer is the first of the series of blackletter folios constituting the early "vulgate" Chaucer. The interest of Chaucerians in these editions has been two-fold: for some, they provide a record of canon formation, with each subsequent edition adding to the canon as defined by its predecessor. For others, the interest is almost exclusively textual-critical, with the value of these late and obviously derivative editions based on the off chance that they may in particular cases serve as independent witness for manuscript readings now lost.

The history of this series of editions was sketched as early as the eighteenth century, and finally presented with uncommon clarity by Thomas R. Lounsbury in 1892.[2] There are a series of editions:

1532 (the Thynne edition) STC 5068 (= TH)
1542 (two variants) STC 5069–70 (= TH2)

[1550] (four variants) STC 5071–5074 (= TH3)
1561 (the Stow editions; three? variants) STC 5075–5076.3 (= ST)
1598 (the Speght edition) STC 5077–79 (= SP1)
1602 STC 5077–79 (= SP2)[3]

What is generally accepted today is the following. The 1542 and 1550 editions (TH2 and TH3) are set from the 1532 edition; the Stow edition of 1561 (ST) is set from the 1550 edition; the Speght edition of 1598 (SP1) is set from the 1561 edition; the Speght edition of 1602 (SP2), although a reprint of 1598, is to some extent based on the 1561 edition as well. This simplified description shows that the relation between the various editions is not strictly linear, but sometimes "leapfrog," although even the most careful scholars of these editions occasionally imply that this is not the case.[4]

The collations by the Variorum editors and my own less systematic collations of the prose sections of the later folios have provided some further clarification of the case with the later folios. Of particular concern here is the importance of format and extraliterary matters: type size and style, line breaks, etc. In W. W. Greg's classic essay, "The Rationale of Copy-Text," the features of a text of most importance to a textual critic are defined as substantives (words and semantic elements) and what Greg defines as accidentals (spelling conventions, punctuation, etc.).[5] Greg was interested primarily in distinguishing an original reading from a later one, and only incidentally in determining relations among later witnesses. Thus matters of format (what might be called "sub-accidental" elements) were of only secondary concern, particularly when they concerned such obviously unoriginal matters as printed line length. Yet on the matter of textual filiation, such elements somewhat paradoxically provide greater evidence than the higher level of substantives.

The importance of these is particularly clear in the case of the Speght editions of 1598 and 1602, which seem not to be set according to what appears to be the most rational procedure. Since the 1602 edition contains revised versions of much of the preliminary matter from the 1598 edition and two texts not in Stow's 1561 edition ("Chaucer's Dream" and "Flower and the Leaf," fols. 355–68), some form of the 1598 text obviously served as printer's copy for these sections in 1602. If we consider the 1602 edition alone, it might seem improbable that Speght would use the 1598 edition as printer's copy to set these sections alone, relying on a copy of the 1561 edition for the remainder of the edition. Yet the evidence proves that he did precisely that.[6]

Because the collations so far done by Lounsbury and by Variorum editors have been confined to the verse sections, the only kind of printing influence that has been detected is a "page-by-page" setup or what Malcolm Andrew calls "articulation" (meaning, I think, headings, section breaks, etc.). It is easy enough to determine, say, that the 1598 edition is set from the 1561 edition (the page length is the same), but since the 1602 edition employs a longer column, it seems to have no relation in terms of page layout to the earlier editions.

A comparison of the uncollated prose sections is, however, decisive. Throughout most of the prose, the 1598 edition is a perfect, line-by-line reprint of the 1561 edition, as it would be expected to be.[7] Only at the end of marked sections in the prose does that correspondence occasionally grow slack. The compositor sets type line for line to make the job of estimating length (casting-off) easier. Thus, in, say, a 50-line unit set from another 50-line unit, line-for-line correspondence will tend to be strict for the first 45 lines or so, slack for the remaining lines.

What is more surprising is that the same holds true for the 1602 edition: it also is set from the 1561 edition.[8] I have checked those particular sections where 1598 and 1602 differ, and here, the 1602 edition often comes into perfect line-for-line correspondence with the edition of 1561. (Had the 1602 edition been set from the 1598 edition, we would expect the two to agree in line composition against the 1561 edition at the end of paragraphs; but they do not.)

For the preliminaries, the situation is more complex, since much of this material appears first in the 1598 edition. The Life of Chaucer and all sections in roman type are thus set directly from 1598. There are correspondences in italicized marginal notes (see for both editions sig. b2r and the marginal note on Canterbury College at the top of sig. b34). Yet not all this material comes from 1598. Much of the preliminary matter differs in content (for example, the dedicatory letter to Cecil and the section "To the Readers"). Behind these is a manuscript of some sort (or manuscript annotations), not the 1598 printed text. More surprising is the introductory letter from Thynne to Henry VIII (reprinted in all sixteenth-century folio editions since TH). The 1602 edition used the 1598 edition for its heading—a margin-to-margin heading in three sizes of roman type, with the same ornaments, then shifted to a copy of the 1561 edition for the printer's copy of the text of that letter; again, the layout is decisive.[9]

As noted earlier, variation in substantives and accidentals seems less im-

portant in determining the material printer's copy than matters of page layout and line composition. And as far as I know, none of these prose sections
(either those of the text or those of the preliminaries) has been thoroughly
collated for such variation. In those prose sections I have collated, I have
found no substantive disagreements in the three editions. If and when such
disagreement is found, it will indicate something other than printer's copy
(possibly a stray hand-written annotation in that printer's copy): because the
1561 and 1598 editions generally correspond line for line, any corrector set to
the task of introducing the readings from a copy of one into a copy of the
other would have a relatively easy time of it.

The collations of the Variorum editors for verse sections of the *Canterbury Tales* support the conclusions above, although some of their claims are
unnecessarily understated. All are based to some extent upon Derek Pearsall's
comments in one of the first volumes of this edition: "The conclusion seems
clear that SP2 was reset from ST . . . but SP2 has been so extensively edited
that the evidence cannot be so decisive as it usually is with early printed
editions" (*Nun's Priest's Tale*, 114). Only Baker in his edition of the Squire's
Tale is categorical about the 1561 edition as printer's copy; yet the evidence is
far stronger than other editors seem to believe.[10] In only one or two instances
is the substantive variation such as even to suggest that either printer's copy
or textual source for the 1602 edition was anything other than a copy of the
1561 edition, and even these examples are capable of alternative explanation.
And despite some occasionally misleading statistics cited in the Variorum,
the same holds true for the General Prologue. In all verse sections where a
text was available, both Speght editions (1598 and 1602) were set from the
Stow edition of 1561.[11]

The Problem of the Fists

The editions under discussion here have a long-noted oddity that bears on
the tradition of printer's copy for these editions. The earlier folios contain
some typographically peculiar marginalia in the *House of Fame*; in the 1561
edition these typographical marks seem to be replaced for the most part with
marginal fists, and they are again confined to the *House of Fame*.[12] The 1598
edition has no marginalia of any kind, but the 1602 edition marks proverbs
and *sententiae* with marginal fists throughout (the two texts printed from

the 1598 edition, texts not found in the 1561 edition, are unmarked). John
Hetherington, in 1964, was the first bibliographer to address these marginalia:

> The earlier Chaucer folios themselves contain some markings which
> could be regarded as anticipating the formal and practical use of the
> fist. Curiously, in each edition these only appear with *The House of
> Fame*. In 1542 and 1561 they only occur in the "middle" margin. In
> 1550 they seem to be "end of line" rather than marginal. I have not
> found any single line to be marked in more than one edition. (8–9)[13]

No explanation of these marginal marks has been offered beyond this. Similar
type ornaments (or constructions) appear frequently in sixteenth-century
books, and there are a number of them the Great Bibles from the early 1540s
printed by Grafton and Whitchurch (Grafton is the printer responsible for
the 1542 Chaucer, although not named in the colophon).[14]

In the first Thynne edition of 1532, three marks occur, all easily reproducible on a keyboard. On fol. 316, *House of Fame*, lines 837, 848, and 858:[15]

(:):)
(:):)
(:(:):)

In 1542, this same section is marked at lines 848 and 853:

(:)(:)
(:)(:)

In 1550, the most heavily marked version, no marks appear in this section.

In the 1542 edition, in the middle sections of *House of Fame*, there are
two more marks of this kind—a *punctus elevatus* (I represent this mark below
with a modern question mark) within parentheses at lines 1108 and 1127.
Toward the beginning and end of the work, several other variously constructed marks occur: three small joined *o*'s, a leaf, and a fist in lines 77, 83,
98 respectively. In the final section, the mark consisting of three *o*'s recurs at
line 1947, and right-pointing fists appear in the interior margin, set with the
left column of type, at lines 1923, 1955, 2130, and 2140.

I will state now that I am not about to offer an explication of the specific
function of these marks. I am certain that if some dozen or so lines in any

text were marked entirely at random, any bibliographer, textual critic, or literary critic worthy of the profession could come up with reasons why those particular lines (and only those lines) were of significance. My argument here is rather that the simple tradition of these marks (their bare existence) was stronger than their perceived function and that only in 1602 were they finally rationalized. In short: sixteenth-century printers had no clearer idea of the original function of these marks than we do.

With that caveat, several aspects of these marks should be noted. I begin with the 1542 edition. Here the right-pointing fists appear in the interior margin, but they are set within the borders of the left column of type. They thus point to lines in the right column, not to the left-column lines with which the typesorts are clearly set. Are they pointing the wrong way? The last two marginal fists seem to point to line 2154 in the right column—a line about stamping for eels (!, see note in Riverside 990)—and a line in the spurious continuation reading "Of that god of Thondre." Eel-stamping may be noteworthy, but these fists almost certainly originate as responses to the lines in the left margin: "With boxes crommed ful of lyes / As euer vessel was with lyes" (lines 2129–30) and "For al mote out late or rathe / Al the sheues in the rathe" (lines 2139–40). Each involves an apparent example of *rime riche*, and such a rhyme type may well have attracted editorial concern. In the second couplet, the rhyme word is clearly an error (for *rathe* read *lathe*). In the first, the rhyme depends in part on the meaning of "boxes"—if, that is, the word *boxes* belongs here. MS F reads *boystes*, MS B *bowgys*. I haven't a clue what lines 2129–30 mean or what Thynne in 1532 thought his variant meant: the gloss in the now standard Riverside edition at p. 373 suggests a rhyme on *lies* and *lees*: "With containers full of lies as ever vessel was with dregs."

The other odd mark, the joined *o*'s at line 1947, is also not a mark for a reader; the reading "In sommer whan they ben grene" reads in other copies "In sommer whan they grene bene." This mark is quite possibly a compositor's rendition of what was intended as a mark of transposition, in other words, an erroneous reading of the copytext.[16] Like the fists at the end of the text, this is something produced during the printing process; it represents (or originates in) notes to a printer or editor. Taken together, these marks are not in any way coherent guides for a reader; any reader taking them seriously would be alternately baffled by the text in the vicinity or left wondering what the fuss was all about.

The 1550 edition contains many complex and bizarre-looking marginal marks and ornaments. Again, they are confined to the *House of Fame*. In some cases, they appear like those in the 1542 edition (there are numerous instances where they are constructed with typesorts, rather than ornamental sorts). For the first two books, these consist almost exclusively of marks formed from parentheses, the *punctus elevatus*, and colons: many are as easily constructed on a keyboard as from a typecase and include the following, at lines 171, 520, 704 and 930:

>):(
> (?)
>)?(
> (?)?(?)

At the end of the second book, with the beginning of a new quire (sig. 3G), these become much more elaborate, formed by multiple commas, inverted commas, colons, etc. Among these are the marks at lines 1185 and 1128 and 1467:

> (,:,:,:,:,)
> (:()?)
> (:)(:)(:

These are consistently well formed and quite carefully done; they are not a haphazard collection of sorts, but formed, for example, with alternating commas and right-facing or left-facing inverted commas, all within parentheses (I will not know, of course, until the typesetting stage of this book, whether they are fairly represented in my own text). The following occurs at line 1429 (the third inverted comma should face right here):

> (,:':,: ':,: ':,:)

I have conjectured a number of functions for these: annotations for inexistent notes, illegible corrections for text, casting-off marks for a projected edition. Most of my conjectures, however, contain the word *inexistent* or a near variant: there are no annotations; the lines marked are in no obvious need of correction; the intervals would not be appropriate for casting off copy. The precise function of the (lost) original marks that inspired the compositor for the 1550 edition to create these variant marks is quite simply lost.

The distribution of these marks, however, does reflect the physical structure of the book, and thus not what must have been the distribution of whatever marks were in the printer's copy (an annotated copy of the 1532 edition). The pattern of their distribution is a product of the creation of this particular edition, not a product of its copytext. The more elaborate marks appear only in a single quire, 3G; the independence of that quire is shown by the initial line, which erroneously repeats the last line of quire 3F and thus makes the catchword inaccurate; some sort of interruption occurs here. Another indication that these are products of processes at the printing house is the presence of marks in quire 3F. They occur only in particular formes: 3F2r/3F5v and 3F3r/3F4v. They do not occur in the reverse formes: 3F2v/3F5r and 3F3r/3F4r. All this indicates that whatever these marks may have represented or have been thought to represent, their presence in the 1550 edition is a function of something in the printer's copy that one compositor could have interpreted as "something to be printed" and another could have interpreted as "something to be ignored" (the hypothetical compositors could of course be one compositor working under a different directive).

When we look at the edition of 1561, we can see another step in the apparent rationalization of an oddity in a printer's copy. For this edition, the printer's copy was a copy of the 1550 edition, containing the bizarre printed marginalia in the *House of Fame*. The 1561 edition puts fists in its text of *House of Fame* (and in no other text). *Pace* Hetherington, there appears to be some relation of these fists to the marks in those in the edition of 1550, and it might be argued that in some cases, they represent an interpretation of the marginalia of 1550.

In the first two books of *House of Fame*, there is no apparent correspondence. There are a number of fists at lines 250ff, but no mark corresponds to them in the 1550 or 1542 editions (at the end of the first book). There are none in the 1561 edition on sig. 3e2r–3e3v (an entire inner and outer forme), whereas numerous marks appear in this section in the 1550 edition. From the beginning of book 3, there are numerous fists in the 1561 edition, and many marks in the edition of 1550. There is some correspondence here: a mark occurs at line 1169 in the 1550 edition and an upward-pointing fist in the 1561 edition; another mark at line 1206 might correspond to an upward-pointing fist in the same line in 1561, and another mark at line 1217 might correspond to an upward-pointing fist at line 1219 in 1561. So also at line 1465, an upward-pointing fist in the 1561 edition is at least in the vicinity of a strange mark in the 1550 edition at line 1467; a downward-pointing fist at line 1479 might

correspond to another mark in the 1550 edition. But of the eleven fists that
follow, there is only a rough correspondence in one or two cases.[17]

A few additional peculiarities about the fists in the 1561 edition are noteworthy. To begin with, there appears to be only one such fist in the typefont,
a right-pointing fist. This is set to point right on only one occasion. In all
other uses, the fist appears between the two columns, set with the left column
of print, and points either up or down. There may be a correspondence with
the text, but trying to find one appears to have the intellectual validity of the
Sortes Virgilianae. What can be said is the same that can be said of the 1550
marginalia: they respond to something noticeable in the printer's copy, but
not to something the compositor fully understood or interpreted in any intelligible way.

What happens in the two Speght editions is a response: in the 1598
edition, no marginal fists appear, although Speght claims in his introductory
note "To the Readers" that he has marked sentences in some unexplained
fashion as one of his eight "undertakings": ". . . Sixtly, Authors by him
cited, declared. Seventhly, Sentences noted." "Sentences," however, are not
included among the seven "Additions" listed on the 1598 title page and "sentences" are in fact not noted in the 1598 text. The title page to Speght's 1602
edition states "Sentences and Prouerbes noted," and Speght adds to the earlier dedicatory letter to Cecil of 1598 the statement that he has "noted withall
most of his Sentences and Prouerbs." Marginal fists appear throughout the
book (with the exception of the two texts that the 1598 edition added to the
contents of earlier editions: "Chaucer's Dream" and "Flower and the Leaf").
And they are perfectly rationalized: sentences and proverbs are marked, precisely what Speght claims on his title page. Yet perhaps because they are
rational, they have no relation whatsoever to the placement of printed marginalia in earlier editions.

The history of these marks confirms other evidence for printer's copy,
supporting the hypothesis of the retention of particular books or manuscripts
as printer's copy, first for the editions of 1542 and 1550, and second for the
edition of 1602. There is no doubt concerning the general relations of the
1542 and 1550 editions: the collations show that both were set from the first
Thynne edition (1532). How, then, does the 1550 edition happen to have so
many marks, some of which correspond exactly to the 1542 edition? And why
do both editions have marks that are formed typographically like the three in
the 1532 edition?

The only explanation for this is that the 1550 and 1542 editions were set not simply from what a textual critic might call TH (the abstract text as represented in the 1532 edition) but rather from a specific copy of that edition, a marked-up copy. Such a specifically marked copy would explain all apparent correspondence with these two editions as far as particular extraneous marginalia are concerned. The relations of the various printers involved in the two editions are close. According to Frank Isaac, the printing of the 1550 edition, in all its variants (or "issues"), is done by Nicholas Hill, who shared type with Whitchurch and Grafton (Grafton is responsible for the 1542 edition); the printers named in the colophons (Bonham and Reynes for 1542; Bonham, Kele, Petit and Toy for 1550) are part of a consortium.[18]

The marginalia also help describe the nature of the printer's copy for the 1602 edition. The 1561 edition served as printer's copy for this edition, and its marginal fists may well have provided the inspiration for the fists in 1602, just as the incoherence of their placement could have inspired the rejection of the fists in 1598. The marginal fists in the 1602 edition, thus, do not represent the marginal fists actually printed in its printer's copy (otherwise they would correspond to those in the 1561 *House of Fame*) but rather indicate lines marked by hand in that copy. This would explain why no such fists appear in those sections of the book set from the edition of 1598; only the printed source text (ST) was marked, not the source text for these two poems. It also can explain why Speght claims in 1598 to have marked the text's *sententiae* ("Seuenthly, sentences noted"), when only the 1602 edition is so marked. The printer's copy used in 1598 may well have been so marked, just as Speght claims, but those handwritten marks were not introduced into the printed text (as marginal fists) until that copy was used again as printer's copy for the 1602 edition.

Conclusion

In 1892, Lounsbury examined lines from the General Prologue, looking primarily for evidence of Speght's claim that he had consulted earlier manuscripts. Although his conclusion was negative, in the process Lounsbury discovered many of the variants that provided an outline for the printing history of these editions, and in particular, the relation of the 1602 edition to the earlier editions of 1561 and 1598. Lounsbury concluded: "A full examination, which has never been made and hardly seems worth making, would be necessary to settle the matter beyond all dispute" (277). The examination "hardly worth making" has now, with the work of the Variorum editors, begun in earnest. Most of the collations confirm the evidence provided by details of layout and line composition, but the interest of editors in possible original manuscript readings contained in these late editions has obscured what the evidence for many of them shows and what Lounsbury suspected: clear and exclusive dependence of later editions on earlier editions whenever those editions were available. Editors, however, are seemingly reluctant to give up the notion of such manuscript sources, and imaginary manuscript readings hypothesized by one scholar are occasionally transformed into actual historical manuscripts for another.[19]

The examination of layout and composition suggests a few areas in which editorial language regarding sources for certain texts could be clarified. Manuscript sigla refer to readings contained in specific material objects. But the sigla for printed editions (TH, ST, SP)—sigla I have of necessity adopted here—refer to entire editions; individual copies of these editions have different readings, either due to ordinary press-variation, or more significantly to the intervention of an annotator. In the present case, one could imagine, say, a copy of the 1561 edition, in which all the readings of the 1598 edition had been entered, or in which numerous changes had been made that were eventually to become the 1598 version (in terms of textual substantives, the two might be identical). Any text copied closely from this might resemble the 1561 edition in details of layout and perhaps in accidentals, but in terms of substantives, it would duplicate the 1598 edition. A textual critic might reasonably claim that the 1598 edition served as *copy text* or *base text*. And under certain understandings of these terms, that could be the case. But it would not serve as printer's copy in any sense, whether we mean by that phrase a physical object in the press room, or more abstractly an edition, one of whose representative copies is in the press room.

Evidence for actual printer's copy is more likely to come from extratextual matters than from the level of textual substantives of interest to most editors—a level to which modern Chaucer editors have found themselves increasingly committed, especially since the publication of John M. Manly and Edith Rickert's Table of Variants in 1940.[20] Yet the precise definition of a substantive, as well as the textual-critical value of such substantives, varies considerably.[21]

The books examined here show that details of layout persist quite apart from their textual or intellectual functions, just as the use of blackletter for medieval texts persisted as the implications of that typeface changed dramatically. Later printers were faced not only with making sense of a text growing increasingly archaic and inaccessible, but with making sense of at least one mystery of their own making.

※

CHAPTER SIX

Editorial and Typographical Diplomacy in the Piers Plowman Archive

The following chapter deals primarily with the Piers Plowman Archive, a digitized editorial project that will eventually make available in facsimile some seventy manuscripts of *Piers Plowman*. Of those CD-ROM volumes published so far, each is focused on a single manuscript represented in both excellent color facsimile and multiple transcriptions. The stated and implied conventions of these transcriptions, called "style sheets," are my primary subject below.

Introduction: From Kane-Donaldson to the Piers Plowman Archive

Piers Plowman presents one of the most difficult editorial problems of medieval literature. It has been the subject of several monumental editions in the past century, beginning with W. W. Skeat's 1885 edition, which defined the now conventional three versions of the text (A, B, and C) and provided an edited version of each. Skeat's edition was not seriously challenged until the Athlone Press edition of 1960; of particular importance was the second volume of this edition, George Kane and E. Talbot Donaldson's edition of the B-Text in 1975, an edition that provided the basis for what then seemed Kane's revolutionary rethinking of editorial theory and procedures.[1]

The Piers Plowman Archive project began as the Athlone Press edition

was being completed, exploiting a technology that could well offer an extension of Kane's theories. Kane, in the B-Text, rejected classical stemmatics.
According to the theory of stemmatics, extant manuscripts of any given text
could be grouped by families through comparison of significant errors; from
these, a stemma could be constructed consisting of past, hypothesized manuscripts, which would in turn lead back to a single, archetypal text that could
be represented in a typeset book.[2] Kane showed that the rigid manuscript
groupings on which classical stemmatics depended were illusory. Like A. E.
Housman, whose voice he often seemed to ventriloquize, Kane considered
variants as individuals rather than as reliable witnesses to coherent families of
manuscripts. In classical editions, the complex variants of manuscripts are
often reduced to mysterious Greek sigla in the bottom margin. These represent manuscript families (an example can be seen in the brief textual notations at the foot of each page in the Oxford Classical Texts series). Kane's
edition uses only roman sigla, each representing a single manuscript. A manuscript reading is thus treated as an individual, and manuscripts are no longer
grouped as stable families; rather, the grouping of manuscripts around their
particular variant readings reveals their constantly shifting relations.[3] Yet
Kane's edition still looks like and functions as a classical edition; evidence in
a series of line-by-line notes remains subordinated to a text, and this text has
all the appearance of being an "authoritative" one, including the magisterial
brackets indicating editorial emendations.[4] An electronic edition could theoretically take Kane's work farther. The electronically constructed text would
shed the mystique of ultimate authority, and reflect rather the variance of
evidence, embodying whatever it is literary scholars mean by textual *mou-
vance*.[5]

     In 2000, the first volume of the Piers Plowman Archive appeared, an
edition of Manuscript F.[6] The title "Archive" spoke to the editorial objective:
what the editorial project would provide was a compendium or repository of
evidence that the reader could use to discover "things" about *Piers* or Langland or medieval culture, without the editorial intervention of the authoritative editor seeking the authoritative text of the authoritative author. This
goal, although often contradicted, was directly stated at several points in the
introductory material to the first few volumes:

     From F: Such an "objective" level of interpretation [the transcrip-
     tion in the "scribal style sheet"] is likely to be useful to scholars
     working on a wide variety of questions . . .

From M: [The corrections] provide striking information about the standards of spelling in Middle English when taken as a whole . . .

From W (in reference to the new layout in W): At the very least this new layout offers a different reading experience; time will tell whether it will have consequences for the appreciation and criticism of the poem.[7]

Like other projects (the Canterbury Tales Project and the William Blake Archive to be discussed briefly below), the Piers Plowman Archive is incomplete, and, given the number of manuscripts, likely to stay incomplete for the lifetimes or careers of its founders.[8] The editors are aware of this, and the possibility of an edition thus remains in the future: "We look at each manuscript text and its documentary edition as a step toward the restoration of an authorial text" (Adams et al., *MS F*) (as this chapter goes to press, an edition of the B archetype text, I am told, is nearly complete). For other subeditors, as well as for reviewers, the question seems left open as to whether that future "authorial text" is to be desired, avoided, transcended, or simply put off until it is forgotten. Perhaps the entire editorial project will be superseded by another one, whose form is unimaginable to us. The following statement from the 1994 Prospectus is representative of this attitude and the contradictions within it: note how the notion of overriding authority (something usually attributed to the final text) has been transferred to the notion of "permanence" claimed now for the level of material evidence:

> An electronic edition does not suppress editorial disagreement or impose spurious notions of authority, as printed editions do. Instead, it embraces the provisional nature of scholarly editing. We shall make permanently available the texts on which future editorial and literary study must be based, and we shall propose a set of solutions to editorial problems without suggesting that they will have final authority. (Prospectus, 1994, from 2007 Archive)

The edition maintains its claim of authority, but now that claim rests on its representation of the materials, not on the reconstructed authorial text.[9]

Such an unqualified claim of permanence seems either naive or purely rhetorical, and this particular statement may well be ironic. Several early electronic databases are usable today only to the degree that, say, my 78 rpm record collection is playable. I can play these records, and sometimes do, even

with wooden needles; but I do that only to demonstrate or experience historical differences in recording conventions or recording technology. This is
never something I do in order to hear what I consider music. I am experienc-
ing not "early music performances," but rather the nostalgia of decades-old
technology and listening conventions.

The Style Sheets

The virtues of the Piers Plowman Archive are obvious: it provides high quality, color images of *Piers Plowman* manuscripts. There is in *Piers* scholarship
nothing to compete with these images, and, if we could disregard its cost, the
project would more than justify itself on the basis of these images alone.[10]
The editors also provide a series of editorial transcriptions of these images,
reducing them to (or interpreting them as) a set of conventional keystrokes
that will form a searchable database at some point in the future. The transcription of the object manuscript is not simple and it is not single. In keeping with the editorial goals, there are multiple methods, conventions, or styles
of transcription that are evolving through the various volumes and will likely
continue to evolve in subsequent volumes.

   When I was first introduced to this project, I was struck by the repeated
description of these four (or five) "style sheets." Although these refer (or
should refer) to editorial conventions of transcription, they are at times conflated with the historical situation of each manuscript; that is, the difference
between various editorial style sheets is equated with the chronologically distinct work of different scribes or correctors. The style sheets and what they
transcribe are referred to in reviews and occasionally in the editions themselves as four or more "levels." It is hard not to see the influence of four
allegorical levels here, beginning with the most literal and moving upward
through more abstract levels, and the style sheets occasionally seem to function that way. But these levels, if they are levels, are not clearly or consistently
defined.[11]

   These style sheets consist of one (or two) purely summary sheets: AllTags
and, in edition F, "NoPals."[12] These two summary sheets are based on the
substantive and highly problematic style sheets that I will discuss below:
Scribal, Diplomatic, Critical. I do not know why these are called "style
sheets." A more accurate if more cumbersome description might be "methods
and special conventions of transcription"; but even by so characterizing these,

I may be misreading their nature and purpose, and it may well have been a desire to avoid such misreading that led the editors to name them as they did.

The term *style sheet* has two meanings, a traditional editorial one and a technical one related to computer technology. In the traditional sense, a style sheet is a list of conventions a printer or publisher and its editorial representatives might give to a subeditor or to an author: these are the conventions *we*, the Institution, follow; this is our house style. Style sheets, in this sense, would be for the Piers Plowman Archive a set of directives to individual editors of each volume. A style sheet in this traditional sense is not addressed to a reader. A reader would only experience or understand such conventions, whether stylistic or editorial, in order to see through them to the unmediated text behind them. If this is the sense and function of the Piers Archive style sheets, they might be thought to invite the same kind of reading: a real, unmediated text is implied somewhere behind them, even if it is one that can never be adequately transcribed or expressed.

As related to computer technology, "style sheet" has a different meaning, one more appropriate for hypertext editions: style sheets in this context have been defined by Susan Hockey simply as "sets of formatting specifications."[13] But that also seems not what "style sheet" means for the Piers Archive; the underlying object (the marked up text) is not simply being formatted for the reader by the blanket application of such a style sheet. The individual components that appear in each style sheet are built into the edition and the editing process. Note that when the editors refer to a style sheet, they are referring not to formatting specifications, but rather to the actual text that appears on the screen as a result of clicking on a particular style sheet. The "levels" to which the term *style sheet* is uncomfortably mapped are similar. They are not moments brought out through the interpretive filter of a style sheet; they are imagined slices of textual history—events that are claimed to have occurred in history (medieval history), not in the computer lab of the edition. The Piers Archive style sheets are thus the result of reconstructing these moments: each is a transcription, not the set of directives for producing a transcription or a way of representing a textual transcription.[14]

These style sheets are described variously, both by individual editors as the editorial project evolves and by reviewers explaining the nature of the edition. I had initially thought it would be an amusing exercise in classical textual-critical methods to collate these variant descriptions and recover O′, the source of all of them; I could also in the process uncover possible review-filiations, that is, I could determine which reviewers copied which particular source in providing their own original descriptions. But there turned out to be no need of that. Since I own a Mac and not a PC, this edition will not function on my computer, or at least, it is predicted to function so erratically that the editors have suggested to me that it might be easier or less frightening to resuscitate my old PC than to try to run it on a newer Mac (the phrase "back up all work before loading or running the program" was decisive in this regard).[15] While waiting for my PC to load Windows, it turned out to be easy to copy the disk onto my Mac and have at my disposal the exceptional JPEG files of facsimile images.[16] Sorting through these files, still waiting for Windows, I inadvertently turned up the "Template" for the description of style sheets. I am not sure this is meant to be available to civilians, but since it was an open file on an open disk, I quote it here (under Folder HmXML, file HmStyleSht.xml):

> org = "uniform" sample = "complete">Presentation of Text: Style Sheets THIS SECTION NEEDS TO BE REVISED AND MADE SPECIFIC TO Hm./(Dug)Using SGML markup and four different style sheets in the Multidoc Pro browser, we offer four different views of the text of Hm. The Scribal style sheet represents as closely as possible the readings and features of the manuscript text. Changes of script are reflected by changes in font. . . . We represent the scribe's habit of accentuating various bits of text by enclosing it in a red box by printing the text so enclosed in red ink inside a black box. The browser does not permit us to display the text in black and the box in red. Scribal lapses are noted by means of purple ink. We have used <SIC> tags to indicate those instances in which we take the scribe not to have written what he intended to write, but we have ignored readings the scribe might reasonably be interpreted as having intended. Eccentric word divisions, e.g., <hi rend = "i-t">atones</hi> for <hi rend = "it">at ones</hi>, or <hi ren-d = "it">anhundred</hi> for <hi rend = "it">an hundred</hi>, are spelled out as written but in lime to call attention to them. We have represented the marginal <foreign lang = "lat"><hi ren-d = "it">notae</hi></foreign> added by an unidentified hand with this icon: <note type = "nota" place = "unspecified" an-chored = "yes"/>. The Critical style sheet is designed to indicate what we believe the scribe intended to have written.

Emendations displayed in the Critical style sheet appear in the conventional square brackets. Since the text displayed in the Critical
style sheet is a reconstructed, putative text, it lacks the color features
that appear in the more nearly diplomatic transcriptions of the
manuscript. We have supplied line references to the Athlone B-text
both for the convenience of readers and to provide a basis for later
machine collation of documentary texts. Eccentric word divisions
are silently, at least in the surface display, corrected in this style
sheet. That is, <hi rend = "it">atones</hi> appears as <hi ren-
d = "it">at ones</hi>, though a scholar who wishes to find all
such divisions can still search for them in the browser as well as in
the underlying SGML text. In addition to the Scribal
and Critical style sheets, we have included a Diplomatic style sheet
that suppresses all notes, marginalia, and indications of error or eccentric word division. Its text is otherwise identical to that presented
in the Scribal style sheet. The AllTags style sheet, as its name implies,
is intended to display the full content of markup in SGML tags.</
p></divı></body></text></TEI.2>

There are variants in all the disks I have examined. Because of the electronic
nature of the edition, it is difficult to know exactly what text existed at what
time, or even what copy a particular editor is using as copytext.

I begin with the difference between Scribal and Critical and the often
fluid meaning of the word "D/diplomatic" in the introductions to selected
Archive volumes:

First we attempt to present the scribal text of F in as unmediated a
form as is practical (digital images). At this least speculative level of
our interpretation, we provide as well an electronically readable,
searchable, and analyzable transcription of F. . . . The F-Critical
style sheet is designed to indicate what we believe F-Scribe intended
to have written and thus to approximate the text of F-Redactor. [It
is] a reconstructed, putative text. . . . F-Scribal style sheet [is a]
diplomatic transcription [with notes]. It presents the scribal text
with all of its corruptions and incompetences. . . . F-Critical style
sheet offers a reading text purging the text of the errors of the F-
Scribe and his immediate predecessors, presenting the text as the F-
Redactor would have wished to see it. This text is, of course, a

hypothetical construct based solely on the criterion of good sense and adherence to the format features of the form. . . . The text has more practical than theoretical justification. (Adams et al., *MS F*)

The Scribal style sheet represents as closely as possible the readings and features of the manuscript text. . . . The Critical style sheet is designed to indicate what we believe the scribe intended to have written. [It is] a reconstructed, putative text. . . . In addition to the Scribal and Critical style sheets, we have included a Diplomatic style sheet that suppresses all notes. . . . Its text is otherwise identical to that presented in the Scribal style sheet. (Turville-Petre and Duggan, *MS W*)

The Scribal style sheet's presentation of the text represents as closely as possible both the readings and features of the manuscript text as well as the most information about editorial interventions. . . . The Diplomatic style sheet suppresses all notes, marginalia not in the text hand, and indications of erroneous or eccentric word division. Its text is otherwise identical to that presented in the Scribal style sheet. The Critical style sheet is designed to indicate the text as it was intended to appear after correction. Since the text displayed is a reconstructed, putative text. . . . (Eliason et al., *MS M*)

The Scribal style sheet's presentation of the text represents as closely as possible both the readings and features of the manuscript text as well as the most information about editorial interventions. . . . The Diplomatic style sheet suppresses all notes, marginalia not in one of the three text hands, and indications of error or eccentric word division. Its text is otherwise identical to that presented in the Scribal style sheet. . . . The Critical style sheet is designed to indicate the text as it was intended to appear after correction. Since the text displayed is a reconstructed, putative text, it lacks the color features that appear in the more nearly diplomatic transcriptions of the manuscript. . . . (Calabrese and Duggan, *MS Hm128*)

There are several noteworthy variants in these descriptions, in particular the order in which the style sheets are presented, and the location of the phrase "putative, reconstructed text," which applies variously to both the Scribal and Critical style sheets. There are also two striking verbal features in the descriptions. The first is the phrase "as closely as possible." This and its many variants are in my experience red flags in editorial projects that indicate the grandest editorial claim and the weakest point in the methodology. Here that phrase, suggesting the closing off of editorial possibility, contradicts one of the most important and innovative claims of the edition, that is, its freedom from the constraints of such a definitive textual base. The second is the word "intention." A major assumption (and the most problematic one) shared by all is that there is an articulable difference between what the scribe "wrote" and what the scribe "intended." The implications of this will be the subject of a later section below.

Comparing Style Sheets I: The Diplomatic Style Sheet

The Diplomatic style sheet is generally listed as the third style sheet. The text is identical to that in the Scribal style sheet, thus "as closely as possible" representing what is in the manuscript, without the hindrance of editorial notes. I don't know why this is listed in the third rather than the second position, and the term itself is problematic.

A diplomatic edition is a particular kind of edition fostered in the nineteenth century; it is most familiar to readers and scholars of medieval literature from works in series such as the Early English Text Society. These editions were responding to a real and immediate problem: how to make unique documents (manuscripts) available to a wider audience. The answer was in a transcription, the so-called diplomatic transcription, that represented not only the text but also the manuscript page itself. In addition to the conventions for reproducing text (keystroke *a* represents variously formed handwritten *a*s), each edition deploys special conventions that allow the reader to reconstruct selected features of that manuscript page. The definition of these features is of course crucial for each edition, but there is no standard definition of what such features should be. Common is the notion of page break, often indicated by a typographical mark, sometimes represented by a physical page break in the edition. Some diplomatic editions represent line breaks of the manuscript as line breaks in the typeset edition, although many diplomatic editions do not; and no diplomatic edition that I have seen represents clearly the vertical arrangement of text, although in the case of some medieval acrostic poems this might be significant.[17] Most diplomatic editions reproduce manuscript spelling, but again, not all of them, and conventions for doing this vary. Every manuscript presents a unique set of problems: how consistently can letterforms of the manuscript be mapped onto the letterforms available on a keyboard or in a printer's typefont? Does the keyboard represent the letter form or the letter function? (this appears in standard diplomatic transcriptions of uppercase *f*, most commonly, and I think absurdly, represented as double-*f*). Are letterform alternatives recognized (for example, the distinctions between *i* and *j* and *u* and *v*)? Should variant forms of *s* be collapsed?[18]

Most important, a diplomatic edition in the late nineteenth century is nearly always a substitute for the manuscript. You make a diplomatic edition and publish it, not because readers are going to use that edition as an aid in studying or reading a medieval manuscript, but rather because they don't have access to that manuscript. The edition is a substitute for the manuscript—an ersatz manuscript.

Although most of these editions are scholarly, many are not. The type facsimile editions of the Malone Society present a diplomatic typesetting of the original in a comparable typeface. The difference between an EETS edition and a Malone Society reprint is one of audience and function. Malone Society editions are belletristic; the typefaces chosen are ahistorical and often represent the original typeface with one from a completely different family of types (in the edition of Heywood's *Pardoner and the Friar*, 1533, the facsimile uses a standard textura for the original bastarda).[19] Again, such editions obviously do not serve as guides to the original. They are rather substitutes for it. To a nineteenth- or twentieth-century reader, a Malone Society reprint "looks" like the original, even though it is not to a bibliographer or a typographer a visually accurate representation of that original.

To call a modern transcription of a manuscript "diplomatic" positions it squarely in one of the branches of this tradition. But the function of the Piers Plowman Archive transcriptions is not the same as the function of transcriptions in these types of editions. The Piers Archive transcriptions are not ersatz texts or manuscripts; they don't look like manuscripts or even like traditional texts, and they are very unlikely to be read as texts even though they may be quoted in scholarly journals as texts. Each text is rather a caption or an interpretative guide to what one sees in the related image of the original manuscript. No one is buying these disks in order to obtain a new text, since texts sufficient for most scholarly purposes are already available. Scholars are buying them to get images of the manuscripts and to obtain a searchable text, essentially an electronic concordance.

Comparing Style Sheets II: Diplomatic Versus Scribal Versus Critical

My original goal was to determine how and where all these style sheets or versions differ. To compare various transcriptions turned out to be relatively easy for the Scribal and Diplomatic style sheets, at least in some of the volumes, since you can put a page on the screen and flip or click between versions, thus creating what amounts to a Poor Man's Hinman Collator version of the two transcriptions. You can do that, that is, unless a folio number appears on the page you are looking at, which for unaccountable reasons is in some volumes (W, but not F) printed in a different font in the two style sheets. In all the passages I checked, my Poor Man's Hinman Collator confirmed what the Archive introduction tells me: the Diplomatic and Scribal style sheets are identical, except that one of them has notes. If this is true throughout, it's hard to see why the two exist. Here is a text of the *Canterbury Tales*. Here is the same one: this has notes. Why not have a single text with a "suppress notes" function?

Armed with this collating technique, I then turned to the Critical style sheet. It quickly became clear to me why the early reviewers of the Piers Plowman Archive did not do what I feel they should have done, that is, catalogue and investigate all those individual cases where editors believe they have been able to distinguish Scribal Act from Scribal Intent. For the Critical text transcriptions in F and W, the editors have included line numbers from the Kane-Donaldson edition (K-D); this is a reasonable decision, since those references make the text easier to compare with that standard edition. But adding those references to the beginning of each line makes it impossible, I think, to conduct a quick Poor Man's Hinman comparison of the two texts, since the K-D references make visual overlay of the images impossible. I thus had no way of finding in any systematic way the cases where editors judge intent and action to be different, and apparently, neither did the scholars who reviewed this edition. What you cannot find, you cannot critique.

Hm128

In the disk of Hm128, the K-D references are less disruptive, and one can thus Hinmanize the different style sheet transcriptions by switching mechanically between them. Their differences are visually obvious. This is a major improvement, in part because it exposes rather than obscures the difficulties of distinguishing between various transcriptional conventions. One difference between the Scribal and Diplomatic style sheets turns out to be the treatment of what are called "erasures." The Diplomatic style sheet shows these erasures; the Scribal style sheet does not. Whatever choice the editors make here will probably be subject to criticism, but confronting this difference in the style sheets, I am suddenly perplexed over the meaning of the word "diplomatic." A diplomatic transcription represents what is in the manuscript or what it looks like. A scribal transcription is what the scribe wrote. Why aren't scribal erasures thus indicated on the Scribal style sheet? Why are they instead on the Diplomatic style sheet, which represents not the history of the manuscript's production but rather the manuscript appearance? Had the editors distinguished these differently, I would likely be asking the reverse question: aren't erasures "diplomatic"? And as I switch through the three style sheets, I suddenly despair of an answer. The problem seems not to be the definition of the various sheets, but the imagining of their very existence.

Note, for example, how the very word *diplomatic* will not stay in place. In F, "diplomatic" means "almost a type facsimile." A type facsimile is, I would think, a typeset version of a typeset original; an example would be the Malone Society editions noted above. Perhaps that is why the qualifier *almost* is used here: it is really not possible to have a diplomatic type facsimile of a manuscript. Yet if the editors believe type facsimile editions of manuscripts are possible, then I do not see why the word *almost* appears here or what qualification it is supposed to indicate. This *is* a type facsimile, not *almost* one. In later volumes, as the Diplomatic (upper case?) style sheet achieves its own autonomy and is no longer simply a version of the Scribal style sheet, editors use the word *diplomatic* somewhat differently:

> The Critical style sheet is designed to indicate the text as it was
> intended to appear after correction. Since the text displayed is a
> reconstructed, putative text, it lacks the color features that appear in
> the more nearly diplomatic transcriptions of the manuscript. (Cala-
> brese and Duggan, *MS Hm128*)

I can only assume from this that the Diplomatic style sheet (with color features) is one of those "more nearly diplomatic transcriptions." But why is a Diplomatic style sheet not *exactly* diplomatic?

I realize one reason for such qualifications is that these are responsible scholars, who recognize the tentative nature of all scholarly assertions. But this is no time for real or false modesty. If you are going to distinguish two transcriptions, scribal and diplomatic, then you must say here is one and there is the other, not "this approximates one, and that is almost the other." An unqualified assertion may be wrong, but it is at least clear and subject to critique. We get no nearer to an imagined scholarly truth or even a consensus on such matters by pussyfooting around.

Text Versus Intention: The Evolving Nature of the Style Sheets

What has struck me most about the difference between these style sheets is the repeated distinction between scribal text and scribal intent. This is a variant of a basic problem of classical textual criticism—how "what is written" (or transmitted) is different from "what is (or was) intended." The author "intended" X, but the scribes "wrote" Y. In the field of textual criticism, this much criticized assumption is most vehemently attacked in modern electronic editions; the occasional condescension shown toward classical critical editions in the various introductions of the Piers Plowman Archive is one reflection of this. The style sheets from the Archive, however, compound the problems associated with the distinction "intention"/"act of writing"; here, "what is intended" does not seem to be placed in the same historical relation to "what is transcribed by the scribe" in the various manuscript situations.

When we look at the description and definition of these style sheets in the volume W, the difference seems utterly banal: what the scribe wrote vs. what we believe that scribe intended to write. This is no more than what classical textual criticism has always wished to record: what someone meant vs. what someone (maybe the same person, maybe a different person) actually set down. But the distinction, so inconsequential in the discussion of manuscript W, has its roots in the situation regarding manuscript F, the first manuscript edition published in the Archive.

Let us look at definitions stated in volume F, first of what are called three "editions," next of five "style sheets." In some formulations, there seems to be no difference between a style sheet and an edition; these distinctions also are blurred by the existence of levels, often six, of transcription (see n. 11 below):

we intend to construct the archetypal (and where necessary, hyperarchetypal) texts of each of the three canonic versions, and eventually, to create critical editions. . . . In this, the first volume of the *Archive*, we offer three editions in one. The first is a diplomatic transcription—almost a type facsimile—of [F], in which we attempt to represent as literally as possible in modern type the readings and significant physical features of the manuscript. We offer at the same time a color facsimile edition of the entire manuscript. . . . Finally, as a kind of textual experiment, we attempt here to edit critically the work of an editorial scribe between the final copying represented in F and the scribe whose efforts created the alpha recension of the B text. . . .

We have attempted to make as close a transcription of the manuscript text as possible, a text that will later serve as a base for machine collation with all of the other B witnesses. This edition, which users of this CD-ROM will access using the "F-Scribe" style sheet is intended to represent the manuscript as closely as print permits. (Duggan, Preface, *MS F*)[20]

If I read these descriptions correctly, the "three editions" or "transcriptions" are the scribal, the facsimile, and the critical, and these are not much different from what one would have in the case of any classical edition. The Scribal style sheet is equivalent to the first and is thus "almost a type facsimile." The Critical style sheet is apparently the last.

These multiple levels are of particular interest in the case of MS F. In the analysis by Kane, largely accepted by the editors of the Piers Archive, there are two manuscript families serving as authorities for the B-text or that constitute the evidence for version B of *Piers Plowman*. Two manuscripts, R and F, are together against all others, and these two form what Schmidt calls the "alpha" branch; the "beta" branch is constituted by all other B-text manuscripts.[21] These two manuscripts R and F also differ from each other, most notably in the structuring of the poem. F is unique among all manuscripts in dividing the poem into sixteen *passus* rather than twenty. The most obvious explanation for this situation involves the hypothesis of a manuscript *alpha*, which then leads to the two extant manuscripts R and F. Somewhere between hypothesized manuscript *alpha* and real manuscript F is an hypothesized action or manuscript or redaction involving or constituting F's unique division or structuring of the poem. This action is attributed to an entity or

person or scribe or editor known as the "F-Redactor," who may or may not
be close to or even identical to the "F-Scribe" who is responsible for the F
manuscript.[22] This situation leads to the Archive editors' "textual experiment," which is to reproduce the text of the "F-Redactor":

> However, when we realized that the immediate scribe who wrote
> the manuscript is not to be identified with the adventurous scribal
> editor who changed the passus structure and revised some thousands
> of lections, we decided to attempt to reconstruct as much as we
> practically could of that revisor's text. It is both in theory and prac-
> tice a text which can only be approximated, but the attempt proved
> sufficiently interesting and, we think, valuable, that we have pre-
> sented a lightly edited text of the revisor's work. That text is accessi-
> ble using the F-Critical style sheet. This model is not likely to prove
> useful in editing other B manuscripts, and we have already adopted
> other editorial practices to display the salient features of those other
> texts. (Duggan, "Preface," *MS F*)

This is an extremely interesting passage. The Critical style sheet attempts to
produce not a "putative" text (one imagined by a scribe), but the *actual text*
(or a "lightly edited" one) from which F was transcribed.[23]

The descriptions of this Critical style sheet are inconsistent. Note in the
passages from the Prefatory material quoted above that the F-Critical style
sheet is first an "approxima[tion of] the text of F-Redactor." In the second
paragraph, it is "the text as the F-Redactor would have wished to see it."
These are two different things. And they are different in precisely the way
that the so-called Scribal and Critical style sheets in all volumes are described
as being different: one sheet represents a real, historical text; the other is an
intended text.

As noted by the editors, the Critical style sheet for F is unique; that is, it
is not the same kind of thing as the Critical style sheets constructed for
other manuscripts. What it reconstructs, or what it was once intended to
reconstruct, is the work of the F-Redactor. It looks backward, to a hypothetical manuscript intermediate between F and hypothesized *alpha*, the source
for readings unique to the two manuscripts R and F. To reconstruct this may
be a useful editorial or intellectual exercise, but the only reason we are really
interested in this manuscript is because of its presumed structuring of the
poem, or *ordinatio*. Among *Piers* manuscripts, this is found only in the manu-

script F. It has nothing to do with the original text B or with Langland; it is "inauthentic" even as far as hypothesized *alpha* is concerned. Not only is there nothing of textual-critical value in this hypothesized manuscript, there is nothing of interest in terms of the reception and transmission of *Piers Plowman* in its "putative" text that is not plainly visible in the real manuscript F.

The Relation of F-Critical Style Sheet to Later Critical Style Sheets

The F-Critical style sheet is not the same as the Critical style sheet in any other volume of the Piers Archive, as the editors state directly. The seemingly close relation between style sheets among the volumes is illusory, and the Template quoted above is thus a source not for the substance of these variant style sheets, but only for the language describing them. In these later volumes (W, M, O, Hm128), the now obligatory style sheets remain, even though they seem to have lost their raison d'être. There is no interesting intermediary between the subject-manuscript and the archetype A, B, or C, nor do the editors at this point seem interested in reconstructing such hypothetical texts, although such a reconstruction is certainly no more difficult and no less problematic than the reconstruction of B itself. For example, W readings are from the subarchetype *beta*; although W is a "good" manuscript by most editorial standards, it is no more an authority for any one of these readings than any other manuscript in this family. The critical invocation of "what the scribe intended" neither answers nor raises important textual-critical questions; it simply raises problems (these problems are of course known to and cited by the editors).

> We have used <SIC> tags to indicate those instances in which we take the scribe not to have written what he intended to write, but we have ignored readings the scribe might reasonably be interpreted as having intended. For instance, at W5.264 the scribe wrote nonsensical *bu* where he intended to write *but*. We print *bu* but flag it with purple. However, the probably erroneous lection, at least in relation to the B archetype, *prechede* for *prayed* is not so marked in W5.43, though a textual note calls attention to this unique reading in W. (Turville-Petre and Duggan, *MS W*)

For the erroneous *bu*, they assume the scribe meant *but*; but for his erroneous *prechede*, the scribe meant exactly that—*prechede*. These may be of theoretical interest, but none of this is of editorial significance.

The notion of what the scribe *meant* or *intended* can only be an important textual-critical concept in cases like this if we assume the word *intended* means "what scribe saw." That is certainly what it means in the case of F, since we are interested in the F-redactor's text that is the basis for F. But in the case of W, it is not at all certain what "intended" means or what purpose the term serves. It might mean "what the scribe saw"; it could also mean "what the scribe thought he saw" or "what he thought was preferable to what he saw." We need to know why the scribe intended what he supposedly did. Only "what the scribe saw"—something that antedates the scribe's work—is of textual-critical interest. "The state in which the scribe wished W to be" post-dates the actual manuscript W and its copytext; in classical textual-critical terms, this is something not to be studied but to be eliminated.

When we turn to the more recent edition of Hm128, we see that the Critical style sheet, at least in its definition, has continued to evolve, and evolve away from the model provided in the edition of MS F. Hm128 contains the work of several hands: two principal scribes and a corrector (I assume this corrector is not contemporary, based on the opinions of Hanna and Doyle, but I do not see the contradiction between this and the notion that he worked with the same exemplar).

> The Critical style sheet is designed to indicate the text as it was intended to appear after correction. Since the text displayed is a reconstructed, putative text, it lacks the color features. (Calabrese and Duggan, *MS Hm128*)

This is a variant of the language that appears in the introduction to volume F. But note that the definition of the Critical style sheet continues to move; editors now unambiguously define this "putative reconstructed text" as one that post-dates the manuscript. Its theoretical existence must be temporally assigned to a date *after* the main scribes worked on the manuscript; it is not something that preexisted the work of these scribes and not something they could have seen. In F, because of the textual situation, the critical text was the work of the "F-Redactor" (this is stated directly); in other words, the manuscript represented in the facsimile and in the Scribal and Diplomatic style sheets was regarded as a deterioration, comparable to all extant witnesses as they are treated in classical textual criticism. Here, however, it is an entity that can only exist following the work of the scribes and perhaps of the corrector.

Conclusion: The Perfect Text

The only way to align the multiple meanings of "putative, reconstructed text" implied by the various Critical style sheets is to assume that "what is intended" by various scribes is a perfect and exact copy of the manuscript they copy: in other words, those scribes intend as a future product a perfect copy of a past product. In this idealized state of textual transmission, even the typographical text is a perfect and exact copy of the handwritten text, and scribal error is not only eliminated but defined out of existence. But if that were ever the case, or even a possible case, past and present editors of *Piers Plowman* would have little to do, and there would be no particular reason for editors to be interested in this text at all. *Piers Plowman* has attracted the interests of serious textual scholars precisely because none of them accepts the notion of the pure and unadulterated copy.

As I noted in the introduction, the editors of this project have shown a willingness to change as possibilities arise, to adapt their methods as new situations present themselves, and to allow the goals and even structure of the edition to evolve. They are in this following the precedent set by the Athlone edition, and in addition establishing quite new standards of editorial openness and (for me) unfailing generosity.[24] But this willingness to change comes with a price. Reviewers for the most part are curiously blind to it, and the editions themselves contradict one of the stated goals of the project.

I have in the past been critical of editions and databases that claim to provide the ground for new questions, while in fact narrowing the range of the kinds of question that can be asked. A database or edition can only be a means for answering questions its editors foresee.[25] The coordinating of the style sheets, which editors obviously see as a desideratum, is in my opinion an error, at least, if we take seriously the stated goal of this edition as producing a new critical edition. The evolution of these sheets will somehow produce a "collatable" *Piers Plowman* B-recension, which ultimately, through the magic of editorialism, will result in a new transcription of a new edition. But the basis of this new edition will be as wonderfully flimsy as Skeat's, built on the fantasy that the scholarly language so perfectly descriptive of one manuscript situation can somehow work equally well for another. The vices of this edition will be exactly its virtues, and the unsatisfactory nature of this typeset edition may well return its users to the manuscript images and unthinkable complexities that are at its base.

Coda on a Coda by Robert N. Essick and Joseph Viscomi: Blake's "Order in Which the Songs of Innocence & of Experience ought to be paged and placed"

The William Blake Archive by Morris Eaves, Robert Essick, and Joseph Viscomi (www.blakearchive.org) is an extension of work begun well before the possibility of an on-line Archive. Blake's works are especially suited for this medium: although they are conventionally described as other books are described (we all have some basic idea of what we mean by "Songs of Innocence"), they do not conform to the terms used in ordinary bibliographical language, nor to the situations described by this language. The texts are not typeset but formed by relief etching, and they are printed using nontraditional methods.[26]

In 2002, in a series of seemingly modest articles on a technical point of printing, Essick and Viscomi reconceived the entire nature of the editorial and bibliographical problem in regard to Blake studies.[27] The ostensible subject of these articles was a technical one, concerning the process of two-color printing. All Blake scholars agree that Blake's work synthesizes (transcends?) many of the basic dichotomies of text and illustration, producing text on the plate rather than in type, combining relief and intaglio methods, combining water and oil-miscible paints. The artistic career of Blake could then be seen as a development within the poles implied by these competing technologies.

The question raised by Essick and Viscomi concerned the method for color printing in *Songs of Innocence* and *Songs of Experience*. This process was described by Martin Butlin as a two-pull method: the plate is inked in one color and a single sheet printed; the plate is washed, a second color applied, and the sheet run through the press again.[28] Yet of the hundreds of variant impressions examined first by Butlin and Michael Phillips and later by Essick and Viscomi, only one shows evidence of having been through a press twice (the plate for "Nurse's Song" from the *Songs of Experience* in the Huntington Library copy, known to Blake scholars as copy E); that evidence is in the obvious misregistration of the images produced with each pull. This plate is often reproduced and the evidence is easily visible; the registration (that is, the two overprinted impressions of the etched lines) is off by at least a quarter of an inch.[29] To Butlin and Phillips, this incontestable evidence suggested that elsewhere, Blake had perfected this process, concealing absolutely the evidence of technique. To Essick and Viscomi, the "Nurse's Song" image is exceptional, and shows that Blake did not really care about the issues for which he receives such praise.

What the articles of Essick and Viscomi show is that such arguments are not neutral, nor are they based on the material evidence they cite. They are, rather, rooted in a Growth and Development narrative that is applied to all aspects of his art, theoretical and technical.

> [Butlin] sees Blake's development as moving from simple to complex, from small relief etchings printed in one pull, to etchings and relief etchings printed in two pulls, to large color prints produced in two pulls and elaborate finished in watercolors and pen and ink. (Essick and Viscomi, "Blake's Method of Color Printing: Some Further Observations," 60)[30]

The history Essick and Viscomi describe is a result of what they find in the images, not what they find in Blake. The arguments by Butlin and Phillips require that Blake's skills as a printer be so great that, in all but one of his images, he absolutely concealed the method of printing—something achieved by no other contemporary printer and in no other work printed in two colors. It is based not on evidence, but on the concealing of evidence—its absence. To a non-Blake scholar who has ever studied two-color printing, however casually, the conclusion is inescapable: those who disagree with Essick and Viscomi do not simply hold competing views; they are flat-out wrong.

The above example is one of several in which the Blake Archive seems the embodiment of the dictum of Henry Bradshaw: "arrange your facts rigorously, and get them plainly before you, & let them speak for themselves." Yet when those facts must be represented in type, they are often less congenial. I close with what amounts to a small footnote in the edition, the almost incidental edition included in the Blake Archive of a manuscript outline or set of notes: "Order in Which the Songs of Innocence & of Experience ought to be paged and placed." This is a two-page manuscript by Blake listing exactly what its title says.[31]

The editorial problem, if it can be characterized as a problem, seems simple: no one in this case would really care about archetypes or filiations or fair copies or *homeoteleuton, lectiones difficiliores,* or any of the usual mystifications found in textual criticism. The only serious questions anyone interested in Blake would have are the following: is this Blake's hand? is it a copy of something else? is it written continuously? is the order of titles here the same as that found in any of the actual copies of the book? what is the function of the check marks (transcribed as *x*'s) in the left-hand margin? Yet these questions cannot be answered by the edition itself, an edition you find by clicking on "textual transcription" on the Archive page; they can only be addressed in a Notes section. Since I am not a Blake scholar, I have the luxury of ignoring such questions; the edition, (happily) by virtue of being an edition, throws such questions completely into the background.

The editors give a facsimile of the page, along with a scrupulously diplomatic transcription, representing typographically the wandering vertical of the checkmarks in the left margins; the transcription also adds some right-facing curled brackets between items 5 and 6 and again between items 8 and 9. I don't know the function of these and I cannot determine what they represent in the manuscript. For most readers, except those who cannot read handwriting of any kind, there is no information in this transcription that is not perfectly obvious from the detailed image reproduced in the Archive. The hand is clear, and there seems no ambiguity of format. The edition, thus, inadvertently poses a new set of questions, not about Blake and his books, but about the function of editions. Perhaps electronic edition-making, where texts such as this can be subjected to classical textual-critical methodology, is far more radical than editors suggest.

The typographical representation of the manuscript requires an intricate set of principles to deal with the most visually obvious of facts. The wandering vertical of the checkmarks is almost certainly intended by Blake to be straight, but visually, it is not, and it is thus represented as curved through a series of discrete keystrokes and spaces in lines 9–12 of the edition. By contrast, the broken vertical formed by punctuation following each numeral is ignored; that is, it is presented as irrelevant in the edition, in accordance with the apparent intentions of Blake. Yet in the transcription of items 19–23, a problem arises: in the original, the initial letters of the titles maintain the vertical; in the edition, they are indented, a function of the interpretation of the period as a typestroke. Furthermore, the right-hand justification (or lack of justification) is a pure function of editorial typography; right-hand justification is thus defined as a matter of indifference, but the decision to define it that way is not a matter of indifference, since that decision is in accord with the implied intentions of the author Blake. Each of these decisions is of course editorially rational, and looking at the edition, we can reconstruct the thinking behind them. Taken together, however, they seem based on thoroughly diverse principles, and I can only assume that having to make such decisions at all was a source of extreme amusement or aggravation to the editors.

The easiest way to confront this selection and editorial decision-making is to attempt to transcribe the transcription in the Archive, something for which my own editors are unlikely to thank me:

```
01  n       page
02  n x x 24.   A Dream
03  n x x 25.   On Anothers Sorrow
04    x x 26.   The Little Boy Lost
```

The columns are straight (or I hope they will be), with the exception of the first column of x's, where the third x is not in vertical alignment with the first and second.

Unlike diplomatic editions of the nineteenth century, the diplomatic transcription in the Archive and my own diplomatic transcription of the Archive do not function for most users as ersatz originals: everyone with access to the Archive transcription has access to an image of the original; everyone with access to my transcription has easy access to the Archive. Nor is the Archive transcription a "trot" or translation of the original, since the original is clear in most of its details, or surely clear enough to anyone who is interested enough in Blake to consider looking at it. Such transcriptions are, rather, sources of errors, many of which the reader is expected to correct. For example, the Archive editors assume quite rightly that a reader looking at the image of the manuscript knows perfectly well that items 52, 53, 54 are written vertically, even though the transcription reproduces them horizontally, respecting the placement of them in the original by printing them in the lower right. The diplomatic edition thus standardizes writing techniques: writing is defined as horizontal, even though the vagaries of other sorts of verticality not defined as writing are scrupulously albeit erroneously represented.

The attempt to reproduce the appearance of the manuscript through a typographical image thus produces something quite different, an interpretation not of Blake but of typography. Readers are now asked to interpret or read as relevant certain keystrokes (spaces), certain anomalies (the wandering verticality); they are instructed to ignore others (no attempt is made to reproduce, say, the different ink colors; the type style chosen in the transcription also has nothing to do with Blake's hand). But there is no consistent way to distinguish these two classes of things. The edition, thus, does not serve ordinary editorial functions of rendering the original more readable, transparent, or accessible. It highlights the oddities of edition-making generally, and thus may well (and rightly) reflect back and comment on the artificiality of the edition-making enterprise, particularly one that involves conventions of type.

The modern literary archive (the Blake Archive is one of the best of them) has competing ideals: one is editorial and heavily mediated; the other is what could be called its iconicity. The imagined repository of evidence unmediated by the machinations of editors in many ways reproduces products or ideals of seventeenth- and eighteenth-century antiquarianism. It becomes an electronic cabinet of curiosities, at best a perfect icon rather than a representation of the past. Among the virtues of both the Blake Archive and the Piers Plowman Archive are those that contradict their apparent aims, those moments when the mediation of their editors comes most strongly to the forefront.

CHAPTER SEVEN

ॐ

The Representation of Representation: Versions of Linear Perspective

The model of linear perspective has been in practical use by drawing manuals for centuries and has been the subject of many recent studies. It is simple in its theory and in its geometry; its construction is equally simple in practice. Yet this simplicity and elegance has not prevented it from being grossly misrepresented, even by those art historians who have studied it closely and by artists who are perfectly competent in using it.[1] Problems associated with this model are an extension of the typographical problem I have been dealing with throughout this study: how does one represent something—an idea, a statement, a three-dimensional object—on a two-dimensional plane? And to what extent do conventional ways of seeing or thinking dominate the sometimes contradictory and recalcitrant facts of objects? Here, our misconstruction of what we see and read seems essential to our understanding of what these things represent.

The present chapter considers three variations: (1) the model itself and traditional misreadings of it; (2) the classical reception by Piero della Francesca and Leonardo and what is known as the three-column paradox; (3) the use of the model in the construction of seventeenth-century stages and contemporary representations of those stages in printed books.

The Classical Model: Alberti and Viator

The model of linear perspective is usually associated with Leon Battista Alberti's *De Pictura* of 1434, first printed in 1540 (in Latin) and 1547 (in Italian).[2]

Neither the earliest manuscripts nor the earliest printed editions of Alberti contain illustrations, although his descriptions are sufficiently clear for a consensus to have developed both on the technique and the pictorial form of the model, which I reproduce in my own variant in Figure 24. In its simplest form, the model of linear perspective is the solution to the problem of how to draw an angled checkerboard on a two-dimensional picture surface. The problem is more complicated than that simple formulation makes it seem, since "how to draw" is a function of "how the picture will be viewed," and that will be one of the subjects of the present chapter.

Among the basic principles of linear perspective are the following: all straight lines in space will be straight when represented in perspective on a two-dimensional surface; a fixed viewpoint implies a horizon on the picture plane and a series of planes emanating from that horizon; any set of parallel lines imagined on any of these planes will intersect at a vanishing point on that horizon.[3]

The checkerboard, the basis for Alberti's discussion, can be constructed purely mechanically, although it is far more cumbersome to describe verbally than to demonstrate in a figure. In Alberti's construction, the checkerboard pattern is imagined as set with one side parallel to (or simply as) the base of the picture. A series of equidistant points is marked on the this baseline: two points are drawn on the arbitrary horizon (one usually the central point of the frame, the other generally outside the frame); a series of lines are drawn from each of the two points to the points on the baseline. A vertical line is drawn from the rightmost point of the checkerboard base to the horizon. The lines of the second horizon point will intersect with that vertical line, and horizontal lines drawn from those intersecting points will determine the receding horizontals of the checkerboard. The correct viewpoint is determined by an imagined perpendicular line from the intersection of the vertical and the horizon; the viewing distance VD will be the distance between the vertical and the second point on the horizon (see Figure 24).

A second, often cited variant of Alberti's procedure is by Viator (Vignola, or Jean Pelèrin).[4] In Viator's method, a series of equidistant points is placed on the base and two points are placed anywhere on the horizon. Here, however, the intersection of the lines with each other determines the proper foreshortening of the horizontals of the checkerboard; the viewing distance VD is equal to the distance between the two horizon points (Figure 25). The two methods of construction by Alberti and Viator are effectively the same; Al-

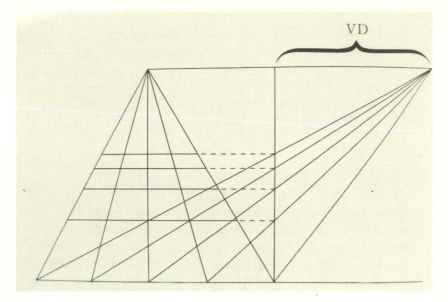

Figure 24. Alberti's model.

berti's vertical line is simply incorporated into the construction in Viator's method.

The easiest check of whether a checkerboard construction follows this model or formula is a simple one: according to the rules of linear perspective, all straight lines in the imagined space will be straight when represented on a two-dimensional plane; thus the diagonals of the checkerboard (straight in space) must also be straight in the two-dimensional representation.[5] In checkerboard floors constructed prior to Alberti, this is never the case. Diagonals commonly curve inward, as seen in the fifteenth-century miniatures of the Limbourg brothers (for example, in the *Très riches heures du Duc de Berry*).

Drawings with curving diagonals are not incorrect, bad, or ineffective; they are hardly noticeable unless one tests for them or is looking for them. The presence of such curved diagonals simply means that the picture is not drawn according to the formulae of Alberti or Viator. Nearly all amateur or freehand drawings of checkerboards in apparent perspective show this feature. Attempts to produce the checkerboard by following an arbitrary arithmetic formula will generally produce this same result. The 1611 English version of Serlio's *Five Books of Architecture*, specifically addressing linear perspective, shows the same thing: the stages pictured in Book II, fols. 25 and

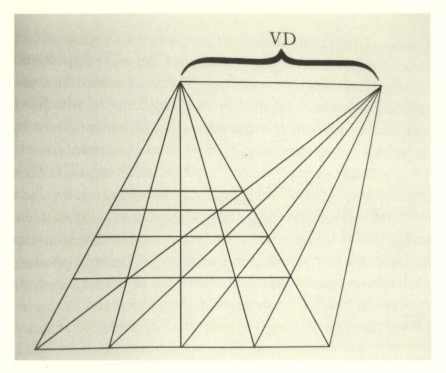

Figure 25. Viator's model.

26 have inwardly curving diagonals, although the earlier drawings (fols. 1–3) show that a true linear perspective model will not produce such things.[6]

The most important feature of the Alberti and Viator model is the requirement of a fixed and determinate viewpoint and viewing distance. The eye must be at the distance VP from the picture plane and perpendicular to the plane at the point X. The eye at this fixed point will presumably "see" the two-dimensional structure precisely as it will "see" such objects in space. A modern *camera oscura* or a pinhole camera will construct or project an image that is identical to one constructed according to the formulae of Alberti or Viator.[7]

The geometry and practical functioning of this model are straightforward, but the fact that it is based on two-dimensional objects in a three-dimensional space creates ambiguities. A checkerboard projected onto a picture plane is the projection of one two-dimensional object onto another. If that checkerboard is on a plane parallel to the plane of the picture, the image is not only the image of the object, but a physical icon of it; as I will discuss below, it is the same as what is called an architectural elevation. This is not the case when three-dimensional objects are at issue.

Traditional Errors

In the reception of this model, there have been a series of errors, some so persistent as to become traditional.

(1) The errant phrase "three-point perspective" and the notion that this has to do with the construction of a cube, with its three sets of parallel planes, oriented obliquely in space, and that this too is somehow, albeit mysteriously, related to the notion of "three-dimensional space." This is a commonplace of drawing manuals, and finds currency even in the article on perspective by B. A. R. Carter in the *Oxford Companion to Art*.[8] These manuals show the edges of a constructed cube extended in apparent space to result in three vanishing points. The notion of "three points" is arbitrary, and a misreading of Viator's own reference to what he calls "third points." Viator's "third points" are the horizon points shown in the diagram above (Figure 25). A cube in perspective can certainly be constructed according to such a misreading of the meaning of Viator's "third points." And thus errors by theorists, by historians, and by artists themselves may have little to do with practical results.

(2) The relation of the linear perspective model to the notion of "curved space." The lineage of this notion is more complex. Obviously, if one stands on railroad tracks and looks east, then west, the tracks are foreshortened in each direction. They must therefore "appear" curved. Wilhelm Schickhardt in the seventeenth century describes this phenomenon in terms of "Sehkurven." Erwin Panofsky, in the twentieth century, tried to relate this both to the physical shape of the retina and to contemporary theories of the curvature of space; in so doing, he misrepresented the problem as well as the simple mathematics of the two geometrical models he provided as illustration.[9]

The paradoxes and occasional confusion here have to do with the difference between what is seen and what should be drawn. The model of Alberti deals only with "what should be drawn": a large mural showing an aerial view of railroad tracks may well be seen by a viewer as a series of foreshortened ties with tracks narrowing left and right. The tracks depicted on that mural therefore must appear curved. But as long as the tracks and ties are imagined as two-dimensional, those tracks will be drawn as two parallel straight lines, with equidistant ties.

(3) Political readings. The most common of what I call the political misinterpretations claims that the model imposes a set of strictures on classical art, which mannerist or postmodern artists break through. The bizarre paintings of Paolo Uccello, or the late twentieth-century constructions of Henri Flocon are seen as freed from the restrictive rules of perspective, which pertain somehow to what is known as realistic or naturalistic art.[10] The reverse is the case: Uccello and Flocon achieve their unsettling effects not by breaking free of the restrictions imposed by the model but by following those rules and restrictions in minute detail, something so-called classical artists did not do. The most radical of art is produced through the paradoxical rigorous application of rules.

Architectural Elevation Versus Perspective Drawing and the Notion of a Fixed Viewpoint

A source of many confusions and errors is the conflation of the linear perspective model with what is called an "architectural elevation" or "floor-plan." In an architectural elevation, a two-dimensional surface is recreated maintaining the proportions of the original. An architectural drawing is a model or icon, not an image or a representation. A checkerboard is recreated, as if on a blueprint, according to its proportionate measurements. A portico, or series of columns of similar size, is constructed as a series of columns of equal width represented in two dimensions; these columns are drawn, not as a portico would be seen in real space, but as if seen from an infinitely distant viewpoint: column widths are identical (the proportions are the same as a cross-section of those columns cut parallel to the picture plane), and no column is closer to the eye than any other. An architectural drawing produces a workable icon of an object that can then be reconstructed physically according to the dimensions in the drawing; it does not represent the way anything might actually be seen in perspective. There are no shadings, light sources, or privileged viewpoints in architectural drawings or in blueprints.[11] An architectural elevation thus is different from a perspective drawing, although in special cases, as noted above, the two are indistinguishable (a two-dimensional checkerboard oriented on a plane parallel to the plane of the picture).

Historically, these types of drawings have been conflated, or their differences rationalized as a progression that often follows quirks of language rather than the logic of geometry. Vitruvius's words *ichnographia, orthographia,* and *scenographia* refer to the construction of a groundplan, the depiction of a façade, and a perspective view of façade and sides. This language was reinterpreted by later writers such as Daniel Barbaro (1669) to refer not to types of drawings but to depictions of increasingly complex objects, such as the doughnut-shaped *mazzocco* or *torus*; Serlio's discussion follows such a progression and ends with a discussion of stages and theatrical scenes (see book 2, "A Treatise of Perspectives," chap. 3).[12] The implications of such a notion of scenography will be discussed below.

The Notion of a Fixed Viewpoint and the Limitations of Optics

In terms of the viewer, the major feature of the perspective model that distinguishes it from an architectural elevation is its assumption of a fixed viewpoint. For the model to work correctly, the viewer is assumed to be a point in space in a fixed location at a fixed distance from the picture. Anyone who spends time in Western museums, or claims to, is aware of this: classical paintings, we are taught, have an implied viewing point, and we imagine we find that point as we view those paintings. Many *trompe l'oeil* paintings seem to rely on the same assumption, whether those are on the ceilings of buildings or in the pages of printed books.[13] Yet this conviction may well be an illusion, a product more of our training in art history than of our experience as viewers.

In a gallery, to maintain such a fixed viewing point is impossible. A gallery is a space in which people move, from painting to painting, from social concern to social concern. Those who are interested in a painting will view it from different distances and angles; often they will view it while they are in motion. Furthermore, any gallery that existed before the advent of electricity is by modern standards a very ill-lit space, as are the seventeenth-century stages I will discuss below; and this will in turn provide severe limitations on the assumptions required for a fixed viewpoint.

Lateral Distortion and the Three-Column Paradox: Piero della Francesca and Leonardo

The problem of the fixed viewpoint and the consequent difference between architectural elevations and perspective drawings are particularly apparent in what is called the three-column paradox, involving the depiction on a picture plane of a series of columns parallel to that plane. A portico of columns drawn as an architectural elevation will be a series of identical rectangles representing these columns across the plane of the drawing. When the same columns parallel to the picture plane are drawn according to the rules of linear perspective, the columns farthest from the axis of the viewpoint (at the margins, if the viewpoint is central) are drawn wider than those nearest the viewpoint; that is, they occupy more space on the canvas. This is a paradox rarely confronted by modern viewers of classical paintings; we are used to seeing such parallel columns drawn as they would be drawn in an architectural elevation or as if seen from an infinite viewing distance: the façades and porticos in the paintings of Canaletto are the most familiar example. Such paintings may appear to be drawn according to rules of perspective and might well be described that way by viewers, since rows of columns depicted obliquely may indeed recede to a definable vanishing point. But they are not.

The problem and its geometry was described with great clarity by Piero della Francesca, whose discussion of this problem occurs as the last chapter in Book 2 of *De Prospectiva pingendi*. The lucidity of this discussion with its accompanying diagram contrasts markedly with the presumably simpler but extraordinarily obscure problem and solution closing book 1—the one section unfortunately canonized for many English readers by its inclusion in Elizabeth G. Holt's *Documentary History of Art*. Both chapters are accounts of the modern paradox sometimes referred to as "lateral foreshortening."[14]

The problem discussed at the end of book 1 involves the portrayal of a row of squares. The problem itself is not clearly defined: a single square moving obliquely across the line of sight does not maintain its visual shape, nor is its distance from the viewpoint easily defined. And the solution Piero proposes—limiting the line of sight and the angle of vision permitted in a drawing of any of the steps of this movement to 90 degrees—seems arbitrary. The only problem Piero's diagram solves is one I have not seen cited in relation to it. Hold a pencil oriented directly along the line of sight so that it appears a point. Move it in a line perpendicular to its shaft. The apparent size will begin to increase. At what point does it begin to decrease? The answer is when it is at a 45-degree angle from the original line of sight; within this 90-degree field it behaves differently from the way it does outside this field.

At the end of book 2, Piero considers the three-column paradox, a more complex variant of the same problem. In a row of columns parallel to a picture plane, the columns farthest from the viewpoint (those at the margins of the picture frame in a picture with a central viewpoint) will appear smaller to a viewer situated at the correct viewpoint; that is, they will have a smaller visual angle when viewed from that point. The viewer will then interpret

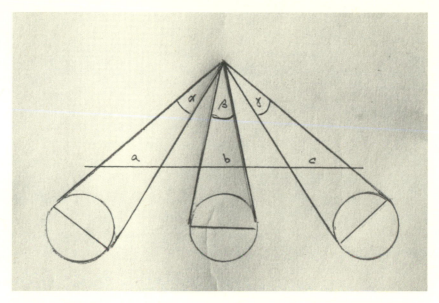

Figure 26. Piero della Francesca's demonstration of three-column paradox. Angle beta is greater than angles alpha or gamma. But line-segments *a* and *c* are greater than *b*.

them as "representing something the same size," since in the real world, things appear smaller when viewed from a greater distance. Yet despite this, the images of these more distant columns will occupy greater space on the picture itself (their represented sizes will be larger).[15] Piero's diagram alone is enough to illustrate this paradox (see Figure 26). The proof that follows the statement is completely straightforward. All that is required is to recognize that what one sees (the diameter of columns perpendicular to the line of sight) is not what is represented on the picture plane (the diameter of columns parallel to the picture plane).[16]

Leonardo, Panofsky, and the Assumption of Coherence

There is one very old source that perhaps requires special mention: Erwin Panofsky's classic *Die Perspective* [sic] *als "symbolische Form"* (1924), available in English as *Perspective as Symbolic Form*, trans. Christopher S. Wood, New York: Zone Books, 1991. The semiotic aspects of the work are still of interest to historians of art. The historical investigation of perspective is very much in the style of the positivistic history of science of the time: it assumes that the "correct" perspective theory of Brunelleschi must have had precursors that were only approximately correct. The nature of the earlier perspective schemes that Panofsky discusses has been deduced by drawing numerous lines over pictures. My misgivings about such investigative procedures have been expressed in the Introduction above. In both style and content this part of Panofsky's work seems [to] me to be too dated to be worth detailed consideration in the present context. (J. V. Field, *Piero della Francesca*, 33, n. 1)[17]

Leonardo's discussion of the three-column paradox occurs in a series of Fragments in his *Notebooks*, fragments 71, 77, and esp. 107–8.[18] Scholars agree on Leonardo's conclusions: he understands but rejects the strictly geometrical solution described by Piero. What is much less clear are the procedures Leonardo uses to reject it, and what his language entails.

The obscurity of these fragments is well attested by the fact that modern scholars have disagreed over the meaning of even the most basic of definitions (on what, for example, "simple perspective" is).[19] Recent scholars seem to be reaching the consensus that Leonardo's discussion of various perspectives in these fragments is either incoherent or impenetrably obscure. Andersen: "These concepts are quite vague and I do not think there is one precise interpretation that can be defended as the correct one" (*Geometry of Art*, 86). This may well be true, but it raises the obvious question: why does Leonardo require such a seemingly tangled argument, even in notebook form, to explain or reject a theory whose basics are set out so clearly in Piero?

Panofsky systematizes the language of these fragments; his discussion remains valuable, at least to me, for the very reasons Field and others reject it. The assumption of coherence (effectively a one-to-one relationship between Leonardo's terms and their conceptual basis) enables us to see more clearly the elements in Leonardo's argument and observations. In other words, we can begin by assuming Leonardo's thinking is coherent, even if that is not likely to be the case, just as we can assume the techniques and events studied in art history are teleological, even if we know they aren't. This is surely no worse than a secular variant of Pascal's wager: what harm can possibly come of it?

What seems uncontroversial is that in these fragments Leonardo defines various types of perspective, or more accurately, uses the word *perspettiva* with at least four qualifiers: simple perspective, natural perspective, artificial perspective, mixed or composite perspective. In Panofsky's analysis, these correspond to four types of perspective. *Perspettiva naturale* is the way things are seen in nature (objects are foreshortened in proportion to the distance from the viewer). *Perspettiva accidentale* is the way things are to be projected onto a flat picture plane through the model of linear perspective; it is essentially the model of Alberti or Viator, and often associated with Brunelleschi. Thus linear perspective in Leonardo's Fragment 99, *la prospectiva liniale*, corresponds to the geometry behind the technique of artificial perspective. When combined, these constitute "mixed" or "composite perspective" (*perspettiva mixta* or *perspettiva conposta*, Fr. 90). And to this mixed perspective is opposed *perspettiva simplice*. Note that these perspectives are different orders of things: artificial perspective is here an artistic technique, natural perspective is a fact of optics. Mixed perspective is then the application of the technique of artificial perspective to the facts of natural perspective.

The most problematic of these terms is, paradoxically, "simple perspective." This is defined in Fragment 90, and the definition is assumed by most scholars to apply to Fragments 107–108, although this may not be Leonardo's intention. Panofsky sees Fragment 90 as a "clear development" of these fragments; it seems rather the foundation for them.

> Frag. 90: La semplicie prospettiua è quella che è fatta dall'arte sopra sito equalmente distante dall-ochio con ogni sua parte,—prospettiua composta è quella che è fatta sopra sito il quale con nessuna sua parte è equalmente distante dall' ochio.

> [Simple perspective is that which made by art on a site where each part is equally distant from the eye; composite perspective is that which is worked on a site where no part is equally distant from the eye.]

There are several possible interpretations.[20] To Panofsky, "simple" perspective is achieved by the adoption of an infinitely distant viewpoint. That does make sense in terms of the first part of Fragment 90: simple perspective is that which treats no point on the picture plane as closer to the eye than any other. This seems to imply a viewpoint so distant that lines drawn from any point on the plane to the viewpoint are effectively parallel and perpendicular to the picture plane. Or it could simply mean that in any particular plane parallel to the picture plane, natural foreshortening is ignored (a legitimate

viewpoint could be imagined as anywhere in space). This interpretation, requiring that *sito* mean a "plane" (of a picture), is the interpretation I will
follow below. But the fragment has also been read as implying a spherical
sito: an eye at the focal point of a sphere is the same distance from any point
on the sphere.[21] Given that this is contrasted with "composite" perspective,
where no part of a "site" are equidistant from the eye, I think Panofsky's
sense of this fragment, even if incorrect, is more useful. Leonardo would then
be talking about those "sites" encountered in all paintings: the plane of the
picture, and perhaps other planes within the picture. Without this condition,
we are forced to consider the two "sites" as (1) a spherical one, rarely encountered in real art, and (2) "all others."

If we accept or assume this interpretation of Fragment 90, then Panofsky's readings of Fragments 107 and 108 follow: "simple perspective" (a technique followed by an artist) is opposed to "composite perspective" (a
competing technique); and "composite" or "mixed perspective" is the result
of the combination of "natural perspective" (a condition of the real world)
and "artificial perspective" (another technique of artists). Fragment 107 distinguishes two "parts" of perspective:

> la prima figura tutte le cose vedute dall'ochio in qualunche distantia
> e questa in se mostra tutte esse cose come l'ochio le uede diminuite,
> e non è obbligato l'omo a stare più in un sito che in un'altro, pure
> che il muro non la riscorti la seconda volta.

My paraphrase: "the first treats things as they are seen by the eye, diminishing
them as they are farthest from the eye. It does not resort to a 'second foreshortening' and does not require that the viewer stand in one point rather
than another."

> Ma la 2ª practica è vna mistione di prospettiva fatta in parte dall'arte
> e in parte dalla natura, et l'opera fatta colle sua regole non à parte
> alcuna che non sia mista colla prospettiva naturale e colla prospettiva
> accidentale.

My paraphrase: "but the second is a mixture of perspectives, made in part by
art and in part by nature. A work constructed according to this rule has no
part which does not mix natural and accidental perspective."

Panofsky claims that the first two perspectives work in contrary fashion

(Wood's translation: they "exactly cancel each other out"),[22] enabling the artist to use simple perspective "in which the [viewing] distance is set so large that the marginal distortions have no importance." Leonardo is talking here specifically about the three-column paradox: the greater (real) width of the columns on the margins of a painting is opposed to the foreshortening of those (wider) columns from the viewpoint. Natural perspective does work exactly "contrary" to artificial perspective ("la prospettiva accidentale cioè quella ch'è fatta dall'arte fa il contrario in se," Fr. 107) although the two perspectives do not as Panofsky's translator implies cancel each other out.

To Panofsky, the rejection of composite perspective leaves simple perspective, as Leonardo seems to claim in Fragment 108.

Ma questa tale inuentione constrignie il ueditore a stare coll'ochio a vno spiracolo e allora da tale spiracolo si dimonstrerà bene; Ma perchè molti occhi s'abbattono a vedere a un medesimo tenpo vna medesima opera fatta con tale arte e solo vn di quelli vede bene l'ufitio di tal prospetiua e li altri tutti restan confusi; Egli è dunque da fuggire tal prospettiva conposta e a tenersi alle senplicie, la qual non uol uedere pariete in scorto, ma più in propia forma che sia possibile.

[But this invention requires that the viewer stand with the eye at a small hole, from which all appears well: but many eyes cannot view the same work at the same time made with such art, and only one of them sees the working of such perspective properly and the others are confused. It is thus best to avoid such composite perspective and hold to simple perspective, which does not depict a plane foreshortened, but rather in the most proper form possible.]

Leonardo then adds in a somewhat more difficult sentence: "this simple perspective is what we constantly experience through the faculty of sight (*dalla virtù visiua*)."[23]

Simple perspective, thus, is anything but simple: if artificial and natural perspective exactly cancelled each other out, then there would be no difference between simple perspective and composite perspective. A real viewer looking at the three columns painted on a picture according to Piero's formula still sees the wider columns on the margins as smaller than those in the center. It is because the two perspectives do not cancel each other out that

Leonardo resorts to simple perspective, where the columns on the painting are the same size, just as they are in nature.

Two points are important. The interpretation of simple perspective in Panofsky's sense (the implication of an infinite viewing distance) is only applicable and workable if we are talking about particular planes in the picture space parallel to the picture plane, and lines of sight drawn to those planes. These planes moreover must be considered singly. Objects on these planes are (simply) constructed in accordance with their "real" proportions. This is in accordance with what Leonardo says. But this solution will not work when these planes are considered together; it will not work in constructing perfectly ordinary architectural objects, and is not used in classical painting.

Imagine a portico of columns parallel to the picture plane. In the middle is a colonnade perpendicular to the picture plane; the viewer standing immediately in front of the picture looks right down through it. In simple perspective understood as involving an infinite viewing distance, none of the columns of this perpendicular colonnade would be visible; all would be obscured by the first pair of columns. We cannot see "down" a hallway unless we are close to the hall opening. So while simple perspective might be responsible for the row of equal columns parallel to the picture plane (something seen in many classical paintings), and might also account for an undistorted sphere placed on the edge of the painting (a sphere that should be distorted if constructed according to the linear perspective model), it cannot account for the fact that in those same pictures, we can see both interior surfaces of a hallway perpendicular to the picture plane or that we can see down two parallel rows of columns forming a colonnade. In other words, the perspective used in such common subjects is almost always mixed.

Second, and more important, Leonardo's main point seems to be the rejection of a fixed viewpoint. Simple perspective (whatever that is) allows viewers from whatever point to "see" the picture correctly, something that absolutely violates all rules of linear perspective.

What Leonardo proposes, then, is not a representative or illusionist picture at all. Each plane is to be constructed according to the principles of architectural elevations: the plane produces an icon, a model of what it represents. This means that the entire picture becomes not an image, but a description, perhaps a description of the (infinite?) parallel planes of a picture. The eye confronts different things in the same picture depending on where the eye is, but the brain is not really fooled or confused by this. It is up the visual virtue to sort this out and translate the details of this picture into an idea of what it represents.

The Scenographia of Stuart Masques: The Perspective of Perspective

A now canonical anecdote cited by several scholars through John Nichols, *The Progresses of James the First* (1828), describes the production of a Latin comedy in Christ Church, Oxford, in 1605. According to Alardyce Nicoll and later John Orrell, the stage was constructed according to the principles used and described in Sabbatini (1638) and in Inigo Jones's often reproduced Ground-Plan of the auditorium and stage for *Florimène* (1635).[24] The auditorium of such stages was conceived as directly related to the scenography. On the level of the pictorial horizon of the stage scenery was a seat called in Ben Jonson's masque "Blackness" the "state." This position provided the ideal viewing distance and viewpoint for a perspective stage constructed as a series of two-dimensional surfaces.[25] In the anecdote from 1605, the placement of the state caused a debate:

> They (but especially Lord Suffolk) utterly disliked the stage at
> Christ Church, and above all, the place appointed for the chair of
> Estate, because it was no higher, and the King so placed that the
> auditory could see but his cheek only; this dislike of the Earle of
> Suffolk much troubled the Vice-chancellor and all the workmen,
> yet they stood in defence of the thing done, and maintained that
> by the art perspective the King should behold all better then if he
> sat higher. In the end, the place was removed, and sett in the midst
> of the Hall, but too far from the stage, viz, 28 foote, so that there
> were many long Speeches delivered which neither the King nor
> any near him could well hear or understand. The stage was built
> close to the upper end of the Hall, as it seemed at the first sight.
> (Nichols, *Progresses*, 1: 538)

As read by Nicoll and Orrell, the debate opposes the ideal of what the king should see to the social realities of who should see the king. The interests of the spectators (who should see the king) seem to have won out.

But there is something wrong with this anecdote: the privileged place

cannot be one that permits the audience to see only "the King's cheek." This
I think implies that the audience is on the same level as the King, and certainly that is not where the privileged "state" is placed in such documents as
the plan for the *Florimène* stage. Nor can a location "28 foote" from the stage
"in the midst of the Hall" be "too far from the stage" for the speeches to be
heard. It appears that the key figures in this anecdote—the reporter (called
by Orrell the "Cambridge spy") and probably the participants in the debate
themselves—do not fully understand the principles of perspective; they do
know, however, that such principles can be usefully invoked to support their
own arguments. Whether the subject is a king, his retinue, workmen, or a
reporter, it is apparently more important to talk about perspective and its
illusions than actually to experience these illusions. There is thus a difference
between perspective and versions of perspective, whether those versions are,
as in the case above, oral and politically charged debates about the matter,
or, as in the cases I discuss below, visual representations of perspective.

    To work as described by Alberti or Piero, a model of linear perspective
requires an ideal viewpoint that is both fixed and monoscopic; it is equivalent
to the point of a pinhole camera. In the human eye, depth of focus is a direct
function of the quantity of light. In a brightly lit environment, the iris closes
so that the eye approaches the situation of a pinhole camera, itself the material embodiment of the theory and model of linear perspective. Theoretically,
in perfect light (whatever that is), the iris could be contracted to a point and
everything would be in perfect focus. When you find yourself without reading glasses, you can read, with difficulty, by poking a small hole through a
piece of paper and looking through it at otherwise illegible print. You cannot
of course see better this way; you can only compensate for the eye's, or iris's,
sacrificing sharpness of focus for light.

    In what I will call the predicament of the seventeenth-century stage, the
human eye is at the mercy of poor lighting. In such a poorly lit environment,
the iris of the human eye widens, and because of this, both the perfect focus
of the pinhole camera and the illusions it supports are lost.[26] Furthermore, as
soon as the viewer moves or employs stereoscopic sight, the perfect illusion
(or what would be a perfect illusion in an ideally lit, pure atmosphere) will
vanish, and must be recreated in the viewer's mind. Neither a king located
in a carefully designed "state" nor any other spectator will overcome these
facts, and, as far as the experience of perfect perspective is concerned, it is a
matter of indifference where these viewers actually sit.

Perspective of Perspective

Figure 27 is an engraving of a Florentine stage and depicts a scene from *Le nozze degli dei* (1637).[27] It appears to illustrate how such a perspective stage might have been seen by the king at Christ Church or perhaps by a king situated where stage designers and perhaps some advisors might want him to be, or, say, an ideal monoscopic king perfectly placed and immobilized in an ideally lit environment. But of course, even with all the qualifications above, this is not what a perspective stage looks like; rather, it is an illustration of one in a printed book, and probably appeared to its viewers as it appears to my own readers here: not an image, but a description of something that might have once been seen or perhaps only imagined. It is fundamentally different from the blueprint-like plans of John Webb; it is not an icon of a stage, but it is not really a picture of one either. Orrell attempts to distinguish these various classes of representation: plans, perspective drawings, sketches, even what he calls "perspective of perspective." Yet particular drawings conflate these classifications, much as Alardyce Nicoll's classic survey of early stages, concerned as it is with the historical stage rather than a critique of representations of it, makes little attempt to distinguish all these classes of drawings: stage-plans, idealized architectural drawings, even artistic sketches.

Of particular interest in the engraving from *Le nozze* is the inclusion of actors; the engraving thus appears to illustrate an actual or imagined performance. These actors, oddly, are drawn the same way; they are roughly of the same proportions no matter where they are placed on stage. They would not be depicted this way in a drawing that followed the rules of linear perspective, where those farthest from the central viewing point would show characteristic marginal distortions. Furthermore, they are foreshortened not as they would be on a stage (since the stage set is itself constructed *as if* foreshortened), but rather as they would be foreshortened if they were part of what that stage depicts. These imagined actors are drawn, thus, whether consciously or no, in some version of Leonardo's "mixed perspective."

Viewers such as those of my Figure 27, or of the book from which I have taken this figure, look at the radical recession of these columns and recognize instantly that they are facing a drawing "in perspective." Yet contrary to that certainty, such representations of the perspective stage, with their perfectly proportioned actors, are clearly not drawn in perspective. Every drawing of the so-called perspective stage that I have seen is drawn not as a perspective drawing but rather as an architectural elevation; that is, the viewpoint as-

Figure 27. Garden of Venus, from *Le nozze degli dei* (Florence, 1637). Courtesy of the Henry E. Huntington Library, San Marino, California.

sumed, despite the strictures on the placement of the viewers in an auditorium, is from an infinite distance. A portico of columns parallel to the picture plane is drawn with equal columns; it is drawn in "simple perspective," imitating an effect produced by the "mixed perspective" used in classical paintings. We can see down an implied perpendicular colonnade without changing the conventions of perspective (as we would have to do in a comparable classical painting), because this is not a real colonnade but a stage representation of one.[28] Actors too are portrayed in the same shape, because we know, in the real world, that is "how they are," and they are foreshortened according to rules that do not apply to the constructed stage in which they appear. The same conventions often seem to apply to sketches *for* these stages, the "blueprints" for their constructions, and to drawings *of* these stages (which presumably depict these stages as seen by real viewers).[29] The sketch of the stage for *Le nozze* could be an architectural elevation of a perspective drawing or a perspective construction of an architectural elevation, what I believe Orrell means by "perspective of perspective." More likely, it is a self-contradictory combination of all these things, which is perfectly at home on the pages of a book, where, despite the conventional limitations imposed on the viewer (how we can physically hold such an object), it cannot be viewed "from the wrong angle."[30]

The viewer of these drawings, the reader who holds the book in one of its multiple copies, is less "fixed" than the viewers in a theater, despite the implied central viewpoint.[31] We know this is a book; human figures on the margins thus will have the same dimensions as a human figure in the center, and will seem to have that no matter how we hold the book. Spheres appear as spheres, no matter where they are on stage, or how they are depicted, just as human actors walking through a Stuart stage will always be "correct" even though their relation to two-dimensional scenery will change. Human beings, we know, are never "incorrect," and neither are the ones shown in a book.

In the 1605 Oxford performance, the political realities of the king proved more important than aesthetic considerations; the situation of the king in 1605 is vulgarized through these later printed engravings. Few viewers are much bothered by the confusions I have noted above, since what the engravings and even the more private sketches accomplish is pure illusion—here, the illusion of a perspective drawing of a perspective stage. From the artist's point of view, such drawings may be examples of what Leonardo calls "mixed" perspective. Considered in terms of audience, they are the inevitable result of human realities: movement, stereoscopic vision, dim lighting, attention, even (in the 1605 production) political concerns—all those aspects of human existence that frustrate any artist's attempt to control them.[32]

Lateral Distortion and Viewer Conventions

A politician is standing before a wall on which a large poster image of that same politician appears. The photographer is at an angle. The photo shows the politician, and it shows a radically distorted view of the poster. Yet despite how the photographer sets up this photo, whether straight on, where the two images of the politician are roughly the same, or from the side, where the mural image is radically distorted, as viewers, we do not find any of this in the least bit disturbing or confusing, no matter what viewing angle we adopt.[33]

Why not?

This is only one of the distortions familiar to most contemporary viewers of photographs. Computer programs, Photoshop, and desktop publishing have made us even more aware of such once abstruse aspects of photographs and perspective: keystoning, barreling, and lateral distortion. Some of these distortions are directly related to peculiarities of camera lenses: straight lines in a fish-eye lens appear curved—a phenomenon not found in classical painting, whatever the conventions followed, nor one justified by the linear-perspective model. Others are predicted by Alberti's model and characteristic of images from pinhole cameras: keystoning, for example, something familiar to those of us with even minimal grasp of Photoshop.

Apparently, we are familiar enough with photographs and the viewing of photographs (perhaps from sitting in a cinema?) that some of these distortions do not bother us no matter what the viewing angle might be. They are, as Panofsky states, "untroubling." Yet others are unacceptable: we seem not to like the marginal distortions we see in a painting by Uccello, even though we confront such distortions with increasing frequency in contemporary journalism. Photographs in modern newspapers often show the radical marginal distortions characteristic of wide-angle lenses, distortions we seem perfectly willing to accept when produced by contemporary professionals, but are far less happy with when we see them in classical paintings or in the products of our own point-and-shoot cameras.

Viewers' perception (Leonardo's *virtù visiua*) is not the same as viewers' perspective; our brains process the signals from our eyes not according to optical realities, but rather according to our understanding of the medium in which they occur; things in the real world, photographs that we might keep

in our wallet, stages, paintings in museums, and engraved images in books—
our brains are dimly (but not perfectly) aware that these are all different
things.

Coda: The Drawing Manual

When we confront a problem, whether ethical or academic, most of us judge
its complexity in terms of our self-interest: a discussion that does not deal
with the complexities with which we are familiar is simplistic or naive; one
that deals with greater complexities than we wish to confront is overly sophisticated and unnecessarily mystified.

I have already noted the paradox of drawing manuals whose instruction
works quite well despite the numerous errors contained in them. With the
help of GoogleBooks, I have chosen two drawing manuals more or less at
random from the nineteenth century. I am not certain these are representative, but they are similar to all those I have seen of whatever date, and more
amusing than most of them. The first is *Practical Perspective: The Course of
Lectures on Linear Perspective*, by Richard Burchett, "Head Master of the
Training and Normal School, Marlborough House" (London: Chapman and
Hall, 1856). Burchett rejects two classes of books: "the profound and abstruse" and its obverse "the simple and unprincipled." According to the author, all books on the subject (except his) fall into one of the two classes.
Burchett has no patience with abstruse instruction manuals:

> [my discussion] does not meddle with curvilinear horizontal lines,
> does not assert that vertical lines converge, nor propose as exercises
> the painting of imitation cupolas upon flat ceilings, which require
> the spectator to lie upon his back on the floor to the detriment of
> clothes and the derangement of his head. (viii)

Nonetheless, the subject requires "thorough understanding"; to understand
perspective, according to Burchett, is to understand reality:

> the appearances of the representations of objects are subject to the
> same optical laws as the appearances of the objects themselves. . . .
> One great value of Perspective most undoubtedly is the power it
> imparts of *seeing correctly.* (ix)

To achieve this power of seeing and drawing correctly, both the laws of perspective and elemental facts of reality are denied, even before the practical instruction begins:

> If, having shut one eye, we keep the other steadily fixed, looking through a square of glass, at any objects beyond it, we shall obtain a perspective view of those objects. (1)

Keeping the eye steadily fixed with "one eye shut" is not as easy as it may sound. But that, apparently, is not a crucial matter, since the problem of stereoscopic vision is finally irrelevant:

> The eye undoubtedly adapts itself to circumstances, whether of limited or extended vision, but the parallelism of the eye may be considered its normal state. (note on p. 2)

That this cannot apply to the real world is indicated by the concept "the eye"; the eye (in whatever sense) cannot be parallel to itself. If this applies to two eyes, it is absolutely untrue. Parallelism of two eyes, if at all possible, would result in the entire world being out of focus.

A second manual is by Charles Hayter, *Perspective Explained: in a series of dialogues between the Author's Children, George, Ann, Eliza, and John.* This is part of Hayter's *Perspective, Drawing, and Painting . . . Illustrated by appropriate plates and diagrams and a sufficiency of Practical Geometry and a compendium of genuine instruction comprising a progressive and complete body of information carefully adapted for the instruction of Females and suited equally to the simplicity of Youth and to mental maturity* (2nd ed., London, 1815; numerous re-editions through the nineteenth century). It is probably not necessary to quote this manual, having quoted its title. The diagrams are complex and abstruse, many of them beyond the capacity of GoogleBooks to reproduce—at least, they cannot be reproduced on any machine I own. Yet despite the accuracy of some diagrams (see the depiction of the three-column paradox in Plate X), others are riddled with errors. Plate V, fig. 3 claims to be a rigorous example of the construction of planes with vanishing points in figs. 1 and 2, but the figure shows the inwardly curving diagonals characteristic of medieval drawings or amateur sketches.

The impatience shown by these authors with other instruction manuals and theorists is presented largely as an impatience with their own competitors, particularly those who rely on what is theoretically valid. Paradoxically, anyone following such manuals, whether the erroneous manuals targeted by these authors, or the erroneous versions produced by these authors, will likely end up drawing far better than any critic who carps at their errors. The problem against which these teachers rail is one that generates the energy which makes these manuals possible. It is the conflict not between theory and practice, but rather between two modes of reality: the real world and the artificial ways in which reality is represented, first when drafted on paper, and second when reproduced in what constitutes print.

❦

CHAPTER EIGHT

Typographical Antiquity in Thomas Frognall Dibdin's *Typographical Antiquities*

Hereby, tongues are known, knowledge groweth, judgment increaseth, books are dispersed, the Scripture is read, stories be opened, times compared, truth discerned, falshood detected and with finger pointed, and all (as I said) through the benefit of printing. (frontispiece to Dibdin, *Typographical Antiquities*, attributed to and mistranscribed from 1641 edition of Foxe's *Book of Martyrs*, 1: 927)

Thomas Frognall Dibdin was the most prolific and influential English bibliographer of the early nineteenth century. Among his more important works are the two-volume *Library Companion*, the three-volume *Bibliographical, Antiquarian and Picturesque Tour in France and Germany*, the seven-volume Spencer catalogue, and a four-volume revision of Joseph Ames's 1749 *Typographical Antiquities*, the principal subject of the present chapter.[1] Nicolas Barker describes young English collectors touring Europe with Dibdin's *Library Companion* in hand, looking to buy the very books recommended by him.[2] He is thus responsible, not only for describing early English books, but in many cases for the material existence of such books in our collections. My primary purpose here is to point out Dibdin's obvious misrepresentation of the very past which his work in some ways has made accessible to us. But that turns out to be inextricably linked to another problem: our own difficulties in describing him.

To study Dibdin requires penetrating the literary style for which he is best remembered, a style that has been described in all the adjectives one would expect from reading even a few selections. My subject here, however, is a specifically nonliterary aspect of Dibdin—the pictorial and illustrative material in *Typographical Antiquities*, material over which Dibdin may not have had complete control. How does he portray and characterize early type? early woodblock initials and illustrations? And what are the issues in which these descriptions are enmeshed?

To a modern bibliographer, there seem to be two Dibdins, and the two could be seen to mark a shift in the understanding of early books. There is first the systematic Dibdin, whose work could be considered foundational in the rise of modern bibliography. Dibdin the bibliographer has as his monument the Spencer catalogue; for bibliographers, this modern Dibdin seems to do roughly what a twentieth-century bibliographer might do. Yet in contrast to this figure (itself a product of the accidents of modern bibliography), there is the far more amusing Dibdin the antiquarian: nostalgic, whimsical, aesthetic, better known for the peculiarities of his style than for his knowledge of books. The conflicting nature of Dibdin is seen everywhere in his work. Here, for example, he is discussing Caxton's *Recuyell of the Historyes of Troye*, the first book printed in English.

> This is the first book printed in the English language. Herbert says it was "not printed in England, yet being printed by Caxton, and being full of information, Mr. Ames began with it, and hoped that it would be favourably received." In his Additions, [p. 1765] he properly observes, that "it is without initial-capital letters, signatures, catchwords, numerals or figures to the leaves or pages: but it contains 778 pages, as told over by Mr. Rundal Minshull, library keeper to the late Earl of Oxford, who published, about the year 1740, 'Proposals for printing by subscription, an account of all the books printed by William Caxton, who was the first printer in England,'" &c. See Bibl. Est. no. 1909.

But immediately after scrupulously, if somewhat garrulously and pedantically, recording this basic information, Dibdin proceeds:

> One Robert Braham, in his Epistle to the Reader prefixed before Lydgate's "Troye Boke," printed by Marshe in 1555, is rather severe

against our venerable typographer for his impression of this work. He says, "If a man studious of that history [the Trojan War] should seek to find the same in the doings of WILLIAM CAXTON, in his leawde [idle] recueil of Troye, what should he then find think you? Assuredly none other thing but a long tedious and brainless babbling, tending to no end, nor having any certain beginning: but proceeding therein as an idiot in his folly, that cannot make an end till he be bidden."

The infectiousness of this sort of thing is too dangerous to allow me to proceed.

Typographical Antiquities

Joseph Ames's *Typographical Antiquities* in 1749 was the first comprehensive bibliography of early English books (the cut-off date was 1600). It was revised as a three-volume work by William Herbert in 1785 and as a four-volume work by Dibdin in 1810–19, following the general framework established by Ames. It is still useful today, in all its editions. Yet what we see as its modern bibliographical purpose is presented even by Ames as almost incidental. Ames's preface concentrates instead on antiquarian matters and a mythological narrative of the rise and progress of printing, a narrative that is retained in all later revisions:

> I have endeavoured to make this book as useful as I could, by shewing the rise, progress, and gradual improvements of this art. In my account of its most eminent men I have added all their privileges, licences, patents, &C. which were granted to them; together with the name of the place, and sign at which they dwelt; the incouragements and discouragements they met with; as also the charter of the company of Stationers. I have likewise adorned it with plates of specimens of their types, marks, rebus's and devices; as also with the heads of some of the most celebrated printers, from the Harleian collection. Their principal performances I have disposed as near as possible into a sort of chronological order of time, beginning with each Printer's first work; then those books of his, which followed;

except those without a date, which are put at the end of each Printer. (Ames's Preface, quoted by Dibdin, 14–15)

The purpose of Ames's book, as seen by Dibdin, is not bibliographical in the modern sense (how to identify or even find early books) but historical and antiquarian.[3] Note in the above quotation, the reproduction of modern (and fantastic) "heads of . . . the most celebrated printers" is placed on the same level as the reproduction of their types and identifying devices. Like all literary works, it should please and instruct; and readerly pleasure is, Dibdin states, an explicit goal of the illustrations:

In the present instance, it has been deemed necessary to lay a broad basis for making the Typographical and Literary Annals of our country as complete as possible; while the fac-similes of Engravings, with which printed works are adorned, may exhibit a pleasing outline of the rise and progress of the sister art in the same country. (Dibdin, "Advertisement," vii)

The question I consider here concerns the relation between that "pleasing outline" and what it refers to, that is, the books, typefaces, and illustrations Dibdin discusses. Just what are Dibdin's "Typographical Antiquities"?

In this Advertisement, Dibdin identifies a certain class of his readers as "resolute lovers of black-letter antiquity":

There is one point in which it is conceived this work will be considered, by resolute lovers of black-letter antiquity, exceedingly vulnerable; and that is, in having generally adopted the modern orthography for the ancient. (viii)

Dibdin assuages the concerns of these supposed readers by claiming to transcribe colophons, titles, and poetry in the ancient spelling such readers love, that is, diplomatically. This might seem unproblematic until we begin to consider the meaning of "blackletter antiquity." Is that period noted only for its capricious orthography? Why does the adjective "blackletter" here not refer to type or examples of that type? Is such "blackletter antiquity" a set of objects (books) produced in history? or is it a transcendent and universal aesthetic quality perceived by a modern audience? When Dibdin reproduces an early text or engraving embodying that "blackletter-ness," what is it he is illustrating? and how Ames or modern bibliographers answer the same question?

Typographical Contexts

To understand or to discuss Dibdin in relation to these issues under the ordinary scholarly conventions I was inadvertently trained in requires placing him within some context or history. In the section below, for convenience, I have reduced those histories to two. First, the history of type, particularly blackletter type, considered in terms of its bibliographical function, and second, a technological history—the means of representing typographical and nontypographical images from early printed books.

Without these histories, Dibdin remains little more than a curiosity. Yet these histories are teleological, and even within this teleology, Dibdin sits uneasily: Dibdin did not know nor did he show any signs of foreseeing later nineteenth-century developments in bibliography. Nor did he take advantage of the technological developments available to him (this is also true of several later nineteenth-century bibliographers). Even when there were coherent histories to be written or enacted, for example, the movement from woodblock to engraving to lithography (histories to which Dibdin occasionally alludes), in the production of his own book, these histories seem to have been ignored.

History #1: The Function of Blackletter Type
Considered in Relation to Bibliographical History

To describe the bibliographical role of type generally and blackletter type in particular, one must begin near the end of this history with the treatment of the fifteenth-century types by such late nineteenth-century bibliographers as Henry Bradshaw, Robert Proctor, and Konrad Haebler, and through the various facsimile projects that supported them. Because of the nature of early type and its methods of manufacture, the English bibliographer Henry Bradshaw was able to envision the early history of printing as a natural history, involving the organization of type impressions and typefonts. Like a biologist, the bibliographer constructs a history of printing by categorizing related forms and species. An arrangement of type impressions is an arrangement and history of the printers who produced them.[4]

This notion of typographical history requires some method of type identification and requires also that this method be quantifiable or reproducible.

The means for doing so was simple measurement of the height of twenty lines of set type. The working assumption behind this method (one that distinguishes it from its analog in biology) is that early typefonts are singular: they are, for the most part, manufactured by or for individual printers, and the identification of a particular typefont is consequently the identification of a particular printer. The 7,000 incunables at the British Library were physically rearranged to embody this system.[5] Even more important were the state-of-the-art facsimiles of early types by the Gesellschaft für Typenkunde and the facsimile volumes of the *British Museum Catalogue*; with these, the evidence for constructing Bradshaw's history was available to any library or incunable collection.[6]

A natural history of type for the fifteenth century was only thinkable because of the later standardization of typefonts and their imagined functions that had taken place in the sixteenth and seventeenth centuries. During this later period, the production of type left the hands of the printer for those of the typefounder, and with this, the simple equation (typefont = printer) was no longer applicable. Late nineteenth-century bibliographers could thus imagine their own work as the endpoint of a particular kind of typographical history: they had defined a period of what I will call "bibliographical typography," which had ended with the institutionalization of type, that is, the separation of type manufacture from actual printing.[7]

Yet Dibdin seems detached from this history, one rooted in the singularity and specificity of early blackletter fonts. The notion of a one-to-one mapping of typefont onto printer did not seem important to contemporary bibliographers and book historians: there were greater bibliographical narratives to be written than the microhistories of minor printers. What these bibliographers inherited from this typographical tradition was what could be called the "antiquarianization" of blackletter. Blackletter was not the material basis of a new bibliographical science; it was simply a mark of something old.

The differences between varieties of blackletter (textura, bastarda, even rotunda) had never functioned coherently in English printing. The page shown in Figure 28 is from the 1554 Gower reprinted by Berthelet from his own 1532 edition; the text, here in textura, is a line-for-line reprint of the 1532 edition, where that same text was printed in rotunda. Even here, bastarda, textura, roman, and even italics (the word *Troie* in col. 1), are losing their specific function: they differ only in being recognizably different:

By the seventeenth century, blackletter was becoming increasingly standardized as a familiar, squarish textura (see Figure 4), what is called "English"

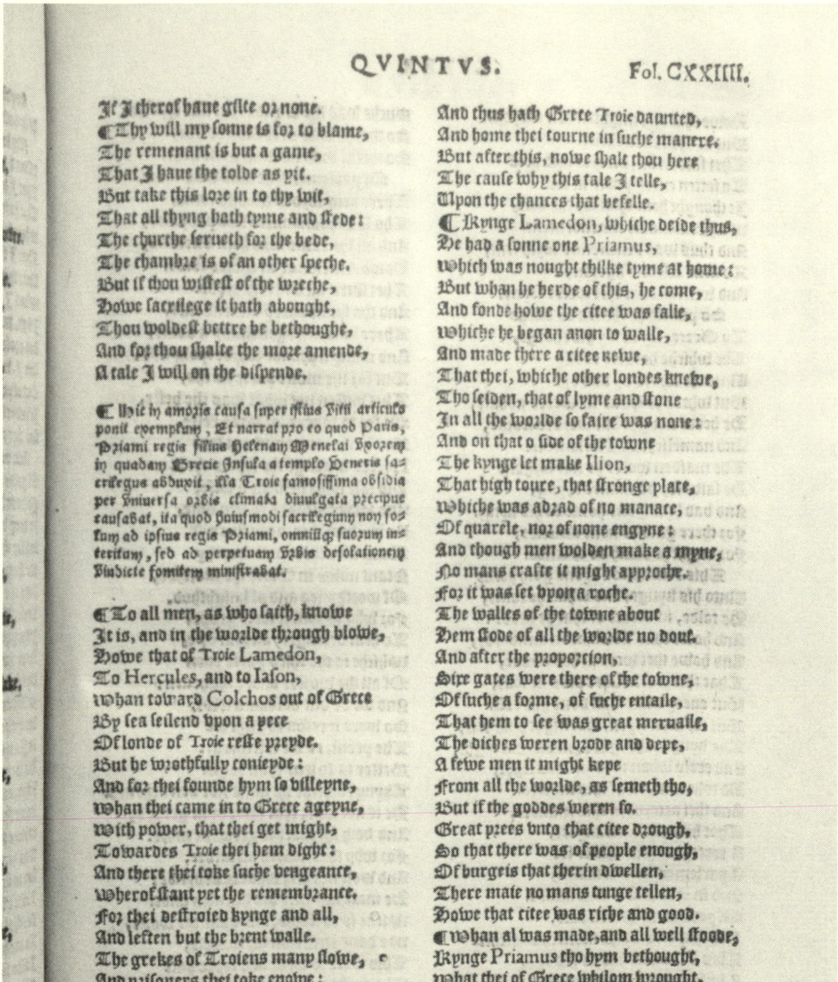

If I therof haue gilte or none.
Thy will my sonne is for to blame,
The remenant is but a game,
That I haue the tolde as yit.
But take this lore in to thy wit,
That all thyng hath tyme and stede:
The churche serueth for the bede,
The chambre is of an other speche.
But if thou wistest of the wreche,
Howe sacrilege it hath abought,
Thou woldest bettre be bethoughe,
And for thou shalte the more amende,
A tale I will on the dispende,

Hic in amoris causa super istius fini articulo ponit exemplum, Et narrat pro eo quod Paris, Priami regis filius Helenam Menelai vxorem in quadam Grecie Insula a templo Veneris sacrilegus abduxit, illa Troie famosissima obsidia per vniuersa orbis climata diuulgata precipue causabat, ita quod huiusmodi sacrilegium non solum ad ipsius regis Priami, omniumque suorum interitum, sed ad perpetuam Vrbis desolationem Iudicie fomitem ministrabat.

To all men, as who saith, knowe
It is, and in the worlde through blowe,
Howe that of Troie Lamedon,
To Hercules, and to Iason,
whan toward Colchos out of Grece
By sea seilend vpon a pece
Of londe of Troie reste preyde,
But he wrothfully coniepde:
And for thei founde hym so villeyne,
whan thei came in to Grece agepne,
with power, that thei get might,
Towardes Troie thei hem dight:
And there thei toke suche vengeance,
wherof stant yet the remembrance.
For thei destroied kynge and all,
And leften but the brent walle.
The grekes of Troiens many slowe,
And prisoners thei toke enowe:
Amonge the whiche there was one,
The kynges doughter Lamedon,
Essiona the faire thynge,
whiche vnto Thelamon the kynge
By Hercules, and by thassent
Of all the holle parliament,
Was at his wille yeue and graunted.

And thus hath Grece Troie daunted,
And home thei tourne in suche manere.
But after this, nowe shalt thou here
The cause why this tale I telle,
Upon the chances that befelle.
Kynge Lamedon, whiche deide thus,
He had a sonne one Priamus,
which was nought thilke tyme at home:
But whan he herde of this, he come,
And fonde howe the citee was falle,
whiche he began anon to walle,
And made there a citee newe,
That thei, whiche other londes knewe,
Tho seiden, that of lyme and stone
In all the worlde so faire was none:
And on that o side of the towne
The kynge let make Ilion,
That high toure, that stronge place,
whiche was adrad of no manace,
Of quarele, nor of none engyne:
And though men wolden make a myne,
No mans crafte it might approche,
For it was set vpon a roche.
The walles of the towne about
Hem stode of all the worlde no dout.
And after the proporcion,
Sixe gates were there of the towne,
Of suche a forme, of suche entaile,
That hem to see was great meruaile,
The diches weren brode and depe,
A fewe men it might kepe
From all the worlde, as semeth tho,
But if the goddes weren so.
Great prees vnto that citee drough,
So that there was of people enough,
Of burgeis that therin dwellen,
There mate no mans tunge tellen,
Howe that citee was riche and good.
Whan al was made, and all well stoode,
Kynge Priamus tho hym bethought,
what thei of Grece whilom wrought,
And what was of her sworde denoured,
And howe his sister dishonoured,
with Thelamon awaie was lad.
And tho thinkende he warte vnglad,
And sette anone a parliment:
To whiche the lordes were assent.
In many a wise there was spoke,

Hou

Figure 28. John Gower, *Confessio Amantis* (London: Berthelet, 1554). Courtesy of the William Andrews Clark Memorial Library, University of California, Los Angeles.

in later typographical manuals and specimen sheets.[8] It was easily enmeshed in persistent *grand récits* of typography such as those discussed above in Chapters 3 and 4 (the Rise of Humanism, the resurgence of the gothic).[9] By the eighteenth century, these grand narratives built around a monolithic conception of a typeface begin to be embodied in type design and book production. In publications of the Sheldon Press, a redesigned blackletter was used for medieval works, and blackletter seemed to be a sign of a certain ill-defined medieval "authenticity." But this authenticity is fraudulent, and the endpoint of such a monolithic conception of blackletter is most strikingly seen in the sweeping but contradictory proclamations concerning it by the National Socialists.[10]

That is my contextual history #1. Note that there is no stable foundation for even this perfunctory sketch of typographical history; there is no perfectly coherent "blackletter" type, no "Blackletterness," no "Type" or "Typography" or even "Bibliography" that moves through this history. There is rather a series of events, physical things, and academic and political fields that can be attached to the same word.

History #2: Technology

The second history in which Dibdin's *Typographical Antiquities* is implicated is technological. The principal illustrations in his book are facsimiles, or what we would today call facsimiles—images of earlier typesorts, type initials, and even early printed initials. How is this subject matter (the illustrations) represented, and what is the relation between the print technologies available to Dibdin and the historical technologies he is describing?

The most obvious history of facsimile production would focus on three methods of printing: relief (woodblock), intaglio (engraving and etching), planographic (lithography). Bibliographically and formally, the distinction between a relief and an intaglio image is one between what is properly typographical and what is not. A relief print can be set with letterpress type, and thus does not interrupt printing procedures in any fundamental way. Intaglio prints require separate printing. But this apparent natural fit of relief block and letterpress does not lead to a seamless history: engravings are found in the earliest examples of printing in books of Colard Mansion and Caxton, and metal relief cuts are in use even before the advent of printing; in the late eighteenth and early nineteenth centuries, woodcuts modeled on engravings are designed by Thomas Bewick, and William Blake's work shows all these methods.

In the early nineteenth century, contemporary with Dibdin, the development of lithography had the potential of changing the way early printing history was represented, as well as changing what that history would later be. Lithography revolutionized what accuracy would mean in the reproduction of early type; in one early method, the very ink of the type page was used to "charge" the image on that plate.[11] By the late nineteenth century, photolithography provided greater flexibility and, by enabling the production of large and accurate facsimiles, dovetailed with the growing study of typefonts by incunabulists (see n. 6).

This is a familiar enough history, yet as with my History #1 above, to place Dibdin within this teleological history seems a falsification. The best bibliographers often ignored newer technological developments and relied on traditional technologies. For their seminal bibliography of William Caxton in 1861, William Blades and his facsimilist G. I. F. Tupper produced their facsimiles by hand, as tracings or as freehand illustrations, without the aid of any of the lithographic methods available to them.[12] Dibdin, a half-century earlier than Blades, seemed even more indifferent to this new technology. And once again, the more I attempt to fit Dibdin into the very histories he invokes—the history of type, blackletter, bibliography, technology—the more elusive he becomes. He seems to exist quite apart from the histories his work defines and in which this work most obviously participates.

Facsimile Production and the Rise and Progress of Printing Techniques

From Ames, Dibdin inherited the idea that the history of printing was a narrative "shewing the rise, progress, and gradual improvements of this art" (Ames, quoted by Dibdin, 14). The production of his own book is of course involved in the processes it is describing and Dibdin was explicit that his images were improvements over those in Ames, images he describes as "scarcely deserving of notice" (15). Dibdin seems to want to map this mythological narrative of improvement onto the technological divisions discussed above: woodblock vs. engraving; relief printing vs. intaglio. But difficulties, like those I encountered in my own discussion, quickly arise.

The initial distinctions Dibdin sets up are exacting. On pages vi–vii, he divides his subject into "Early Engraving" and "Ornamental engraving."

This is already Borgesian, since it is like distinguishing "animals owned by the Emperor" from "those that tremble as if they were mad":

> In pursuing the subjects of early ENGRAVING and ORNAMEN-
> TAL PRINTING in this country, I purpose to consider the first
> under the two following heads or divisions: I. *Impressions from
> Wooden Blocks*: II. *Impressions from Copper Plates*: the second subject,
> or Ornamental Printing, [which is, in fact, a branch of the former]
> I shall consider under the following: I. *Capital Initials*, or the first
> letter to the first page of a work: II. *Title Pages*, or the designation
> of the subject of the work on a separate, preceding, page. (vi–vii)

Dibdin's primary division (engraving versus ornamental printing) is functional; his secondary division (wooden blocks versus copper plates) is technical and equivalent to the modern division between relief and intaglio printing. In his prose, however, the apparently technical terms "engraving" and "cuts" can refer indifferently to either woodblocks or copper engravings; they can even refer to bronze castings—a technique that may be involved in some of these initials, but one acknowledged by Dibdin only in his notes.

> I am aware that it has long been a curious and keenly agitated ques-
> tion among connoisseurs, whether many engravings of the 15th, and
> early part of the 16th, century, professed to be cut in wood, are not,
> in fact, cut upon "some other material"—such as brass, or steel, or
> silver—or "from the substance (whatever it may have been) that was
> originally used for letter types." Mr. Landseer, from whom the pas-
> sages within inverted commas are taken, thinks that "from the free-
> dom and frequency of the dark crossings which distinguish these
> works from modern wood engravings, and from this mode of work-
> ing being obviously the easiest mode of producing the effects which
> their authors had in view, they are either etchings—the lights being
> corroded away; or, which is yet more likely, that a prototype or
> matrix was cut in intaglio, probably with the graver, in which the
> tablets, from whence the prints were taken, are cast in the matter of
> letter-types." (*Lectures on Engraving*, 202–3; Dibdin, *Typographical
> Antiquities*, n. on xxii–xxiii)[13]

Compounding this apparent slippage in terminology are the printing processes used in Dibdin's edition to facsimilize early woodblocks and engravings. Although Dibdin's printer uses the same techniques as early printers (intaglio and relief), the particular technique used in each illustration has no necessary relation to the technique used in the original. This is specifically noted by Dibdin, who illustrates many early copperplates in woodblock "for the convenience of press-work" (xxv).[14]

The "thing described" in *Typographical Antiquities* is thus an image divorced from the means used to produce it. In a passage quoted in full below, it is the "idea of that peculiar species or character of wooden-block engraving" (xviii). If we follow Dibdin and consider the object of his history to be that particular and very abstract "character," his typographical antiquities become things not of the historical past but things produced in *Typographical Antiquities*. The much-praised Rise and Progress of Printing, thus, finds no endpoint in the techniques of printing employed in Dibdin's own book.

Examples (I): Initials and Woodcuts

Let us look at some of the facsimiles in *Typographical Antiquities*, first for the typefaces of Caxton. The facsimile representations of these types in Ames (Figure 29), dismissed by Dibdin as "scarcely deserving of notice," seem to me to be reasonably good descriptions of them; that is, they are sufficient for distinguishing Caxton's various typefaces from each other, although they may not be sufficient for identification of those typefaces in the wild. It is hard to critique Ames's specimen plates without knowing which of these functions Ames believed they were serving.

Ames's plates, both those of individual types and those of complete pages, appear to be drawn freehand and engraved, a process involving more than one artist or technician.[15] In the early nineteenth century, such facsimiles were often traced before being transferred to woodblock or plate. A traced facsimile will (or should) have the same text-block measurement as the original and should have the same 20-line measurement as well. It is of course possible for a hand-drawn page to achieve the same thing (by writing within a page-block constructed in the exact dimensions of the original), but I am not certain this was ever done, nor can I see the advantage to such a technique.

The illustrations in Dibdin were produced by combinations of these methods, although he does not distinguish them clearly, as Blades would do a half-century later. Page 1 gives a table of initials: "Fac-similes of Initial

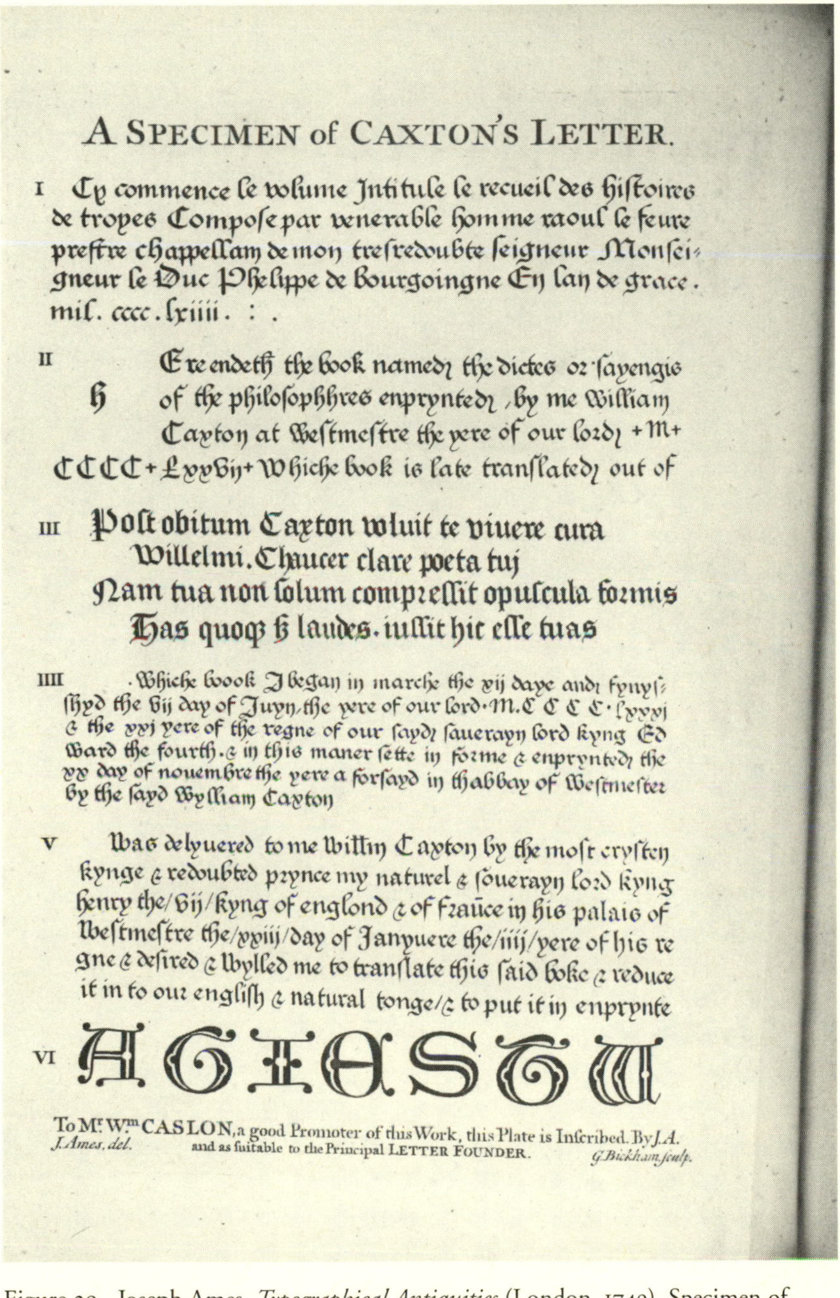

A Specimen of Caxton's Letter.

I   Cy commence le volume Jntitule le recueil des histoires
de tropes Compose par venerable homme raoul le feure
prestre chappellam de mon tresredoubte seigneur Monsei=
gneur le Duc Phelippe de Bourgoingne En lan de grace.
mil. cccc. lxiiii. : .

II   Ere endeth the book named the dictes or sayengis
of the philosophhres enprynted / by me William
Cayton at Westmestre the yere of our lord + M +
CCCC + Lyxvij + Whiche book is late translated out of

III   Post obitum Cayton voluit te viuere cura
Willelmi. Chaucer clare poeta tuj
Nam tua non solum compressit opuscula formis
Has quoqʒ ʒ laudes. iussit hic esse tuas

IIII   .Whiche book J began in marche the vij daye and fynys=
shyd the vij day of Juyn, the yere of our lord· M·C·C·C·Lyyvj
ʒ the vyj yere of the regne of our sayd sauerayn lord kyng Ed
Ward the fourth. ʒ in this maner sette in forme ʒ enprynted the
vy day of nouembre the yere a forsayd in thabbay of Westmestre
by the sayd Wylliam Cayton

V   Was delyuered to me Willm Cayton by the most crysten
kynge ʒ redoubted prynce my naturel ʒ souerayn lord kyng
henry the/vij/kyng of englond ʒ of Frauce in his palais of
Westmestre the/vyiij/day of Janyuere the/iiij/yere of his re
gne ʒ desired ʒ Wylled me to translate this said boke ʒ reduce
it in to our english ʒ natural tonge/ʒ to put it in enprynte

VI   A G I H S T W

To Mr Wm CASLON, a good Promoter of this Work, this Plate is Inscribed. By J.A.
J.Ames, del.   and as suitable to the Principal LETTER FOUNDER.   G.Bickham sculp.

Figure 29. Joseph Ames, *Typographical Antiquities* (London, 1749), Specimen of
Caxton. Courtesy of the William Andrews Clark Memorial Library, University of
California, Los Angeles.

Capitals Used by our Early Printers from 1471 to 1550." These are woodblocks, and I believe they are from tracings, although I am not certain of this.
There is no caption identifying the printers of the rows of initials here, although as you read through the chapter, you will eventually find reference to
them. Some distance from the introductory plate, page xvi refers to a "sump-
tuous edition [of the Bible] during the reign of Henry VIII" and on the
following page a "quarto edition, printed in the black letter, which belonged
to the late Reverend Mr. George Ashby of Bury, in Suffolk; who supposed
that the edition came from the press of either Grafton or Whitchurch, or of
both" (xvii). A reference on page xxxvi identifies the initials in the middle
rows as by De Worde.

   These initials are all actual size, something of paramount importance for
a modern bibliographer. Fifteenth- and sixteenth-century woodblock initials
were originally produced in unique sets, with each block of the series the
same size; the dimensions of these blocks alone are often sufficient to identify
the set of blocks from which those images come, and this in turn can often
identify a particular printer.[16] Dibdin does not even note this, perhaps because "actual size" was, for the nineteenth-century printer reproducing such
images, the norm, not, as for a twentieth-century printer, an extra burden at
each step of the printing process. A nineteenth-century printer transfers images using physical plates. Thus, an image traced by a nineteenth-century
illustrator will be reproduced through physical contact with successive sheets
all the way to the leaves in the final printed book; "actual size" will be maintained throughout this process without any thought given to the matter.
What we consider accuracy (proper measurement) is for a nineteenth-century
facsimilist a pure accident of production. What a nineteenth-century bibliographer considers accuracy may be something else entirely.

   Even though the traced reproductions in Dibdin are sufficient to identify
most early woodblocks or initials, these versions do not meet ordinary twentieth-century standards of accuracy. Figure 31 compares an image in Dibdin
with a photographic image from the original. The changes effected by Dibdin's artist in such details as shading are fairly easy to see, even in casual
comparison. Clearly, the images have been cleaned up or rationalized. Dibdin's *grand récit* concerning the "Rise and Progress" of the arts of engraving
and woodblock printing has been taken over by his facsimilist, who has himself improved the appearance of the original.

   A more elaborate illustration is from the 1527 *Polychronicon* (Treveris),
fol. clxxxii (Figure 32). Dibdin is proud enough of this image to credit his

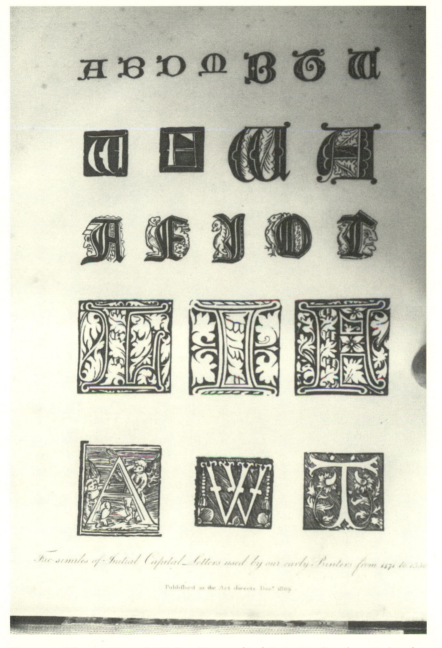

Figure 30. Thomas Frognall Dibdin, *Typographical Antiquities* (London, 1810), vol. 1. Facsimile of initials. Courtesy of the William Andrews Clark Memorial Library, University of California, Los Angeles.

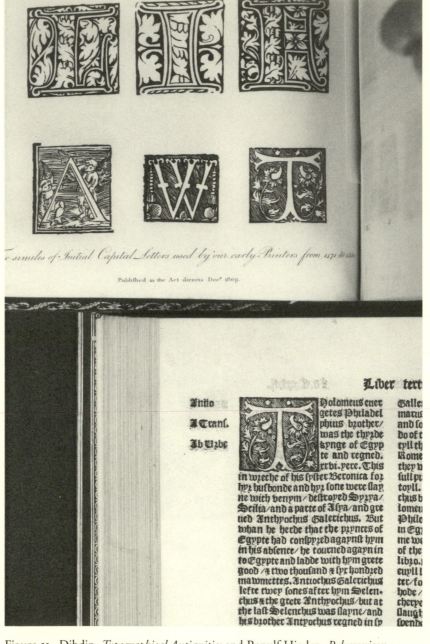

Figure 31. Dibdin, *Typographical Antiquities* and Ranulf Higden, *Polycronicon* (London: Peter Treveris, 1527). Courtesy of the William Andrews Clark Memorial Library, University of California, Los Angeles.

own facsimilist (not the facsimilist responsible for other images in the book): "The skill and fidelity of Mr. John Nesbit, the artist who traced and engraved it, will be acknowledged by the most fastidious critic" (Dibdin, xv). The subject here is suddenly nineteenth-century artistry (the skill of Mr. John Nesbit), not sixteenth-century artistry. This artistry can again be judged by placing Nesbit's illustration next to the original. The same qualities distinguishing the original initial (or rather, my modern photographic facsimile of it) and Dibdin's version (or a modern version of that), can be found here.

Finally, I note an elaborate initial of Queen Elizabeth reproduced from Foxe's *Book of Martyrs*, 1563 (Figures 33 and 34). To Dibdin, the art of woodblock printing culminated during the reign of Elizabeth and then suffered a decline, due to the rise of copper engraving:

> Borders to pages of the body of a work, or different manners of setting up a page, is also another department of ORNAMENTAL PRINTING: and of this, the Prayer Book before mentioned [xxi], published in the reign of Queen Elizabeth, is probably the most splendid examples which this country ever produced. (xlvii)

In Dibdin's view of this history, the reign of Elizabeth constitutes the highpoint of the tradition of woodblock printing, and here, Elizabeth serves appropriately as the subject of the woodblock itself. When we compare Dibdin's version to the original, we can see that this history of perfection has again been embodied in the modern reproduction. Dibdin's Elizabeth is far more perfectly and carefully portrayed than the Elizabeth of the original woodblock.

Examples (II): Type Facsimiles

Dibdin states his purpose as follows:

> My object in laying these fac-similes before the reader is, to impress him with an idea of that peculiar species or character of wooden-block engraving, which may be traced in a variety of productions that signalised the typographical annals of Elizabeth's reign. And even those who are accustomed to the productions of ancient artists,

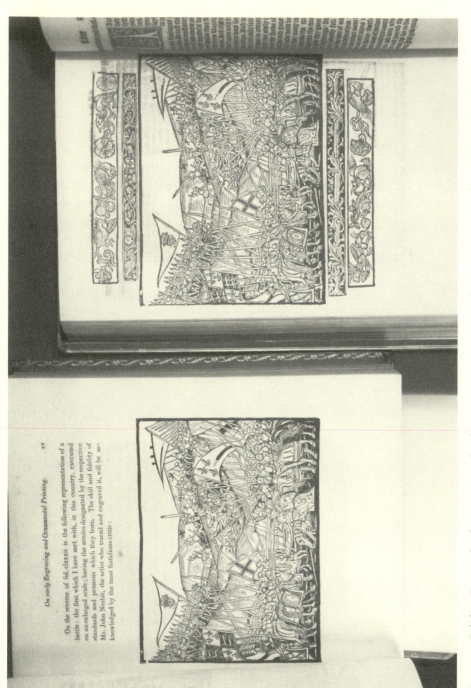

Figure 32. Dibdin, *Typographical Antiquities* and *Polycronicon* (1527). Courtesy of the William Andrews Clark Memorial Library, University of California, Los Angeles.

Figure 33. Dibdin, *Typographical Antiquities*, 1: xxxv. Courtesy of the William Andrews Clark Memorial Library, University of California, Los Angeles.

may probably receive some gratification in observing the spirit and truth with which they are executed. (xviii)

What is the "object" or purpose spoken of in this paragraph? What is the "peculiar species or character" of engraving? And what is the "spirit and truth" of such illustrations? We might perhaps recognize or agree upon what constitutes the "spirit" of an historical art work, but this is different from what the "truth" of that artwork might be. "Truth" cannot in this passage mean "validity," since Dibdin's readers cannot compare the reproduction to the original. "Truth" to make any sense in this context must refer to some transcendent abstraction that is as much known, or potentially known, to the nineteenth-century viewer as it was to the fifteenth- or sixteenth-century artist.

Figure 34. John Foxe, *Actes and monuments of these latter and perillous dayes* (London: John Day, 1563). Courtesy of the Henry E. Huntington Library, University of California, Los Angeles.

This notion of a transcendent truth or stability then plays back into Dibdin's own typographical representation of the past. At the end of this section Dibdin reproduces a series of title pages (xliv ff). Here, the techniques of reproduction are the same as those in the original illustrations: type is physically set within woodblock borders. Yet the standards of accuracy are by any modern standards far worse than in all the other illustrations.

The use of ordinary type set within woodblock borders is the same procedure that would have been used to produce such title pages in the sixteenth century. These are not, therefore, facsimiles in the modern sense; that is, they do not reproduce accurately the appearance of the original. They are what is known as type facsimiles, imitations or mere allusions to an original using a typeface that under modern type classifications would be the same family of typeface as the original. They are the equivalent of the Malone Society type facsimiles spoken of in Chapter 6, where printed texts are reproduced line-for-line and letter-by-letter using a modern blackletter typefont in place of the original. The convention of representation seems unscholarly in this context, but it is the same followed in bibliographical catalogues such as Ludwig Hain's contemporary *Repertorium bibliographicum* of 1810 or the twentieth-century *Gesamtkatalog der Wiegendrucke*, whose brief descriptions of early books broadly distinguish in their own transcriptions of incipits or colophons the type family of the original: blackletter for blackletter, roman for roman.

In Dibdin's facsimiles, the typeface is immediately recognizable as modern, or at least to a modern bibliographer it should be. The roman shows the exaggerated distinction of wide and narrow strokes characteristic of early nineteenth-century "Modern face" type, and is remarkably unlike early typefaces or even contemporary versions of early typefaces (those typefaces known as Old Style).[17] The highly ornamented blackletter is also unlike anything found in the sixteenth century. Any modern reader can recognize these differences, and having recognized them, can see similar peculiarities of detail in the framing woodblock facsimiles. The attempt to reproduce visual detail is specious and misleading: in the Thomas More title page pictured here, the thin diagonal "river of white" in the lower left reproduces not a characteristic of the original woodblock, but rather a fold in the paper in the original impression from which this facsimile is copied.

Dibdin has thus produced a modern version of typographical antiquities, a testament to the *telos* of the rise and progress narrative he claims to be writing, but a *telos* quite different from what a modern bibliographer, trained in photographic facsimiles, might see. The early typefaces he is describing

Figures 35–37. Dibdin, *Typographical Antiquities*, facsimiles of title pages. Courtesy of the University of Southern California, on behalf of USC Libraries.

The Actes of the Apo=
stels, wrytten by Saynt Luke the Euangelyst, whiche was present at the doynges of them .

The fyrst Chapter.

The Ascention of Christ, Mathias is chosen jn the steade of Iudas.

¶ I the former trea=

A ¶ The pistle on Ascention

develop in a straight-line evolution to the refined blackletter types of the early nineteenth century, typefaces that Dibdin then uses as descriptors of the ancient typefaces from which they developed. The modern representations of title pages, then, are not really representations at all. They are, like the much later and more self-conscious imitations and facsimiles of Caxton typefaces by Blades in 1861, bibliographical descriptions, but, unlike the descriptions in Blades, they are what modern bibliographers must describe as bad descriptions. The aesthetic function served by these reproductions completely obscures the bibliographical one, in that they serve neither as accurate descriptions nor as representations of history, but rather as representatives of what that history could have been had it included (and ended with) the soon-to-be-obsolete technology and aesthetics of the early nineteenth century.

Conclusion: A Bibliographical Tour of a Bibliographical Tour

During the publication of *Typographical Antiquities*, Dibdin toured European libraries with his illustrator George Lewis, the result of which was his three-volume, heavily illustrated *A Bibliographical, Antiquarian, and Picturesque Tour in France and Germany* (1821). This was followed by another tour and another set of volumes: *A Bibliographical Antiquarian and Picturesque Tour in the Northern Counties of England and in Scotland*, 2 vols. (London, 1838). In these volumes, Dibdin claims to have two objects, bibliographical and antiquarian, that is, (1) books and manuscripts and (2) architectural antiquities. In regard to books, Didbin claims to be recovering a past unknown even to those who own the volumes that record it:

> My object has been to select, and bear away, many of the curious, splendid, and interesting specimens of ART, of the *"olden time,"*[18] contained in these volumes; and which, till their present appearance, were probably scarcely known—even to their possessors. (*Bibliographical Tour . . . France and Germany*, iii–iv)

Dibdin provides lavish praise for his illustrator:

> It is therefore but a necessary consequence of the foregoing premises, to introduce the name of the Artist, to whom, after all, these pages are probably indebted for their chief source of attraction. Mr.

George Lewis, who accompanied me, has here given such proofs of
a varied and happy talent, that I hardly know ("absit invidia") where
to look for a *union* of such attainments in any other living artist. . . .
The reader will cast his eye upon the views included in the Antiquarian department of this work, and he will perceive that Mr. Lewis is
nearly as powerful in the delineation of Gothic remains, as of picturesque appearances of nature, and of national character in groups of
the common people. It was due to talents of this description, and
more especially was it due to a liberal public, that the copies from
such a pencil should be worthy of the originals. (viii–ix)

That such a project is implicated in the history it records is stated explicitly
by Dibdin:

I am willing to hope that, as no expense has been spared, and no
pains and exertions have been withheld, the ENGRAVINGS in
these volumes may, upon the whole, be considered a splendid and
permanent monument of the progress of British Art. (ix)

We can analyze some of these illustrations exactly as we did those in
Typographical Antiquities, reproducing Dibdin's own reproduction of a
printed book page or initial and reproducing beside it the original, or a more
modern reproduction of that original. The same qualities we see in the images
from *Typographical Antiquities* would be seen in these cases. The Bayeux
Tapestry illustration (1:378) is cartoonish, as are many of the illustrations of
manuscript pages. In other cases, there seems no original to be had: the
illustration on 1:137, I believe, is supposed to represent an entire class of books
produced for Catholic children in Rouen from the sixteenth to the nineteenth century.

The most striking illustrations in *Bibliographical Tour*, however, are not
of books but of architectural monuments, such as Caen Cathedral in Figure
38. As a modern viewer looking at such a reproduction, I see not a monument, but rather a nineteenth-century illustration. What I see are quaint
nineteenth-century personages dressed in medieval costume with appropriately sublime cloud formations in the background.[19] I cannot date the figures;
they seem to be wearing what a friend once described as nondescript opera
costumes. The cathedral could be Notre Dame; it could be Rheims, or any
other cathedral—the individual characteristics are lost to me in the conven-

Figure 38. Thomas Frognall Dibdin, *Bibliographical, Antiquarian and Picturesque Tour in France and Germany* (London, 1821), 1:297. Caen.

tions of the reproduction. I see these reproductive qualities not because I am comparing this in my mind to the "original"; in most cases, I have not seen the original monument, and even in those cases where I have, my memory can hardly be trusted to provide a meaningful image of comparison. I am, rather, comparing them to modern images. Having been trained in the conventions of two-dimensional photography, I interpret Dibdin's images as something other than representations. They refer not to an object, but to a period in the history of illustration: the crisp lines of steel engravings, the signs of etching, even the hand-coloring and the faded pigments characteristic of such coloring from this period. If I compare this with a modern photograph of the scene, whether in color or in black and white, I only highlight these features. I cannot describe the characteristics of the photograph because I cannot see them—I see right through them, ignoring the false perspective, the keystoning, the artificiality of the focus. There is to me, nothing to compare in any serious way: it is Dibdin on the one hand, and it is reality on the other, embodied in that zero degree of representation I find in a skilled photograph.

When I turn back to the representation of typographical images, I am suddenly unsettled by this realization. For no matter how many times I look at these early books, how many times I have examined them, as soon as I begin to discuss them, or to write about them, or to consider which illustrations in these books I can use, I begin to judge these mental images in terms of my own understanding of images generally. My mental images are not of books, but of framed photographs of books, and, in terms of the images I have used here, not even images of books (which should properly be three-dimensional holograms) but images of pages of books—that artificial and illusory two-dimensional surface that modern photographic techniques can reproduce with crisp, 90-degree corners characteristic of an impossible, infinite focal length. Looking at Dibdin's versions, I see thus what Dibdin himself claimed to see looking at Ames's images produced some sixty years earlier—something whose "intrinsic merit [seems] scarcely deserving of attention," even though I am giving it my full attention here.

Print Culture Redivivus

A persistent theme in this book has been the lack of control: Dibdin does not control his illustrators, Herbert his engravers, Gutenberg his typesetters, or Chaucer his later annotators. I began this thinking of this work as an extension of a polemic I have been conducting for several years. I would critique, as in the first chapters, the notion of the bibliographical *grand récit,* that large general abstraction within which all material evidence is placed, and which defines out of existence the very possibility of counter-evidence. But I have discovered, of course, my own version of the narrative I have critiqued elsewhere; I have kept some familiar topics (Chapters 4 and parts of 7), discarded others (an earlier chapter 5), added others that have been irritating me for some time (elements of the Piers Plowman Archive) and some that once seemed to fit my narrative and now seem to be in the hands of others ("Interlude"). Here, as elsewhere, chance trumps intent.

I have called this collection *Out of Sorts* because I am not entirely satisfied with this situation. I did not go into literary studies because I wanted to study ink or paper or typesorts or binding structures, the conventions of book description, editorial inanities, or the squabblings of bibliographers, cataloguers, and career professors. Even as a bibliographer, I avoided the Gutenberg Bible, read Dibdin only for pleasure, and never looked at a seventeenth-century poem unless I had to teach it. Certain things—they simply do not work out as they should.

And as I sit at this computer keyboard, or imagine myself staring at proofs, I think of sitting at another keyboard. Decades ago, I earned a living typing term papers and moot court briefs for students at various colleges and universities in New Orleans, essentially translating their illegible hands, their half-sentences, their arrows and cross-outs and heated marginalia into key-strokes of an IBM selectric typewriter—at the time, the cutting edge in tech-nology and an investment the equivalent of nearly a year's rent. I typed the paragraphs they had written and the ones they had plagiarized amateurishly from textbooks, reformatting as the typewriter space demanded. I typed lewd notes for the hell of it, midway through the papers, where neither the author nor the professor grading the paper would ever read them, and sometimes, as an experiment, I typed these on the last page to see who would be the first to discover them. I rewrote notes and sentence fragments, thesis statements, and sometimes paragraphs, because there were many times when it was easier simply to compose something intelligible than to decipher what was before me.

At times, my typing became composition, and I wrote papers on Beckett, on baseball gloves, on contemporary philosophy, on early American duels, on art history. I constructed each as a five- to fifteen-page packet with the notes at the back and its purchaser's name typed in my own special formula on the title page. Plagiarism is of course a serious academic offense, but since the evidence suggests that only students and bad people who hold nefarious political views are punished for it, I can safely admit to it here. Every page I typed was my own, whether I wrote that page or copied it, and you could if you cared recognize my work at a glance—the erasable paper, the number of typeover corrections, the exactly calculated margins to ensure a decent hourly wage, and finally the style, that inaudible and professional voice that found expression even in the most formulaic of legal briefs, even in the most absurd of student poetry analysis.

I think also of the former binder for the former librarians at the William Andrews Clark Library in Los Angeles. When the Clark Library once sent books to the bindery, with explicit instructions on retaining the endpapers, the books came back from the binder with those endpapers neatly cut away (the incalculable loss of notes of provenance!) and his exquisite endpapers in their place. That unnamed but famous binder doubtless thinking, in a parody of Scott Montcrieff: you collect; I bind. And yes, you write, and I type.

It is conventional to lament such things, the evils of the bindery, the unscrupulous nature of the amanuensis, the outright plagiarist. But in the end, all these actions redound to our advantage, whether we see ourselves as perpetrators or victims. I can now, thanks to unscrupulous or egomaniacal binders, reconstruct the histories their workings obscure, and even write a paragraph about it, as here. And I can also take joy in what I did for those overworked professors at Tulane, or Loyola, or University of New Orleans, now safely retired: for some, how much easier their lives briefly were when dealing with the bland invisibility of my formulaic papers; for others, more conscientious, there were even greater pleasures, as they saw their hard work rewarded when, surely thanks to their instruction, a once illiterate student became what seemed to be a passably competent writer of prose.

Note on a Note by Walt Whitman

> As there are now several editions of L. of G., different texts and dates, I wish to say that I prefer and recommend this present one, complete, for future printing, if there should be any; a copy and fac-simile, indeed, of the text of these 438 pages. The subsequent adjusting interval which is so important to form'd and launch'd work, books especially, has pass'd; and waiting till fully after that, I have given (pages 423–438) my concluding words. W.W. (Copyrights, & c. [p. 2] *Leaves of Grass* , Philadelphia: David McKay, 1891–92)

Leaves of Grass went through multiple editions during Whitman's lifetime. Poems were added, and re-arranged in terms of what Whitman called "clusters." According to Whitman's own testimony, the 1891–92 edition, known as the "Deathbed Edition," is the definitive copy, containing his "concluding words." This is the "preferred and recommended" one. Future editions should contain "a copy and fac-simile" of the text of these 438 pages.

Whitman's wishes were not fulfilled, nor does his statement, if taken seriously or literally, seem feasible. His "preferred and recommended" edition is certainly accessible to readers, but only in libraries in copies of the original print run, and on the Web in the Walt Whitman Archive (www.whitmanar-chive.org). My casual survey of the UCLA catalogue shows (I think) some 57 editions, or editions of significant selections, in addition to several sound recordings and translations (one in German, three in Yiddish). Many of these of course are in multiple copies. I cannot from the library catalog determine the precise nature of many of these editions, although many claim to be "authoritative"; I do not know the typefonts used, and often I have to guess at the order of poems or the number included. But even the brief descriptions here show that the only ones that could be said to obey Whitman's strictures are the two McKay editions (the Clark Library has a copy of each; UCLA has an additional copy of 1891–92). Some of these later, twentieth-century editions claim to follow the 1892 "arrangement"; most follow or facsimilize other editions.

There are likely economic reasons to prefer the earlier editions: an editor who does not have to follow slavishly a particular copytext can work more efficiently. But the somewhat unfocussed defense of the 1881–82 edition by Dennis K. Renner in 1998, reprinted in the Whitman Archive, suggests that at least some objections to Whitman's later editions were made on what I think are imagined to have been aesthetic grounds:

> Even granting the coherence of Whitman's final design, the superior literary standing of prewar poems and clusters will probably endure. However, instead of blaming the abstractness of postwar poems and programmatic clusters in the 1881–1882 edition on a waning of poetic powers—a subtle form of ageism—critics can recognize the logic of the volume as Whitman designed it, acknowledging that twentieth-century readers have admired Whitman's achievement as a lyric poet more than the larger communal and national purposes he envisioned for his work.[1]

There are further objections to these various editions on bibliographical or editorial grounds: what Whitman considers a "version" or "edition" is apparently, from a bibliographical point of view, often nothing of the sort. R. W. French, as quoted also in the Whitman Archive, claims that the 1891 "text" is "not an edition at all, but an IMPRESSION." "It does not qualify as an edition . . . since it contained no significant new material." Thus, the only authentic editions are those of 1855, 1856, 1860, 1867, 1871, 1881. See also Gay Wilson Allen, in the 1975 *Walt Whitman Handbook*:

> The 1891–92 issue of *Leaves of Grass* is widely known as the "death-bed edition" but it is not, as defined at the beginning of this chapter . . ., a new *edition*, and the book which his intimate friends called the "death-bed edition" was a book hastily assembled in December, 1891, from unbound sheets of the 1889 reprint so that Whitman might hold the promised "new edition" in his hands before he died. A few copies were bound for the poet's friends, but it was, in

a sense, a fake, and certainly not the projected final and definitive 1892 *Leaves of Grass*.[2]

In other words the nonexistent "1892 *Leaves of Grass*" is more "final and definitive" than the actual 1891–92 *Leaves of Grass* printed with Whitman's own authorizing words.

If I am reading Whitman's comments and those of his editors correctly (and I likely am not, since I do not pretend to be a Whitman scholar), what is defined as an edition here is fluid. At times it is an edition in the textual-critical sense: the change or addition of texts (the existence of "significant new material"). But the definition of edition occasionally shifts to a bibliographical one; it is defined on the basis of "plates"; a century earlier, these plates might be roughly equivalent to preserved typeset formes; in the twentieth century, the same function might be served by an imagined photographic reprint. An abstract text and a typographical one are fundamentally different things: an abstract text is something to be read, not seen; it thus can be reproduced on a keyboard; a typographical text is what can only be reproduced as an image. It can be read, but it cannot be reproduced in different visual forms or shapes.

What Whitman seems to have been referring to or imagining is these physical plates, containing the text and its arrangement as well as the typesetting and formatting; these would be the source of any later "copy and facsimile of the text." Modern textual critics and Whitman scholars are concerned with the abstract text, not the material plates (the physical things that cause impressions in paper); this text is something grander, something disembodied and abstracted from the plates that may produce it. These plates are not, as they were to Whitman, definitive; they are rather only one of many witnesses to that text, just as Whitman's printed words in the 1891–92 edition are only one expression in a lifetime's worth of expressions of his intentions.

Let us look at the result of a late twentieth-century editor's conscientious attempt to follow Whitman's statements, this from the Library of America edition.[3] I consider here the text alone, ignoring the visual impediments of the nineteenth-century typeface. It is not necessary to provide images to see differences: I transcribe the 1892 edition against the version in the Library of America, both in "diplomatic" editions. First, the 1892 text:

INSCRIPTIONS.

ONE'S-SELF I SING.

ONE'S-SELF I sing, a simple separate person,
Yet utter the word Democratic, the word En-Masse.

Of physiology from top to toe I sing,
Not physiognomy alone nor brain alone is worthy for the Muse, I
        say the Form complete is worthier far,
The Female equally with the Male I sing.

If my own typesetters assume that what I have constructed as line breaks are relevant (but the precise vertical arrangement is not), then I can explain the differences in a diplomatic transcription. The Library of America version is as follows:

Inscriptions

One's-Self I Sing

ONE'S-SELF I sing, a simple separate person,
Yet utter the word Democratic, the word En-Masse.

Of physiology from top to toe I sing,
Not physiognomy alone nor brain alone is worthy for the
        Muse, I say the Form complete is worthier far,
The Female equally with the Male I sing.

If these texts appear as I hope they do, it should be obvious what "accuracy" to the Library of America editors means: textual accuracy, with the entire poem reduced to house style. We have italics for titles, no punctuation following titles, no lines dividing title from text; the conventions regarding line length are those used in ordinary verse—lines too long for the printer are wrapped without comment; it is thus indifferent where conventional "line 2" (in fact lines 2 and 3) of stanza 2 are broken. What the editors represent is their understanding of Whitman's text, not, as he claimed to want, all visual aspects of that text. We really do not know how important these differences might be to Whitman, since we cannot be certain how important was the difference between text and facsimile, nor whether by "facsimile" he foresaw the preservation of the appearance of his text in a dated, obsolete typefont: that is, we do not know whether Whitman preferred Whitman to be living or dead.

There are many ironies in Whitman's remarks, and it may be these that legitimize the disparaging of these remarks by many Whitman scholars, and the ignoring of them by his best editors. First, the notion that the multifarious poem itself, *Leaves of Grass*, which for most readers owes a large part of its essence to its variability, is to be fixed—the living poem becomes an actual poem that can be contained in a book. Second, the attempted fossilization of that poem in a form (typographical and visual) for which Whitman himself could have been only partially responsible. A facsimile produced during the twentieth century according to Whitman's stated wishes would reproduce not Whitman's radical poem, but rather the most banal of Whitman's contemporary conventions—the typeface instantly recognizable as late nineteenth-century, for many of us, more reminiscent of the revoltingly sentimental and moralistic texts associated with the tongue-clucking admonitions of our grandmothers.

Only if we read Whitman as we want to read him (for me, in one of the physically satisfying and generally heavily discounted American Library editions), not as he says we should read him, can we avoid this. I do not have to gaze through the maddening screen of my grandmother's moral system, nor do I have to confront the unpleasant notion that this is all an illusion— America was doubtless much less grand than the version of it Whitman presents. The histories that Whitman tells are sanitized and universalized in my edition. They are marked by the legitimacy conferred by literary history, and appear in that same excellent typeface that serves for Melville, Stevens, Poe; it is American literature, after all, not America, and probably no longer Whitman at all.[4]

NOTES

✺

INTRODUCTION

1. In English, Douglas C. McMurtrie and Karl Schorbach, *The Gutenberg Documents, with Translations of the Texts into English* (New York: Oxford University Press, 1941).

2. For a list of these early references, see Jan Hendrik Hessels, "Typography," in the 1911 *Encyclopedia Britannica*, www.1911encyclopedia.org.

3. Text and translation from Alfred W. Pollard, *An Essay on Colophons with Specimens and Translations* (Chicago: Caxton Club, 1905), 37.

4. W. J. B. Crotch, ed., *The Prologues and Epilogues of William Caxton*, EETS, OS, 176 (London, 1928), 7–8.

5. For examples, see below, Chapters 1 and 2.

6. This feature of the manuscript is oddly far more obvious in the black-and-white facsimile by Israel Gollanz, ed., *Pearl, Cleanness, Patience and Sir Gawain, reproduced in facsimile from the unique ms. Cotton Nero A.x of the British Museum* (London: EETS, 1923) (reproduced here) than in the excellent images provided by the British Library.

7. Gottfried Zedler, *Die älteste Gutenbergtype, mit 13 Tafeln in Lichtdruck,* VGG, 1 (Mainz: Gutenberg Gesellschaft, 1902).

8. See my "The Cataloguing of Early Book Fragments," in *The Myth of Print Culture: Essays on Evidence, Textuality, and Bibliographical Method* (Toronto: University of Toronto Press, 2003), 57–82.

9. For problems in this simple assumption, see my *Abstractions of Evidence in the Study of Manuscripts and Early Printed Books* (Aldershot: Ashgate, 2009), 19–23.

10. See Albert Derolez, *The Palaeography of Gothic Manuscript Books, from the Twelfth to the Early Sixteenth Century* (Cambridge: Cambridge University Press, 2003), passim.

11. Daniel Berkeley Updike, *Printing Types: Their History, Forms, and Use: A Study in Survivals*, 2 vols. (Cambridge, Mass.: Harvard University Press, 1937), 1:57; cf. A. F. Johnson, *Type Designs: Their History and Development*, 3rd ed. (1934; Norwich: Andre Deutsch, 1966), chap. 1.

12. *BMC*, XI: *England* (2008), 335.

13. The term from Roland Barthes has been applied to typography most accessibly in the polemics surrounding the late twentieth-century use of Helvetica: see the 2007 documentary "Helvetica" dir. Gary Hustwit.

14. A. F. Johnson, "The Classification of Gothic Types" (1929), in *Selected Essays on Books and Printing*, ed. Percy H. Muir (Amsterdam: Van Gendt, 1970), 4: "The term Gotico-antique is new in typography, and even, I believe, in paleography. Not only that, but it represents an entirely new grouping of types, among which are the type of the Catholicon, and several standard types of Schoeffer, Gunther Zainer, Augsburg and his school, and the first printers at Basle." See also Derolez, *Gothic Script*, 177.

15. See my "Bibliographical History Versus Bibliographical Evidence: The Plowman's Tale and Early Chaucer Editions," *Bulletin of the John Rylands University Library of Manchester* 78 (1996): 47–61.

16. B. L. Ullman, *The Origin and Development of Humanistic Script* (Rome: Edizioni di Storia e Letteratura, 1960), 1–20.

17. G. W. Prothero, *A Memoir of Henry Bradshaw* (London: Kegan, Paul, Trench, 1888), 349; Paul Needham, *The Bradshaw Method: Henry Bradshaw's Contribution to Bibliography* (Chapel Hill, N.C.: Hanes Foundation, 1998), 8.

18. Carl Wehmer, *Mainzer Probedrucke in der Type des sogenannten Astronomischen Kalenders für 1448: Ein Beitrag zur Gutenbergforschung* (Munich: Leipniz, 1948), 31; Gottfried Zedler, *Gutenbergs älteste Type und die mit ihr hergestellten Drucke* , VGG, 23 (Mainz: Gutenberg Gesellschaft, 1934), 23–25, and below, Chapter 4; the passage is translated word for word by Hessels, "Typography."

19. Paul Schwenke, *Die Donat- und Kalender-Type: Nachtrag und Übersicht*, VGG, 2 (Mainz: Gutenberg Gesellschaft, 1903), "Vorwort."

20. Lucien Febvre and Henri-Jean Martin, *L'Apparition du livre* (1958), trans. David Gerard, *The Coming of the Book: The Impact of Printing 1450–1800* (London: Verso, 1976), 9.

21. Elizabeth Eisenstein, *The Printing Press as an Agent of Change*, 2 vols. (Cambridge: Cambridge University Press, 1979), 1: 4.

22. Nicholas Barker, "Reflections on the History of the Book" (1990), rpt, in *Form and Meaning in the History of Books: Selected Essays* (London: British Library, 2003), 270.

23. William Sherman, *Used Books: Marking Readers in Renaissance England* (Philadelphia: University of Pennsylvania Press, 2008): "Anyone who turns to marginalia with high hopes of easy answers quickly discovers that the evidence they contain turns out to be (if not always thin, scattered, and ambiguous) peculiarly difficult to locate, decipher, and interpret" (xiii).

CHAPTER 1. ON THE CONTINUITY OF CONTINUITY: PRINT CULTURE MYTHOLOGY AND THE TYPE OF THE GUTENBERG BIBLE (B42)

1. Joseph A. Dane, *The Myth of Print Culture: Essays on Evidence, Textuality, and Bibliographical Method* (Toronto: University of Toronto Press, 2003), chap. 1, 10–21.

2. A classic study of this nature concerns the two-color initials of the Mainz Psalter; Heinrich Wallau, "Die zweifarbigen Initialen der Psalterdrucke von Joh. Fust und Peter Schöffer," in *Festschrift zum fünfhundertjährigen Geburtstage von Johann Gutenberg* (Leipzig: Harrassowitz, 1900), 325–79, esp. 350ff.

3. The word "unimpeachable" describing such evidence is from William Blades, *Life and Typography of William Caxton*, 2 vols. (London: J. Lilly, 1861), 1: viii.

4. Lucien Febvre and Henri-Jean Martin, *The Coming of the Book* (1958), trans. David Gerard (London: Verso, 1976), 54. Febvre and Martin relied to some extent on Charles Mortet, *Les origines et les débuts de l'imprimerie* (Paris: Picard, 1922), who dismissed the studies from the Gutenberg Gesellschaft "à cause d'un certain nombre d'idées précon- çues inspirées par l'orgueil national" (vi). Yet the most obvious twentieth-century offender was Gottfried Zedler, who paradoxically supported the "Coster" theory of a Dutch origin of printing, one also supported by Mortet.

5. Elizabeth Eisenstein, *The Printing Press as an Agent of Change*, 2 vols. (Cambridge: Cambridge University Press, 1979), 1: xi and 4.

6. Much of the most important early twentieth-century work appeared in the series Veröffentlichungen der Gutenberg Gesellschaft (VGG) from 1902 to 1929, building on earlier studies by Karl Dziatko and Paul Schwenke. The state of the art in late nineteenth- century studies was well described for English readers in various publications by Jan Hen- drik Hessels, including his article in the 1911 *Encyclopedia Britannica* (www.1911encyclo pedia.org).

7. Brian Leister and Nancy Willard, *Gutenberg's Gift: A Book-Lover's Pop-Up Book* (Baltimore: Wild Honey, 1995). Houghton, who now owns copyright, has refused permis- sion to have this reproduced here.

8. Stephen Füssell, *Gutenberg and the Impact of Printing* (1999), trans. Douglas Mar- tin (Aldershot: Ashgate, 2003), 8; Maurice Audin, *Histoire de l'imprimerie: radioscopie d'une ère, de Gutenberg à l'informatique* (Paris: Picard,1972), 95; Henri-Jean Martin, *Pour une histoire du livre: cinq conférences* (Naples: Bibliopolis, 1987), 12; Ronald B. McKerrow, *An Introduction to Bibliography for Literary Students* (Oxford: Oxford University Press, 1927), 6; so also Silvia Werfel, "Einrichtung und Betrieb einer Druckerei der Handpres- senzeit," in Helmut Gier and Johannes Janota, eds., *Augsburger Buchdruck und Verlagswe- sen* (Wiesbaden: Harrassowitz, 1997), 98–99. The statement is a commonplace, but a warning about this sort of thinking in relation to early printing was issued as early as 1861 by Blades, *Caxton*, 2: xxiii–iv; Blades drew on his practical experience as a printer for many of his conclusions (1: vii).

9. Joseph Moxon, *Mechanick Exercises on the Whole Art of Printing (1683–4)*, ed. Herbert Davis and Harry Carter, 2 vols. (Oxford: Oxford University Press, 1958).

10. *Pour une histoire du livre*; ref. to Philip Gaskell, *A New Introduction to Bibliogra- phy* (Oxford: Oxford University Press, 1972).

11. Carl Wehmer, *Mainzer Probedrucke in der Type des sogenannten Astronomischen Kalenders: Ein Beitrag zur Gutenbergforschung* (Munich: Leibniz, 1948); Gottfried Zedler, *Die älteste Gutenbergtype mit 13 Tafeln in Lichtdruck*, VGG, 1 (Mainz: Gutenberg Gesell-

schaft,1902); Paul Schwenke, *Die Donat- und Kalendertype: Nachtrag und Übersicht*, VGG, 2 (Mainz: Gutenberg Gesellschaft, 1903).

12. Image from Clark Library copy, *A Noble Fragment: Being a Leaf of the Gutenberg Bible (1453–1455), with a Bibliographical Essay by A. Edward Newton* (New York: Wells, 1921).

13. Gottfried Zedler, *Die sogenannte Gutenbergbibel, sowie die mit der 42-zeiligen Bibeltype ausgeführten kleineren Drucke*, VGG, 20 (Mainz: Gutenberg Gesellschaft, 1929), 10–13. These letters do not occur in Latin and would have been necessary only for proper names.

14. The fragments in Figures 3, 10, and 11 represent both early and perfected states of the type; see discussion below in Chap. 2.

15. Paul Schwenke, *Untersuchungen zur Geschichte des ersten Buchdrucks* (Berlin: Hopfer, 1900).

16. S. Leigh Sotheby, *The Typography of the Fifteenth Century, being specimens of the productions of the early continental printers, exemplified in a collection of fac-similes from one hundred works* (London, 1845), 52ff.

17. Schwenke's table (*Untersuchungen*, 53–54) is more complicated, indicating four and eventually six simultaneous settings, but only two are involved in these early sections. See more recently, Severin Corsten, "Die Drucklegung der zweiundvierzigzeiligen Bibel: Technische und chronologische Probleme," in *Johannes Gutenbergs zweiundvierzigzeilen Bibel: Faksimile Ausgabe nach dem Exemplar der Staatsbibliothek Preußischer Kulturbesitz Berlin* (Munich: Idion, 1979), *Kommentarband*, 35–38, 44–47; Paul Needham, "The Compositor's Hand in the Gutenberg Bible: A Review of the Todd Thesis," *PBSA* 77 (1983) 341–71; "Division of Copy in the Gutenberg Bible: Three Glosses on the Ink Evidence," *PBSA* 79 (1985): 411–26; "The Paper Supply of the Gutenberg Bible," *PBSA* 79 (1985): 303–74.

18. See, however, the qualifications of Martin Boghardt, "Partial Duplicate Setting: Means of Rationalization or Complicating Factor in Textual Transmission," *The Library* ser. 6, 15 (1993): 306–31, and my "A Ghostly Twin Terence (Venice, 21 July 1475; IGI 9422, 9433)," *The Library* ser. 6, 21 (1999): 99–107.

19. A fragment of a Donatus in this state is at Scheide library; see Paul Needham, *The Invention and Early Spread of European Printing as Represented in the Scheide Library* (Princeton, N.J.: Princeton University Library, 2007), illustration 2, pp. 15, 13.

20. Enthusiasts for this theory claimed they could see the file-marks in the impressions left by the type, and perhaps they could; see the criticisms of G. P. Winship by William B. Todd, *The Gutenberg Bible: New Evidence of the Original Printing* (Chapel Hill, N.C.: Hanes Foundation, 1982), 11–18.

21. *Johannes Gutenbergs zweiundvierzigzeilige Bibel: Erganzungsband* (Leipzig, 1923). Some of these modified positions concerned the number of presses used to print the Bible. Although Schwenke himself changed his earlier theory of six operating presses, those who have cited him in support over the last fifty years have ignored this change or attributed it to others. See discussion in Todd, *Gutenberg Bible*, 17.

22. Guy Bechtel, *Gutenberg et l'invention de l'imprimerie: une enquête* (Paris: Fayard, 1992), 434–36, claims the 41-line setting is artificial in the sense that it is intended only to blur the transition from the earlier to later settings. I assume by this he means that it was not the result of a physical manipulation of type.

23. Theodore L. De Vinne, *The Invention of Printing: A Collection of Facts And Opinions Descriptive of Early Prints and Playing Cards, the Block-Books of the Fifteenth Century, the Legend of Lourens Janszoon Coster, of Haarlem, and the Work of John Gutenberg and His Associates* (1876; rpt. Detroit: Gale, 1969), esp. 49–67. C. F. Gessner, *Die so nöthig als nützliche Buchdruckerkunst und Schriftgiesserei* (Leipzig, 1740), 2: 174 also emphasizes this; see Werfel, "Einrichtung," 114.

24. Antonius van der Linde, *Geschichte der Erfindung der Buchdruckkunst*, 3 vols. (Berlin, 1886), 682, also attributes the invention of printing to the metalworker.

25. Zedler, for the earliest type (DK-type and B42 type), proposed several different methods of typecasting (see below, Chapter 3); steel punches and copper-matrices, along with the hand-mold, are then attributed to Peter Schoeffer (*Die älteste Gutenbergtype*, 24–26). Prior to the twentieth century, discussions of various methods of producing early type and type-pages were common—sand-casting, wooden punches, even stereotyping. The question of method became enmeshed in nationalistic histories of the origin of printing (see summary in Hessels, "Typography," 1911). Febvre and Martin, by dismissing these discussions as "puerile," inadvertently cut themselves off from scholarship focused on the technological issues in which they claimed to be more interested.

26. Colin Clair, *A History of European Printing* (London: Academic Press, 1976), notes on Jost and a nearly contemporary depiction: "The mould held by the caster would have been recognisable by his nineteenth-century counterpart" (13).

27. Albert Kapr, *Johann Gutenberg: The Man and His Invention* (1996), trans. Douglas Martin (Aldershot: Ashgate, 1996), 126: "The ladle shown in Amman's illustration for pouring in the molten lead is almost ten times larger than it would have been in reality." Kapr then turns for evidence to Gessner's description in 1740 (Kapr, 148, claims Gutenberg had invented the mold by 1440). See further, posts by James Mosley to Typefoundry.blogspot.com (2007).

28. Paul Needham, "Johann Gutenberg and the Catholicon Press," *PBSA* 76 (1982): 395–456. Needham did not follow this up in any detailed publication, but reasserts the theory strongly in 2007: *The Invention and Early Spread of European Printing*, 29. See also Paul Needham, "Corrective Notes on the Date of the Catholicon Press," *Gutenberg Jahrbuch* 1990, 46–64; "Further Corrective Notes on the Date of the Catholicon Press," *Gutenberg Jahrbuch* 1991, 101–26; and "Slipped Lines in the Mainz Catholicon: A Second Opinion," *Gutenberg Jahrbuch* 1993, 25–29.

29. Blaise Aguera y Arcas, "Computational Analytical Bibliography," Bibliopolis Conference: The Future History of the Book, 7–9 November 2002, The Hague; "Temporary Matrices and Elemental Punches in Gutenberg's DK Type," in Kristian Jensen, ed., *Incunabula and their Readers* (London: British Library, 2003), 1–12.

30. See my "Note on Some Fifteenth-Century Types of Johannes Koelhoff," *PBSA* 97 (2003): 167–82.

31. The other identifying feature is type family: roman, gothic, bastarda, semi-gothic. Thus the conventional description 134G means a gothic type measuring 134mm per 20 lines. For the challenge these variations in measurement pose to early type-identification, see my *Myth of Print Culture*, 75–82.

32. Francis Jenkinson, "Ulrich Zell's Early Quartos," *The Library* ser. 4, 7 (1926): 46–66; Severin Corsten, "Ulrich Zells früheste Produktion," *Gutenberg Jahrbuch* 2007, 68–76.

33. Dane, "A Ghostly Twin Terence."

34. Fernand Braudel, "Histoire et sciences sociales: la longue durée" (1958), rpt. in *Écrits sur l'histoire* (Paris: Flammarion, 1969), 41–84.

35. Janet Ing pointed out in a review of the *Histoire de l'édition français* "if one doesn't know where and when printing was invented, how does one determine which larger historical themes may have a bearing on the invention"; *Johann Gutenberg and His Bible: An Historical Study* (New York: Typophiles, 1988), 14–15.

CHAPTER 2. GOTTFRIED ZEDLER AND THE
TWENTIETH-CENTURY HISTORY OF DK TYPE

1. Otto W. Fuhrmann, "The Gutenberg Donatus Fragments at Columbia University, One of the oldest Mainz Imprints," *Gutenberg Jahrbuch* 1954, 36–46.

2. The *Astronomical Calendar* is now in ISTC known as the "Planeten Tafel, sive Ephemerides 1448." I retain the earlier title, since this is how it is known in most twentieth-century discussion.

3. The most straightforward discussions of these, although relying on a misdated *AK*, are Seymour DeRicci, *Catalogue raisonné des premières impressions de Mayence (1445–1467)* VGG, 8–9 (Mainz: Gutenberg Gesellschaft, 1911), and Aloys Ruppel, *Johannes Gutenberg: Sein Leben und sein Werk* (Berlin: Mann, 1939).

4. For example, the photographs in the seminal studies of Gottfried Zedler, *Die älteste Gutenbergtype mit 13 Tafeln in Lichtdruck*, VGG, 1 (Mainz: Gutenberg Gesellschaft, 1902); Paul Schwenke, *Die Donat- und Kalender Type: Nachtrag und Übersicht*, VGG, 2 (Mainz: Gutenberg Gesellschaft, 1903) (hereafter *DK Type*). Better reproductions are scattered throughout the secondary literature; see the excellent photographs from the Scheide collection in Paul Needham, *The Invention and Early Spread of European Printing, as Represented in the Scheide Library* (Princeton, N.J.: Princeton University Library, 2007), also available online: diglib.princeton.edu. For the *Astronomical Calendar*, see the color reproduction by Konrad Burger, *Monumenta Germaniae et Italiae typographica: Deutsche und italienische Inkunabeln in getreuen Nachbildungen* (Berlin: Reichsdruckerei, 1892–1913), pl. 184 (reprinted here as Figure 11). The microfilm collection "The Printing Revolution in Europe" (Gale), is not in my experience available in many top research libraries.

5. See my *The Myth of Print Culture: Essays on Evidence, Textuality, and Bibliographical Method* (Toronto: University of Toronto Press, 2003), chap. 3, 57–82.

6. Carl Wehmer, *Mainzer Probedrucke in der type des sogenannten Astronomischen*

Kalenders für 1448: Ein Beitrag zur Gutenbergforschung, mit einer Untersuchung der Astronomische Kalender, eine Planetentafel für Laienastrologen, von Viktor Stegemann (Munich: Leibniz, 1948).

7. J. H. Hessels, trans., *The Haarlem Legend of the Invention of Printing by Lourens Janszoon Coster, critically examined by A. Van der Linde* (London, 1871), introduction, xxv.

8. Karl Dziatzko, *Gutenbergs früheste Druckerpraxis* (Berlin: Asher, 1890), 19–87.

9. Paul Needham, *The Bradshaw Method: Henry Bradshaw's Contribution to Bibliography* (Chapel Hill, N.C.: Hanes Foundation, 1988), 8, 13–17.

10. Examples datable by external means seem to be in the perfected form; in the *Bulla Thurcorum*, and the *Türkenbulle*, lines are straight, and irregular letterforms are infrequent.

11. Those sections of a Donatus fragment where the typesetter seems to run out of sorts provide less evidence as to the state of a typeface than to the actual number of particular typesorts in the case. See Zedler, *Die älteste Gutenbergtype*, 18; many examples noted by Schwenke.

12. Schwenke, *DK Type*, 5, notes that Dziatzko's method involved both typeforms and setting conventions. Fuhrmann's statement quoted at the beginning of this chapter, that Zedler's method depended on the presence or absence of secondary forms alone, is not correct.

13. Paul Needham, "Preface," in Janet Thompson Ing, *Johann Gutenberg and His Bible: A Historical Study* (New York: Typophiles, 1988), 12–13. Among the more prominent curiosities of Zedler's work for which Needham criticizes him is the responsibility for both the highest and the lowest estimate of the size of the B42 print run; Paul Needham, "The Paper Supply of the Gutenberg Bible," *PBSA* 79 (1985): 308; noted also by Ruppel, *Gutenberg*, 150.

14. Zedler's publications that bear specifically on DK type include *Die älteste Gutenbergtype* (1902); *Die sogenannte Gutenbergbibel, sowie die mit der 42-zeiligen bibeltype ausgeführten kleineren Drucke*, VGG, 20 (Mainz: Gutenberg Gesellschaft, 1929); *Von Coster zu Gutenberg: Der holländische Frühdruck und die Erfindung des Buchdrucks* (Leipzig: Hiersemann, 1921); *Gutenbergs älteste Type, und die mit ihr hergestellten Drucke*, VGG, 23 (Mainz: Gutenberg Gesellschaft, 1934); *Der älteste Buchdruck und das frühholländische Doktrinale von Alexander de Villa Dei* (Leiden: Sitjhoff, 1936).

15. Cologne Chronicle quoted by Hessels, *Haarlem Legend*, xix, and translated on p. 8. See also Jacqueline Glomski, "Seventeenth-Century Views on Early Printing," *The Library* ser. 7, 2 (2001): 336–48, and for early variants on this myth, Adrian Johns, *The Nature of the Book: Print and Knowledge in the Making* (Chicago: University of Chicago Press, 1998), 329–32.

16. See esp. Wytze Hellinga and Lotte Hellinga, *The Fifteenth-Century Printing Types of the Low Countries*, trans. D. A. S. Reid, 2 vols. (Amsterdam: Hertzberger, 1966).

17. Because these lines do not appear in any handwritten script that might have served for a model, they were products of the typecasting process itself. Later scholars, appealing to the same class of experts as those used by Zedler, denied that such marks were

possible under the casting methods he hypothesized; Victor Scholderer, "The Invention of Printing" (1941), in *Fifty Essays in Fifteenth- and Sixteenth-Century Bibliography*, ed. Dennis E. Rhodes (Amsterdam: Hertzberger, 1966), 156–68, esp. 157.

18. "The idea that Gutenberg as the inventor of printing also invented type-casting has so far established itself, that scholars have assumed that the problem of type-casting is itself solved through the 'genial discovery' of the Hand-Mould" (Zedler, *Die sogenannte Gutenbergbibel*, 25); see also Zedler, *Von Coster zu Gutenberg*, "Das Handgiessinstrument," 174–87.

19. "An ihr erkenne wir, dass Gutenberg auch, als er sine Erfindung praktisch zu verwerten begann, also das Handgiessinstrument und seine zugleich damit entstandene älteste Type fertigvorlagen, jahrlang noch schwer gerungen und dass es ihn unablässige Mühen und Versuche gekostet hat, bis es ihn gelang, gleicherweise das Giessinstrument auf die Höhe der Vollendung zu bringen und seiner ältesten Schrift die Form zu geben, in der wir sie im Astronomischen Kalender für 1448 vor uns sehen" (*Gutenbergs älteste Type* [1934], 1). Zedler's view, at least in 1934, seems to be that a wooden model was used to sand-cast a new "punch," which in turn was used to form a lead matrix (13–14).

20. Charles Enschedé, *Technisch Onderzoek naar de Uitvinding van de Boekdrukkunst* (Haarlem: Bohn, 1901). For a summary of some of the procedures, see Harry Carter, *A View of Early Typography, up to About 1600* (Oxford: Oxford University Press, 1969), 5–22.

21. I quote Hessels's full description here, interspersing a few of Zedler's sentences. All other sentences in Hessels's account have a corresponding sentence in Zedler. Most, of course, have corresponding statements in Enschedé, but obviously not those noted here:

From the types of B36 and B42 Enschedé concludes that Gutenberg's punches (patrices) were made, like the bookbinders' stamps, of yellow copper (brass, Germ. *Messing). [Nach Enschedé ist die bei Herstellung der Bibeltypen, der 36- sowie der 42zeiligen, angewendete Patrize graviert und zwar in Messing.]* With such patrices only leaden matrices could be made, but the latter could be produced in two ways: the lead can be poured over the patrix, or the patrix be pressed into cold lead. *[Mit einer Patrize aus Messing lässt sich nur eine bleierne Matrize herstellen. Letztere kann man sich auf zweierlei Art vershaffen: . . .]* The first mode is somewhat complex, but the matrix would have a smooth surface, and need no further adjustment. The second mode is more simple, but requires great force, although lead is a soft metal. Moreover, the surface of the matrix has to be trimmed, as the impression forces the lead downwards and sidewards, which makes the surface uneven, though by this pressure the lead becomes firmer and more compact, to the advantage of the type-founder. Enschedé thinks that Gutenberg's letters must have been sharp, and that he obtained his matrices by the second mode; *[Enschedé möchte angesichts des schönen Druckes, der mit einer scharf gegossenen Letter hergestellt sein müsse, glauben, dass Gutenberg seine bleierne Matrize auf die zweite Art verfertigt habe. . . .]* he had each letter

engraved on a brass plate, 2mm. thick, therefore a mere letter without anything
underneath it. This letter (patrix) was pressed, by means of a small flat plate, so
far into the metal that its back formed one surface with the top part of the lead,
and then removed. After the patrix and matrix had been made in this way, the
letter was to be cast, and Enschedé believes that for this work Gutenberg used
what in Germany is called the *Abklatsch-method,* which, after having been
gradually improved, was at last superseded by more perfect machinery. By this
method the letter was cast in two tempos. [*Beim Abklatschen wurde jede Letter
in zwei Tempi gegossen . . .*] First the letter itself on a small plate; then the plate
placed underneath a castingform, to fix it to a small shank, which was to be
cast into the form and would make, with the plate, the exact height of the
letter. The letter on the plate was made not by pouring the metal into the
matrix, but by beating the latter into the molten metal. When lead is heated so
as to be a soft mass it easily assumes the form of any object which falls on or in
it, therefore also of the matrix, which is the *image* of the engraved type. When
the metal is not overheated it will immediately cool down by contact with the
cold matrix, so that the latter will not be injured, although it consists of the
same substance as the molten metal. In this way a great many letters can be cast
from one matrix. Enschedé describes various difficulties connected with this
method, and tells us that only large letters, like those of B 36 and B 42, could
be made by it, as the operation of adding the shank to the letter becomes
impossible in the case of smaller letters. (Hessels, "Typography," *Encyclopedia
Britannica,* 1911).

22. Guy Bechtel claims, without reference, that Hessels was not proficient in German; *Gutenberg et l'invention de l'imprimerie: une enquête* (Paris: Fayard, 1992), 36. This is
obviously untrue, unless Bechtel is referring only to the German in the early Gutenberg
documents.

23. Zedler, *Die älteste Gutenbergtype* (1902), chap. 1: "Ein neu entdeckter astronomi-
scher Kalender für das Jahr 1448"; Wehmer, *Mainzer Probedrucke* (1948). The proofsheet
was among printed fragments in a binding from Mainz; included is a leaf of a 40-line
Bible in DK type, not otherwise known.

24. Evidence for the deterioration (*Abnutzung*) of type was seen in B36 itself; the
type used in later sections is more "worn-down" than that used for sections printed earlier.

25. Wehmer: "Man trennte also Drucke, die einen ähnlichen typographischen Zustand aufweisen, durch den Zwischenraum fast eines Jahrzehnts" (*Probedrucke*, 19). Skepticism over the 1447 date was voiced by Otto Hupp and by Konrad Haebler for these
reasons (see references in Wehmer, *Probedrucke*), but no concerted critique developed
against it.

26. The clearest bibliographical expression of the state-of-the-art chronological history incorporating this dating of *AK* is to be found in DeRicci, *Catalogue raisonné des
premières impressions de Mayence (1445–1467).* Dericci's four states are A: primitive charac-

ters, "dits du Donat" 1445–47 (*Weltgericht*, three examples of 27-line Donatus—Paris, Heiligenstadt, 1 and 2); B: "Caractères dits "Du Calendrier" 1447–57: (*AK*; 26-, 27-, 28-, and 30-line Donatus; *TK*); C: "Caractères Pfisterians" (B36); D: impressions of Pfister (28-line Donatus, *Edelstein*).

27. Ruppel, *Gutenberg*, 125: "Dieser *AK* . . . zeigt einen sehr fortgeschrittenen und genauen Typenguss und eine grosse Beherrschung der Satztechnik auf." The type is identical (?) to that in the Donatus, and thus must be the result of an "improved casting-instrument" (126). "Somit bedeutet der Typenzustand des astronomischen Kalenders einen Höhepunkt, der später nur noch in der 36zeiligen Bibel übertroffen wurde" (126).

28. Ruppel claims on the basis of the "left leaning *d*" that shows up in examples throughout this history (see n. 33 below) that no new punch (*Stempel*) is cut through this history; but this particular letterform, because it exists in more than one sort, also seems to indicate that there is no new matrix either.

29. Ruppel, *Gutenberg*, 130ff. The type of the *Laxierkalender* (1457) is "nicht mehr so scharf wie im *Türkenkalender*" (for 1454/55) (130). That of *Cisianus* (um 1457) ragged; the *Türkenbulle* (dated 1455/56) shows ragged right, like the earlier *Weltgericht*). Cf. the 26-line Donatus with perfectly justified right margin.

30. Albert Kapr, *Johannes Gutenberg: The Man and his Invention* (1988), tr. Douglas Martin (Aldershot: Ashgate, 1996), 220; the title suggests that Kapr or his publishers intended this book to replace the standard history of Ruppel.

31. Charles Mortet, *Les Origines et les débuts de l'imprimerie* (Paris: Picard, 1922), vi-vii. See above, chap. 1, n. 3.

32. This was noted by several scholars; see n. 25 above.

33. In Zedler's Taf. XIII, I believe this *d* is represented as the first *d* on line 3 of I. I believe it is also the first of the *d*'s listed in II.b. If Zedler is correct that type is "continuously recast" using fresh matrices, it is difficult to explain the recurrence of such an obviously flawed letterform.

34. The word used by Schwenke is "verschwommen" (blurred) as opposed to "sharf" (sharp); so Zedler, *Die älteste Gutenbergtype*, 16: "Verschwommenheit"; see above, pp. 00–00.

35. Zedler even speaks of "broken matrices" (16), which frankly, I cannot see in his Table IIIb. It is impossible to see a "broken matrix" unless one sees the appearance of a number of cases of "broken typesorts" (Zedler only identifies a few).

36. See Figures 10 and 11.

37. Gottfried Zedler, "Die Technik und Urheberschaft der Psalterinitial," *Gutenberg Jahrbuch* 1937, 30–33: here Zedler is arguing against Wallau, who (he claims) is following Hupp's opinion of 1900, which Hupp himself later reversed.

38. On these initials, see esp. Irvine Masson, *The Mainz Psalters and Canon Missae 1457–1459* (London: Bibliographical Society, 1954), 50–58, and Heinrich Wallau, "Die zweifarbigen Initialen der Psalterdrucke von Joh. Fust und Peter Schöffer," in *Festschrift zum fünfhundertjährigen Geburtstage von Johann Gutenberg* (Leipzig: Harrassowitz, 1900), 325–79, esp. 350ff.

39. "Dass die Initialen mit der Hand eingemalt sind, wurde von Juchhoff, ZfB 57 (1940), S. 213, Anm. 1, gegen Zedler, VGG XX (1920), S. 20f.; XXIII (1934), S. 53 und GJ 1937, S. 31 nach Einsichtnahme des Originals einwandfrei festgestellt." I thank Paul Needham for pointing out to me this note, which should have been obvious.

40. That the initials were painted is a statement often made in scholarship, but many of these follow the apparent consensus of 1903, not that of 1948. Konrad F. Bauer, *Aventur und Kunst: Eine Chronik des Buchdruckgewerbes von der Erfindung der beweglichen Letter bis zur Gegenwart* (Frankfurt a. M.: Bauersche Gießerei, 1940), 6, is cited by Wehmer as an authority, but as far as I can determine, Bauer offers nothing more than a casual although categorical statement in an introductory note: "die Initialen in Gutenberg astronomischen Kalender auf das Jahr 1448 sind nicht gedruckt, sondern eingemalt, weshalb sie nicht, wie bislang geschehen, als früheste Druckinitialen und früheste Farbendrucke Erwähnung fanden."

41. Reproductions of Burger's plate (although rarely identified as such) are available in numerous standard texts on Gutenberg.

CHAPTER 3. THE VOODOO ECONOMICS OF SPACE: FROM GOTHIC TO ROMAN

1. Horatio Brown, *The Venetian Printing Press: An Historical study based upon Documents for the most part hitherto unpublished* (New York: G.P. Putnam's Sons, 1891), 18, and n. 3.

2. Michel Maittaire, *Annales Typographici ab artis inventae origine ad annum MD* (The Hague, 1719).

3. Giacomo Sardini, *Esame sui principj della francese ed italiana tipografia ovvero storia critica di Nicolao Jenson*, 3 vols. (Lucca: Stamperia Bonsignori, 1796–98).

4. Daniel Berkeley Updike, *Printing Types: Their History, Forms, and Use: A Study in Survivals*, 2 vols. (Cambridge, Mass.: Harvard University Press, 1937), 1, plate 27, at 74–75. For Morris's use of Jenson, see William S. Peterson, *The Kelmscott Press: A History of William Morris's Typographical Adventure* (Berkeley: University of California Press, 1991), 82–87.

5. For biographical details, see *Inventario dell'Archivio di Stato di Lucca*, vol. VI, Archivio Sardini, 52–54, and esp. Moneti E. Amico, "Giacomo Sardini, patrizio lucchese, erudito e bibliografo," in *Miscellanea in memoria di A. Gallo* (Florence: Olschki, 1956), 47–78.

6. Antonio Orlandi had repeated (in passing) Maittaire's charge in 1722 (Sardini refers to him in his marginal notes); *Origine e progressi della stampa o sia dell'arte impressoria e notizie dell'opera stampate dall'anno m.cccc.lvi. sino all' anno MD* (Bologna, 1722), 16–19. Orlandi always credits Jenson with a better gothic: better than that used in Mainz or Rome (16) and better than that later used by John and Wendelin da Spira in Venice

(19). Orlandi never mentions gothic in his prose discussions (and eulogies) of Jenson, only in reference to particular books.

7. Franciscus Saver. Laire, *Specimen historicum typographiae romanae xv saeculi* (Rome, 1778), 42–43, n. 66: "Hunc quidem characterem Gothicum usurpavit JENSON-IUS, non tamen prius invexit, quod nonnullis scribere placuit." The passage quoted here is translated by Sardini (54).

8. Sardini distinguishes three typefaces more or less as they are distinguished today: gothic, roman, and fere-humanistica or gotico-roman. "In questa maniera si aprì la strada a quei primi libri di Roma, che dir si possono veramente gotici." See above, Introduction. For a twentieth-century version of the assumptions behind this argument, see Bernhard A. Uhlendorf, "The Invention of Printing and Its Spread till 1470 with Special Reference to Social and Economic Factors," *Library Quarterly* 2 (1932): 225: "Had Ulrich Han . . . been a printer of the caliber which Haebler assumes of all early printers, he would most likely never have been guilty of the tastelessness which he showed in printing the texts of several law books with Gothic characters and the accompanying commentaries in a Roman font."

9. "Ma erano eglino questi caratteri gotici meritevoli di tutti quei rimproveri, co i quali si unisce ora il consenso dei Bibliografi ad ingiurarli? se cio fosse, il nostro Artefice co i suoi Compagni di gran lunga sarebbesi ingannato. . . . Non sia mai che, noi vogliamo quì tesser l'elogio di un depravato costume, che passò nella Tipografia per mezzo del barbaro consiso modo, onde scrivevasi allora in tutte le severe discipline, le quali quasi giurato aveano inimicizia alle Muse, introduzione poi, che troppo adottata dai torchj, servì a vicenda per fomentare un idioma fatale tra gli Scrittori."

10. On Sardini's own association with these presses in 1785 and in 1792, see Moneti, "Sardini," 55–56.

11. For the importance and variants of this measurement, see my *The Myth of Print Culture: Essays on Evidence, Textuality, and Bibliographical Method* (Toronto: University of Toronto Press, 2003), 80–82.

12. Moneti, "Sardini," 53–56. In *Esame*, Sardini offers thanks to Sig. Gio. Battista Bodoni diretore della Reale Stamperia di Parma and Sig. Aurelio Nannei of the Camerale stamperia Cambiagi of Florence. It is thus possible he had the type page physically typeset in these fonts, although that is not what his language implies.

13. The type used in *Mammotrectus* is described by Sardini as a "small gothic" (carattere gotico minore) (*Esame*, 3:55), again measured by lines per page: "Le linee sono 38, e talore 39 per pagina."

14. According to *BMC*, this font is the same as Jenson's 85G (that is, in other books, this "gothic" type has a 20-line measurement of 85 mm); it is cut down for this book. I am not sure I accept the explanation in *BMC*, but the two typefaces seem identical.

15. The apparent precision of this figure (one that impressed at least some later bibliographers) is illusory; it is produced by combining measurements of completely different standards of exactness. The Bodoni Silvio (a real typeface) might be measurable as 4 percent larger than the Parma Silvio (another real typeface); but the calculation "double"

comparing the typesetting of the Jenson text with the Parma typeface is not precise. The figure given for the Bodoni should *also* be "double."

16. Paul Needham has passed on to me figures for early Bibles showing that roman type results in the use of 25% more space.

17. Joseph A. Dane and Alexandra Gillespie, "The Myth of the Cheap Quarto," in John King, ed., *Tudor Books and Readers* (Cambridge: Cambridge University Press, 2009), 25–45. A variant of this myth can be seen in the often cited but laconic essay by Charles C. Mish, "Black Letter as a Social Discriminant in the Seventeenth Century," *PMLA* 68 (1953): 627–30 (esp. 629), where blackletter in the seventeenth century is associated with cheap presswork, indicating a lower-class readership.

18. Martin Lowry, *Nicholas Jenson and the Rise of Venetian Publishing in Renaissance Europe* (Oxford: Blackwell, 1991), viii.

19. Lowry, *Nicholas Jenson*, Appendix 3: "Short Bibliography of Jenson Editions," 117–18. Lowry claims Sardini overestimated the number of editions in roman type; this may be true, but the claim is not borne out by the list Lowry gives, which by and large conforms to that of Sardini.

20. Lucien Febvre and Henri-Jean Martin, *L'apparition du livre* (Paris: Michel, 1958), trans. David Gerard, *The Coming of the Book: The Impact of Printing 1450–1800* (London: Verso, 1976). See my *Myth of Print Culture*, 22–29.

21. Georg Panzer, *Annales typographici ab artis inventae origine ad annum MD . . .* (Nuremberg: Zeh, 1793–). Robert Proctor, *Index to Early Printed Books in the British Museum . . . to the year 1500* (London: Kegan Paul, 1898); the system developed by Proctor is the basis for the order of books in *BMC*, by far the most useful incunable catalogue at the time of Febvre and Martin's *L'apparition du livre*.

CHAPTER 4. THE TYPOGRAPHICAL GOTHIC: A CAUTIONARY NOTE ON THE TITLE PAGE TO PERCY'S *RELIQUES OF ANCIENT ENGLISH POETRY*

1. See the polemical essay by D. F. McKenzie, "Typography and Meaning: The Case of William Congreve," in Giles Barber and Bernhard Fabian, eds., *Buch und Buchhandel in Europa im achtzehnten Jahrhundert* (Hamburg: Hauswedell, 1981), 81–126.

2. ESTC lists four self-styled London editions (1765, 1767, 1775, 1794) in addition to editions of Dublin 1766, and London and Frankfort, 1770. The 1765 edition is reprinted with an introduction by Nick Groom, "The Formation of Percy's *Reliques*" (London: Routledge, 1996), 1: 1–68.

3. Nick Groom, *The Making of Percy's "Reliques"* (Oxford: Clarendon Press, 1999), 202; Christine Baatz, "'A Strange Collection of Trash'? The Re-Evaluation of Medieval Literature in Thomas Percy's *Reliques of Ancient English Poetry* (1765)," in Barbara Korte, Ralf Schneider, and Stefanie Lethbridge, eds., *Anthologies of British Poetry: Critical Perspectives from Literary and Cultural Studies* (Amsterdam: Rodopi, 2000), 105–24, quotation

116; Nicholas Barker, "Typography and the Meaning of Words: The Revolution in the Layout of Books in the Eighteenth Century," in Barber and Fabian, eds., *Buch und Buchhandel*, 127–66.

4. James Macpherson, *Fingal: An Ancient Epic Poem, in Six Books* (London, 1762). See discussion in Thomas Warton, "Dissertation I: On the Origin of Romantic Fiction in Europe," in *The History of English Poetry*, 3 vols. (London, 1778–81), vol. 1.

5. See esp. Groom, *Making of Percy's Reliques*, chap. 3: "Macpherson and Percy," 61–105.

6. Baatz describes the change from folio to "smaller" formats such as quarto, octavo, duodecimo ("Strange Collection of Trash," 110). Macpherson's quarto, typical of those of the eighteenth century, is difficult to fit into such a narrative, since eighteenth-century quartos tend to be not "small" in the history of book sizes, but roughly the same size as seventeenth-century folios.

7. Baatz, "Strange Collection of Trash," 117–18 and n. 52. Reference to Wale's engravings for books can be found in *DNB*, the source for the references to Wale in most standard biographical histories of artists and engravers.

8. See, e.g., Warton, "Dissertation I," sig. g3r–v.

9. These seemingly anachronistic details may owe something to the description of a minstrel "minutely described" in a document quoted by Percy: the document concerns a pageant for Queen Elizabeth, entertained at Killingworth Castle by the Earl of Leicester; see Percy "An Essay on the Ancient English Minstrels," in *Reliques*, 1: xix–xx.

10. See Diane Dugaw, "The Popular Marketing of 'Old Ballads': The Ballad Revival and Eighteenth-century Antiquarianism Revisited," *Eighteenth-Century Studies* 21 (1987): 71–90. The titles are cited by Groom, *Making of Percy's Reliques*, 42–43, from the study of Stephen Vartin, "Thomas Percy's *Reliques*: Its Structure and Organization" (Ph.D. dissertation, New York University, 1972). We have chosen the editions themselves with an element of randomness: they are those most readily available on the Clark Library shelves.

11. See further David Foxon, *Pope and the Early Eighteenth-Century Book Trade* (Oxford: Clarendon, 1991), 25.

12. John Carter and Percy H. Muir, eds., *Printing and the Mind of Man: A Descriptive Catalogue Illustrating the Impact of Print on the Evolution of Western Civilization During Five Centuries* (London: Cassell, 1967); Joseph Blumenthal, *Art of the Printed Book, 1455–1955: Masterpieces of Typography Through Five Centuries from the Collections of the Pierpont Morgan Library, New York* (New York: Pierpont Morgan Library, 1973); see also Alexander Nesbitt, *Two Hundred Decorative Title Pages* (New York: Dover, 1964); A. F. Johnson, *One Hundred Title Pages, 1500–1800* (New York: John Lane, 1928).

13. See Cleanth Brooks, ed., *The Percy Letters*, vol. 7, *The Correspondence of Thomas Percy and William Shenston* (New Haven, Conn.: Yale University Press, 1977), 99, 123, 147–48. The classical simplicity often associated with and sought in printed classical texts is not always to be found in them. See the engraved title page of the Horace printed (entirely in engraved pages) by Pine (London, 1733); see reproduction in Blumenthal, *Art of the Printed Book*, fig. 72, or the relatively cluttered title page to Pope's *The Odyssey of*

Homer, printed by Lintot (London, 1725), reproduced Barker, "Typography and the Meaning of Words," fig. 31.

14. Other bibliographical arguments, employing similar logical fallacies, could easily be imagined: e.g., *because* the opposition good/evil is fundamental to eighteenth-century thought, *therefore* it is manifested typographically in the intrusive black ink on the otherwise white page.

15. See, however, Figure 18 above, the title page to the 1719 edition of *Wit and Mirth*. The title page to the 1707 edition is similar, with the title and subtitle printed in a variety of upper and lower case fonts. The only difference is in the key word "Melancholy"; in the 1707 edition, this word is printed in blackletter. That the same word is printed in italic in 1719 suggests that both fonts are seen simply as "display" fonts.

16. See, for example, Daniel Berkeley Updike, *Printing Types: Their History, Forms, and Use, a Study in Survivals*, 2 vols. (Cambridge, Mass.: Harvard University Press, 1937), 2: 131, fig. 285, from the 1581 edition of Ascham's *Scolemaster*.

17. See the series of historical texts edited by Thomas Hearne, for example, *The Chronicle of Robert of Gloucester* (Oxford, 1724). Blackletter is occasionally used in Percy's notes when he is citing early English words used in dictionaries.

18. See Joseph A. Dane, *Who Is Buried in Chaucer's Tomb?: Studies in the Reception of Chaucer's Book* (East Lansing: Michigan State University Press, 1999), 51–74, 115–35.

19. See Caslon's type specimen of 1734, rpt. Updike, *Printing Types*, vol. 2, fig. 262. Of the 46 fonts in this specimen, only two are "black" (i.e., blackletter); the text printed is a legal statute: "And be it further enacted by the Authority . . ." See also the 1782 specimens in Edward Rowe Mores, *A Dissertation Upon English Typographical Founders and Founderies (1778), with A Catalogue and Specimen of the Typefoundry of John James 1782*, ed. Harry Carter and Christopher Ricks (London: Oxford University Press, 1961), 21–41. See also the Oxford Specimen sheets of 1693 and 1706, in Stanley Morison and Harry Carter, *John Fell: The University Press and the "Fell" Types* (Oxford: Clarendon, 1967), 115, 118, figs. 5, 6, and essay "The Uses of Black Letter," 113–14.

20. See further Updike, *Printing Types*, 2: 188–219. Martin Antonetti, "Typographic Ekphrasis: The Description of Typographic Forms in the Nineteenth Century," *Word and Image* 15 (1999): 44–45.

INTERLUDE. AT THE TYPOGRAPHICAL ALTAR:
INTERLUDE FOR RANDALL MCLEOD

1. Randall McLeod, "FIAT fLUX," in Randall McLeod, ed., *Crisis in Editing: Texts of the English Renaissance* (New York: AMS Press, 1994), 61–172; Random Cloud, "Enter Reader," in Paul Eggert and Margaret Sankey, eds., *The Editorial Gaze: Mediating Texts in Literature and the Arts* (New York: Garland, 1998), 3–50. See further Randall McLeod, "Gerard Hopkins and the Shapes of His Sonnets," in Raimonda Modiano, ed., *VoiceTextHypertext: Emerging Practices in Textual Studies* (Seattle: University of Washington Press, 2003), 177–297.

2. For the convenience of typesetting, over which I have little control, I do not reproduce this title in the correct typographical form: for McLeod's italic *f,* I employ a lower-case roman f. Among other roman variants commonly used by bibliographers to cite this title: "fLux" "Flux" "FLUX."

3. Again, I am mistranscribing this title, by not accepting McLeod's blackletter transcription (or representation) of the word *Reader.* For my reasoning, see Introduction.

4. "[it is] part of this essay I left out because the editors, I thought, would not give me another 100 pages to lay it out" ("Cloud on Dane," December 2009).

5. The Jones manuscript reads under "Perirranterium" a four-line stanza "Thou unborn and former precepts . . ." on a verso, and on the facing recto a four-line stanza entitled "Superliminare" beginning "Avoid Profaneness . . ." The Tanner manuscript has these in the same order on the same page, but under the single title "Superliminare." In the 1633 edition, versions of these four-line stanzas "Thou, whom the former precepts . . ." and "Avoid profanenesse . . ." appear under the single title "Superliminare." The title "Perirranterium" belongs to a different seven-stanza poem. Both manuscripts are reproduced in "Enter Reader," 6–11.

6. McLeod shows that these were cancelled and replaced in the 1674 edition, only to reappear as variants in a few copies of the 1695 edition.

7. McLeod sees them as "merely ignorant" ("Cloud on Dane," 2009).

CHAPTER 5. FISTS AND FILIATIONS IN EARLY CHAUCER FOLIOS, 1532–1602

1. William Sherman, *Used Books: Marking Readers in Renaissance England* (Philadelphia: University of Pennsylvania Press, 2008), esp. chap. 2, "Toward a History of the Manicule," 25–52.

2. Thomas R. Lounsbury, *Studies in Chaucer,* 3 vols. (New York: Harper, 1892), 1: 265–80, based in large part on Francis Thynne, *Animadversions uppon the Annotacions and Corrections of some imperfections of impressiones of Chaucers workes* (1598), ed. G. H. Kingsley, rev. J. F. Furnivall (London: Trübner, 1875). See the excellent bibliographies by Eleanor Prescott Hammond, *Chaucer: A Bibliographical Manual* (New York: Macmillan, 1908), 116–27 and John R. Hetherington, *Chaucer, 1532–1602: Notes and Facsimile Texts* (Birmingham: Vernon House, 1964), and the discussion by Charles Muscatine, *The Book of Geoffrey Chaucer* (San Francisco: Book Club of California, 1963) and Derek Pearsall, "Thomas Speght (ca. 1550-?)," in Paul G. Ruggiers, ed., *Editing Chaucer: The Great Tradition* (Norman: University of Oklahoma Press, 1984), 71–92. See also W. W. Greg, "The Early Printed Editions of the Canterbury Tales," *PMLA* 39 (1924): 737–61; Tim William Machan, "Speght's Works and the Invention of Chaucer," *Text* 8 (1995): 145–70. The importance of Lounsbury is often underestimated, but the influence of his narrative and the infectiousness of his style are easily seen, as in the following statement on the relation of Speght to William and Francis Thynne: "In return Speght spoke with the profoundest deference of the Thynnes, father and son" (273); the sentence finds its way into Pearsall virtually unchanged: "He speaks with the profoundest deference of the Thynnes, father

and son" (Pearsall, 85). The word then reappears in the Variorum Chaucer: "Perhaps in deference to Thynne . . ."; Malcolm Andrew et al., *The General Prologue*, Variorum Chaucer II, 1 (Norman: University of Oklahoma Press, 1993), 100.

3. I will use the now standard abbreviations adopted by the Variorum Chaucer, although I have reservations (expressed in my conclusion below) about what these abbreviations sometimes mean: TH1 TH2 TH3 (= the Thynne editions of 1532, 1542, 1550), ST (= Stow's edition of 1561), and SP1 and SP2 (= the two Speght editions of 1598 and 1602).

4. "They are set up, line by line, from their predecessor, diverging from it only insofar as the text undergoes the usual mechanical degeneration at the hands of the compositor" (Pearsall, "Speght," 71).

5. W. W. Greg, "The Rationale of Copy-Text," *Studies in Bibliography* 3 (1950–51): 19–36. For my qualifications of this term in relation to Chaucer, see my "Copy-Text and Its Variants in some Recent Chaucer Editions," *Studies in Bibliography* 44 (1991): 163–83. No specific document exists in the sense of those studied long ago by Gavin Bone, "Extant MSS. Printed from by Wynkyn de Worde," *The Library* ser. 4, 12 (1931): 284–306, or more recently by James E. Blodgett, "Some Printer's Copy for William Thynne's 1532 Edition of Chaucer," *The Library* ser. 6, 1 (1979): 97–113, and N. F. Blake, "Aftermath: Manuscript to Print," in Jeremy Griffiths and Derek Pearsall, eds., *Book Production and Publishing in Britain, 1375–1475* (Cambridge: Cambridge University Press, 1989), Appendix A: "Caxton Prints for Which a Copy-Text Survives or Which Were Used as copy," 419–25 (Blake's word "copy" has the meaning "printer's copy").

6. For the bibliographical details supporting this, see the earlier version of this article in *Studies in Bibliography* 51 (1998): esp. 51–52. The volumes of the Variorum referred to here are the following (all from University of Oklahoma Press): Derek Pearsall, *The Nun's Priest's Tale* (1984); Thomas W. Ross, *The Miller's Tale* (1983); Donald C. Baker, *The Manciple's Tale* (1984); Helen Storm Corsa, *The Physician's Tale* (1987); Beverly Boyd, *The Prioress's Tale* (1987); Donald C. Baker, *The Squire's Tale* (1990); Malcolm Andrew et al., *General Prologue* (1993); John F. Plummer, III, *The Summoner's Tale* (1995). In his notes (267, n. 26), Pearsall cites collations by Charles Moorman on the General Prologue; I assume these are what is included in the published version, although Daniel Ransom seems to be claiming to have thoroughly revised them (Andrew et al., *General Prologue*, xv). Ransom's statement is none too clear here, and I am uncertain as to whose "Collations," Ransom's or Moorman's, were checked by "Dr. Levy." I will refer to this edition simply as Andrew's. On the setting of the 1598 edition, see Pearsall, "Speght," 79, 84–85, with reference to collations contained in his excellent edition of *The Floure and the Leafe and The Assembly of Ladies* (London: Nelson, 1962).

7. Since the 1561 and 1598 editions are so similar, any apparent relation of the 1602 edition to either is meaningless. Consequently, some Chaucerians have concluded that the printer's copy cannot be determined for individual sections (so Plummer, *Summoner's Tale*, 85). Yet examination of the compositing details in these prose sections proves absolutely that the 1602 edition used the edition of 1561 as a printer's copy, just as did the 1598 edition.

8. See, e.g., the first paragraphs of "Pars secunda penitencie" of the Parson's Tale in ST and SP1 (sig. S5r). The second paragraph of SP2 (1602, sig. R6r) is a line-for-line reprint of ST, not SP1. See also, ST and SP1, sig. T2va. Again, SP2 (sig. S2va) agrees with ST only. The same correspondences exist in the *Testament of Love*.

9. For the most part, the three editions of 1561, 1598, and 1602 vary in layout in the Preliminaries. But at the end of paragraph sections in the letter to Thynne on sig. C5v, the line lengths and breaks for the 1602 edition are identical to those of 1561 and bear no relation to those of 1598. This cannot be fortuitous; the prose of the 1602 edition, both in text and in its preliminaries, was set from the 1561 edition whenever a 1561 text was available.

10. Baker, *Squire's Tale*, 106; Baker cites as reference the somewhat variable statements in Pearsall, *Nun's Priest's Tale*, 114, Corsa, *Physician's Tale*, 78, and Boyd, *Prioress's Tale*, 102. Cf. Plummer: "Because ST and SP1 are nearly identical, one cannot demonstrate beyond doubt which of the two served as copytext for SP2" (*Summoner's Tale*, 85); and Corsa, *Physician's Tale*, "The making of SP2's text . . . remains a mystery" (79).

11. See my "Fists and Filiations," *SB* 51, notes 13–18.

12. There is at least one exception to this in Stow, and there may be more. On fol. 243r of ST (sig. Y3r), there are five small ornaments in the inner margin. I have not found these elsewhere in the edition.

13. The statement that these marks occur in the 1542 and 1561 editions only in the middle margin is not accurate.

14. See the 1539 Bible (STC 5068), and the series of Great Bibles printed by Grafton and/or Whitchurch from 1540–1541 (STC 2070–76). Ornaments constructed from type-sorts much like those in the Chaucer editions appear frequently in the prefatory matter, with no discernible relation from edition to edition. For a convenient overview, see Francis Fry, *A Description of the Great Bible, 1539, and the Six Editions of Cranmer's Bible, 1540 and 1541, printed by Grafton and Whitchurch* (London: Sotheran, 1865), plates 2–4. Later Bibles printed by Whitchurch in 1549 (STC 2079) and 1550 (STC 2081) contain sporadic ornaments and marginal fists, but nothing similar to those discussed here. Stephen Tabor of the Clark Library has pointed out to me as well the signature marks indicating half-sheet collation noted by David J. Shaw, "Quire and Sheet Numbers in Sixteenth-Century France," *The Library* ser. 6, 17 (1995): 311–320..

15. For ease of reference, I cite these by the line reference in Larry D. Benson, ed., *The Riverside Chaucer* (Boston: Houghton Mifflin, 1987).

16. For marks of transposition in early printers, see the examples in Peter W. M. Blayney, *The Texts of King Lear and Their Origins*, vol. 1, *Nicholas Okes and the First Quarto* (Cambridge: Cambridge University Press, 1982), 224, fig. 17d, 225 n.1, and 237, figs. 31, 32.

17. See, however, the downward pointing fist at "So gyue hem ioye that it here" in the 1561 edition; there is a leaf there in 1542, but nothing in 1550. Yet 1542 is not the printer's copy, and it may be that relations between the 1550 and 1561 placement of marginalia are products of pure chance. Anne Hudson, "John Stow (1525?-1605)," in Ruggiers,

ed., *Editing Chaucer,* 60, rightly concludes that the 1550 edition is the source for that of 1561, but collates, unnecessarily, against various earlier "issues" of 1542 and 1550 for press-variants. There is no likelihood that divergences among various issues in terms of press variation will be any greater than divergences in individual copies of the same issue, since issue is not defined by variant sheets.

18. Frank Isaac, *English and Scottish Printing Types, 1535–58, 1552–58,* 2 vols. (London: Oxford University Press, 1932), see Appendix: William Bonham, Robert Toy, and entry under Richard Kele, Richard Grafton, 29–39, Edward Whitchurch, 40–50 and Nicholas Hill, 88–91 (for 94T, see figs. 50 and 88a). The type identification and size is the same (94T; see figs. 50 and 88a), and the two are very similar (the upper case is different). See, however, the notes by Hetherington, 3–4, and discussion in Muscatine, *Book of Geoffrey Chaucer,* 23–24. The Variorum editors often refer to unspecified evidence in favor of the later date for the third Thynne edition (1550, instead of the 1545 date in the first edition of STC), but none has detailed what that evidence is. See, e.g., Andrew, 94. (I believe the reference is to Hetherington, 3–4, although Andrew, unlike other Variorum editors, does not include Hetherington in his bibliography). Isaac's work is cited by Muscatine, but not by any of the Variorum editors.

19. Where Pearsall spoke of possible manuscript readings in Speght (readings he characterizes as "commonplace"), Corsa, citing Pearsall, speaks of specific manuscripts: "The difficulty in such research, however, is increased by Speght's inconsistent use of more than one manuscript" (Corsa, 79, with reference to Pearsall, "Speght," 87). There is no evidence that Speght used any manuscript, unless we include as manuscript hand-written notes (perhaps his own) in a copy of the 1561 edition.

20. John M. Manly and Edith Rickert, *The Text of the Canterbury Tales,* 8 vols. (Chicago: University of Chicago Press, 1940); Andrew, 122–24, and notes on 122. Andrew is the first Variorum editor to provide a clear presentation along with examples of what Manly-Rickert and later Variorum editors define as a variant. Some points of value can also be extracted (with difficulty) from an earlier study by Kurt Rydland, "The Meaning of 'Variant Reading' in the Manly-Rickert Canterbury Tales," *Neuphilologische Mitteilungen* 73 (1972): 805–14.

21. A transposition such as *he said/said he* is common in Chaucer texts and by definition classified as a substantive; the textual-critical value of such variation is equivalent to that of accidentals.

CHAPTER 6. EDITORIAL AND TYPOGRAPHICAL DIPLOMACY
IN THE PIERS PLOWMAN ARCHIVE

1. Walter W. Skeat, ed., *The Vision of William concerning Piers Plowman together with Vita de Dowel, Dobet et Dobest, and Richard the Redeles, by William Langland,* 2 vols. (London: Oxford University Press, 1885), now superseded by A. C. Schmidt, ed., *William Langland: A Parallel-Text Edition of the A, B, C, and Z Versions,* 2 vols. (London: Longman 1995; Kalamazoo, Mich.: Medieval Institute Publications, 2009); George Kane, *William*

Langland's Piers Plowman: The A-Version (London: Athlone, 1960); George Kane and E. Talbot Donaldson, *William Langland's Piers Plowman: The B-Version* (London: Athlone, 1975). A number of Kane's essays are usefully reprinted in George Kane, *Chaucer and Langland: History and Textual Approaches* (Berkeley: University of California Press, 1989).

2. The circularity of the reasoning behind such theories was often critiqued by Kane; see e.g., Kane-Donaldson, *B-Version*, 17–18; such circularity leads to the "ultimate absurdity of recension as an editorial method."

3. These groupings are discussed in a detailed, but unindexed, introduction.

4. This sense of authority seems extolled and in turn transferred to the often cited review by Lee Patterson, "The Logic of Textual Criticism and the Way of Genius: The Kane-Donaldson *Piers Plowman* in Historical Perspective," in Jerome J. McGann, ed., *Textual Criticism and Literary Interpretation* (Chicago: University of Chicago Press, 1985), 55–91.

5. The term originated in Paul Zumthor's *Essai de poétique médiévale* (Paris: Seuil, 1972), e.g., 73, and is now a catchall for describing unstable texts. The type of editing theory that results is sometimes, and not always coherently, characterized as "rhizomic"; see, e.g., David Greetham, "Phylum-Tree-Rhizome," *Huntington Library Quarterly* 58 (1996): 99–126.

6. Robert Adams et al, eds., *MS 201, Corpus Christi College, Oxford (F)*, Seenet Ser. A.1 (Ann Arbor: University of Michigan Press, 2000). For summary of available publications and introductory discussion, see Piers Plowman Electronic Archive, Seenet, www.iath.virginia.edu/seenet/piers/. Discussion below based on Thorlac Turville-Petre and Hoyt N. Duggan, eds., *MS B.15.17, Trinity College, Cambridge (W)*, Seenet Ser. A.2 (Ann Arbor: University of Michigan Press, 2000); Katherine Heinrichs, ed., *MS Oriel College, Oxford 79 (O)*, Seenet Ser. A.5 (Cambridge, Mass.: Medieval Academy, 2004); Eric Eliason, Thorlac Turville-Petre, and Hoyt N. Duggan, eds., *London, British Library Additional 35287 (M)*, Seenet Ser. A.7 (Cambridge, Mass.: Medieval Academy, 2005); Michael Calebrese, Hoyt N. Duggan, and Thorlac Turvlle-Petre, eds., *Huntington Library MS Hm 128 (Hm, Hm2)*, Seenet Ser. A.9 (Cambridge, Mass.: Medieval Academy, 2008).

7. See also the rhetoric of reviewers, for which the Archive editors are not of course responsible: Stephen Shepherd, rev. Adams et al., *MS F.*, *YLS* 14 (2000): 199: "The next obvious thing to say, then, is that the PP Electronic Archive, when complete, will bring us closer to Langland's 'making,' both product and process, than any printed edition can"; Andrew Galloway, "Reading *Piers Plowman* in the Fifteenth and the Twenty-First Centuries: Notes on Manuscripts F and W in the Piers Plowman Electronic Archive," *JEGP* 103 (2004): 232–52, the Archive "will be the supreme tool for carrying forward textual work on *Piers Plowman*"; with the Athlone edition are "monuments of daring and shrewd Middle English textual criticism."

8. The Canterbury Tales Project has organized the project by textual unit (the individual) tale, rather than by manuscript. For overview, see www.canterburytalesproject.org.

9. The reinstatement of the concept of authority discredited in conventional editing is seen frequently in Jerome J. McGann, "The Rationale of Hypertext," *Radiant Textuality: Literature After the World Wide Web* (New York: Palgrave, 2001), 38–74.

10. The cost of these volumes is not inconsequential. It appears to me that it might be in the $5000–6000 range, which is 60x greater than the present cost of, say, the Skeat edition, and more than 10x greater than either the Athlone edition or the two-volume Schmidt edition.

11. The Preface to F speaks of five "levels of description" and "layers of description," which I believe are to be associated with the six (!) "layers" or "levels" listed as author, B-archetype, alpha family, F-redactor, F-scribe, and "Nachleben" scribes, rather than the "five" style sheets, although the distinction (as here) is blurred. Later volumes (for example, M), keep these distinctions clear, referring to two "layers" (scribe and corrector), which are subsequently and variously represented in the four style sheets.

12. AllTags, the least technical or traditional of terms, incorporates all style sheets. The amusingly named NoPals, dropped in subsequent volumes, means a transcription in which paleographical notes are suppressed.

13. Susan Hockey, "The Reality of Electronic Editions," in Raimonda Modiano, Leroy F. Searle, and Peter Shillingsburg, eds., *Voice, Text, Hypertext* (Seattle: University of Washington Press, 2004), 366–67.

14. In the electronic archive, the section "Transcriptional Protocols" is clearly directed toward editors and subeditors. Individual volumes do not detail the decisions involved in constructing their transcriptions and style sheets.

15. The warning about the use of this with Macs is confirmed by Simon Horobin, rev. Piers Plowman Archive vols. 3 and 4 (MSS O and L), *Yearbook of Langland Studies* 19 (2005): 223.

16. For reasons that I do not understand, I can load all the images of each edition on my Mac without the risk of catastrophe, even though I cannot run the programs that control the edition. On my older PC, the editorial programs work, but only some of the volumes function as they are supposed to; in others, I was unable to view the images associated with the transcriptions.

17. This might be relevant both for poems intended to be read vertically (examples occur in Sidney's *Arcadia*) and also for determining scribal features due to immediately surrounding text. See, for example, Randall McLeod, "UnEditing Shak-speare," *Substance* 10 (1981): 26–55. See further "Coda on a Coda" below.

18. Translating these distinctions into modern type poses problems. The distinction *i* and *j* on a modern keyboard is a distinction of letters, while earlier it was a distinction of letter position. The distinction between *u/v* is similar, and it is incorrect to claim that that distinction is "maintained" or "followed" or "respected" in a diplomatic transcription since *u/v* means something completely different in a modern transcription from what it means in, say, a medieval manuscript.

19. John Heywood, *The Pardoner and the Friar, 1533*, Malone Society Reprints (Oxford: Oxford University Press, 1984).

20. Note that grammatically "the text" and "style sheet" are different, as indicated by the word "access." Although I understand why editors may say use this circumlocution, this is a distinction without a difference. In all uses of the phrase "to access" a text through a style sheet, text and "style sheet" are effectively the same (see quotation below).

21. A. V. C. Schmidt, ed., *The Vision of Piers Plowman: A Critical Edition of the B-Text*, 2nd ed. (London: Dent, 1995), lxff. See also A. V. C. Schmidt, rev. C. David Benson and Lynne S. Blanchfield, *The Manuscripts of Piers Plowman* (1997), *Medium Aevum* 68 (1999): 322–23.

22. See Galloway's call for "sustained literary criticism," of the F-redactor (rev. *MS F*, pp. 238–40), and reference to James Weldon, "Ordination and Genre in MS CCC201: A Mediaeval Reading of the B-Text of *Piers Plowman*," *Florilegium* 12 (1993): 159–75. Note the uncertainty over whether the redactor is a reader or a poet; see further my "Scribes as Critics," in *Who Is Buried in Chaucer's Tomb? Studies in the Reception of Chaucer's Book* (East Lansing: Michigan State University Press, 1998), 195–213.

23. Editors qualify this assertion; see discussion in Adams et al., *MS F*, Presentation of Text: "Initially we intended to present texts of the last two such layers of scribe labor, the one a diplomatic transcription of the text of the final copyist (F-Scribe) and the other a lightly annotated critical text of the work of a scribal-editor . . . which we have designated as F-Redactor. We are now convinced that F-Redactor's text cannot be distinguished from that of the immediate scribe." The text they present, however, seems to contradict these later convictions.

24. I am particularly grateful to Hoyt Duggan in this regard, and I take this opportunity to thank him again.

25. *The Myth of Print Culture: Essays in Evidence, Textuality, and Bibliographical Method* (Toronto: University of Toronto Press, 2003), 7–8.

26. Thus the variety of seemingly unsystematic terms used by Essick and Viscomi to describe individual copies: section, copy, set, impression, print-run, even session. Bibliographically, the problem is similar to that found in some of the earliest colored blockbooks of the mid-fifteenth century. For discussion, see many studies by Nigel F. Palmer, including "Blockbooks, Woodcut and Metalcut Single Sheets," in Alan Coates et al., *A Catalogue of Books Printed in the Fifteenth Century Now in the Bodleian Library*, vol. 1 (Oxford: Oxford University Press, 2005), 1–50.

27. Robert N. Essick and Joseph Viscomi,"An Inquiry into William Blake's Method of Color Printing," *Blake: An Illustrated Quarterly* 35 (2002): 74–103; "Blake's Method of Color Printing: Some Responses and Further Observations," *Blake: An Illustrated Quarterly* 36 (2002): 49–64.

28. Martin Butlin, "Is This a Private War or Can Anyone Join In? A Plea for a Broader Look at Blake's Color-Printing Techniques," *Blake: An Illustrated Quarterly* 36 (2002): 45–49; "William Blake, S. W. Hayter, and Color Printing," on-line article from *Blake: An Illustrated Quarterly*; rev. of Joseph Viscomi, *Blake and the Idea of the Book*, *Burlington Magazine* 137 (1995): 123. See also Michael Phillips, *William Blake: The Creation of the Songs From Manuscript to Illuminated Printing* (Princeton, N.J.: Princeton University Press, 2001).

29. See, most conveniently, the reproduction Robert N. Essick, ed., *William Blake: Songs of Innocence and of Experience* (San Marino, Calif.: Huntington Library Press, 2008), pl. 44; see also illustrations 65–70 in Viscomi and Essick, "Inquiry."

30. See further, "Blake's Method," n. 14 and references. Essick and Viscomi by contrast see what amounts to a reverse Growth and Development process: "[Blake's] development . . . was towards greater simplicity, from printing a combination of oil-based ink and water-based colors from two levels of one plate to the planographic printing of just water-based colors from the surface of a support."

31. Easy as it would be to reproduce these figures, I will do readers a service by referring them to the readily accessible Archive itself. For the full image and transcription: www.blakearchive.org/blake/indexworks.htm > Manuscript and Typographic Works > The Order . . .

CHAPTER 7. THE REPRESENTATION OF REPRESENTATION:
VERSIONS OF LINEAR PERSPECTIVE

1. See my "Linear Perspective and the Obliquities of Reception," in Sandra P. Prior and Robert M. Stein, eds., *Reading Medieval Culture: Essays in Honor of Robert W. Hanning* (Notre Dame, Ind.: University of Notre Dame Press, 2005), 428–53, and references. Among recent studies, see esp. Hubert Damisch, *The Origin of Perspective* (1987), trans. John Goodman (Cambridge, Mass.: Harvard University Press, 1994); M. J. Kemp, *The Science of Art: Optical Themes in Western Art from Brunelleschi to Seurat* (New Haven, Conn.: Yale University Press, 1990), various studies by J. V. Field, esp. "Alberti, the Abacus, and Piero della Francesca's Proof of Perspective," *Renaissance Studies* 11 (1997): 61–88, and *Piero della Francesca: A Mathematician's Art* (New Haven, Conn.: Yale University Press, 2005).

2. John R. Spencer, *Leon Battista Alberti: On Painting* (New Haven, Conn.: Yale University Press, 1966), book 1; Italian text from Luigi Malle, ed., *Leon Battista Alberti: Della pittura* (Florence: Sansoni, 1950). Among many recent studies, J. V. Field, "Alberti on Painting," in *Piero della Francesca*, 35–42; Kirsti Andersen, *The Geometry of an Art: The History of the Mathematical Theory of Perspective from Alberti to Monge* (New York: Springer, 2007), 19 and n. 3, and Appendix IV: "The Perspective Sources Listed Country-wise in Chronological Order," 739–46.

3. One of the clearest and earliest statements of these principles in English is Brook Taylor, *New Principles of Linear Perspective of the Art of Designing on a Plane*, 3rd ed. rev. John Colson (London, 1749).

4. Jean Pèlerin (Viator), *De artificiali Perspective* (1505); the basic and most lucid study is William M. Ivins, Jr., *On the Rationalization of Sight* (1938; rpt. New York: Da Capo Press, 1973). See also Timothy K. Kitao, "Prejudice in Perspective: A Study of Vignola's Perspective Treatise," *Art Bulletin* 44 (1960): 173–94.

5. Andersen, *Geometry of an Art*, 31, credits Alberti with this rule, which as Field notes is simply a matter of common sense (*Piero della Francesca*, 55–57).

6. Sebastiano Serlio, *The Five Books of Architecture* (1584; English trans. 1611; rpt. New York: Dover, 1982).

7. A real eye, of course, will not "see" the image in that ideal fashion, due to the

density of air and narrowness of focus. On the *camera oscura*, see Joel Snyder, "Picturing Vision," *Critical Inquiry* 6 (1980): 507–11; John H. Hammond, *The Camera Obscura: A Chronicle* (Bristol: Hilger, 1981); and pinhole camera images in M. H. Pirenne, *Optics, Painting, and Photography* (Cambridge: Cambridge University Press, 1970), 95–115; David Lindberg, "The Theory of Pinhole Images from Antiquity to the Thirteenth Century," and "A Reconsideration of Roger Bacon's Theory of Pinhole Images," *Archive for the History of Exact Sciences* 5 (1968): 154–62; 6 (1970): 214–23.

8. B. A. R. Carter, "Perspective," in Harold Osborne, ed., *Oxford Companion to Art* (Oxford: Oxford University Press, 1970), 843–51. I believe the same error appears in a casual remark by otherwise reliable John Orrell, *The Human Stage: English Theatre Design, 1567–1640* (Cambridge: Cambridge University Press, 1988), 232, who sees the oblique placement of an architectural structure on a plane an example of "two point" perspective. All these are examples of single-point perspective. The principle is that any set of parallel lines however oriented in space depicted on a picture plane will have a single vanishing point. A drawing with x sets of parallel lines (sets whose lines are not parallel to those in other sets) is not an example of "x-point perspective."

9. Erwin Panofsky, *Die Perspektive als symbolische Form*, Vorträge der Bibliothek Warburg, 1924–25 (Leipzig, 1927), 258–330; trans. Christopher S. Wood, *Perspective as Symbolic Form* (New York: Zone Books, 1991). For Panofsky's misreading of his own diagrams, see my discussion, "Linear Perspective and the Obliquities of Reception," 436–42.

10. Albert Flocon and André Barre, *Curvilinear Perspective: From Visual Space to the Constructed Image* (Berkeley: University of California Press, 1987), 58–59; see also, remarks of Andersen, *Geometry of an Art*, 110.

11. Dynamic computer-generated plans or images are no exception here; any computer-generated image must be one or the other—either an "elevation" or a "perspective" image. The movement of the image may give the illusion that the rules of architectural elevations and three-dimensional perspective are being followed simultaneously; but to work effectively, it must violate the rules of one or the other (or both).

12. Vitruvius, *On Architecture*, I.2.2., ed. Frank Granger, 2 vols. (Cambridge, Mass.: Harvard University Press, 1931); Danielle Barbaro, *La practica della perspettiva* (1669). Serlio's apparent reconception of "scenographia" ignores his correct translation of Vitruvius' term: "Perspective is that, which Vitruuius calleth Scenographie, that is, the vpright part and sides of any building or of any Superficies or bodies." See further, on importance of both Serlio and Barbaro to Jones, John Orrell, *The Theatres of Inigo Jones and John Webb* (Cambridge: Cambridge University Press, 1985), chaps. 1 and 2, 1–38.

13. See, e.g., Stan Parchin, "Art and Illusions: Masterpieces of Trompe l'oeil at Palazzo Strozzi," (2009) reviewed *Art Museum Journal*, artmuseumjournal.com. See also Andrea Pozzo, *Rules and examples of perspective proper for painters and architects* (Rome, 1693; trans. London, 1707).

14. Piero della Francesca, *De prospectiva pingendi*, ed. G. Nicco Fasola (Florence, 1942; rpt. Florence: Le Lettere, 1984); facsimile edition, Piero della Francesca, *De prospect-*

iva pingendi; facs. Parma Biblioteca Palatina, MS 1576 (New York: Broude, 1992). See Elizabeth G. Holt, *A Documentary History of Art*, vol. 1, *The Middle Ages and the Renaissance* (Princeton, N.J.: Princeton University Press, 1947), 261–63. For discussion, see Field, *Piero della Francesca*, 54–60, and "Alberti, the Abacus, and Piero della Francesca's Proof of Perspective."

15. "Se nel piano degradato se mena la equidistante al termine, et quelle se devida in più parti equali, et in quelle devisioni se ponghi basi equali, ciascuna oposta ortogonalmente a l'ochio, la più remota se rapresenterà nel termine magiore che la più propinqua, niente di meno se rapresenterà nell'ochio socto menore angolo che la più propinqua" [Given a plane viewed from a central viewpoint, divided into equal parts, and in these divisions are placed equal columns, each opposed to the eye, the most remote will be depicted as greater (on the plane) than the nearer, even though it occupies a smaller angle than the nearer one].

16. Panofsky, *Perspektive*, sees this as a difference between "reality" and "perspective," although perspective is surely by any standard a part of reality and the distinction is misleading. Panofsky, n. 8: "The rigorous Piero della Francesca, for one, decides the dispute between perspective and reality without hesitation in favor of the former. . . . Piero recognizes the fact of marginal distortions and adduces the example . . . of the exact perspectival construction of a frontal portico. . . . But so far from proposing a remedy, Piero proves rather that it *must* be so" [Piero: "Non che mancho necessaria"].

17. Field, I think, does not express such misgivings in the Introduction, and I assume they are stated here in the note. The dismissal of Panofsky as "naïve" (which of course he is not) but characteristic of his time (nor is he that), is also found in Damisch, *Origin of Perspective*, 14.

18. Jean Paul Richter, ed., *The Notebooks of Leonardo da Vinci* (1883; rpt. New York: Dover, 1970), #107 and 108 = Notebook E, 16a and b. Translations mine, correcting (I think) the sometimes maddeningly obscure translations of this edition.

19. Among disputants, see James S. Ackermann, "Leonardo's Eye," *Journal of the Warburg and Courtault Institutes* 41 (1978): 108–13; Martin Kemp, "Leonardo and the Visual Pyramid," *Journal of the Warburg and Courtault Institutes* 40 (1977): 128–49; Thomas Frangenberg, "The Angle of Vision: Problems of Perspectival Representation in the Fifteenth and Sixteenth Centuries," *Renaissance Studies* 6 (1992): 1–45.

20. The word "groundplan" introduced in the English translation adds even more. Ackermann, "Leonardo's Eye," considers simple perspective the same as *construzione legitimma*.

21. So Frangenberg, "Angle of Vision," 19–22; "Leonardo refers to spherical intersections as 'pariete' and 'sito'; either term can refer to pictorial surfaces" (22). Frangenberg does not show that Leonardo ever produced a practical example of this. James Elkins, "Did Leonardo Develop a Theory of Curvilinear Perspective, Together with some Remarks on the 'Angle' and 'Distance' Axioms," *Journal of the Warburg and Courtault Institutes* 51 (1988): 190–96, also sees Leonardo as dealing here with curvilinear perspective.

22. Panofsky, *Perspektive*, 294, n. 8: "Diese beide Perspektiven wirken in genau entgegengesetztem Sinne."

23. "E di questa prospettiua senplicie, della quale la pariete taglia le piramidi porta-tricie delle spetie all'ocio equalmente distanti dall virtù visiua ci ne dà sperientia la curva lucie del l'ochio sopra la quale tali piramidi si tagliano equalmente distanti dalla virtù visiua ecc." I think the notion of equal distance applies to several things: the columns are interpreted as "equally" wide, that is, the brain interprets them (through the faculty of sight) as the same size as they would be if seen from the same distance. Although the curvature of the retina is involved, the retinal images of the three columns are not the same size, and whether Panofsky is talking about those images or perspective in general, there is no geometric correspondent to the notion of equal size.

24. John Nichols, *The Progresses, Processions, and Magnificent Festivities of King James the First*, 4 vols. (1828; rpt. New York: B. Franklin, 1967), 1: 538. See Alardyce Nicoll, *Stuart Masques and the Renaissance Stage* (New York: Harcourt Brace, 1938), 32–35, and more recently chapters in Orrell, *Theatres of Inigo Jones* and *Human Stage*. See also Martin Butler, *The Stuart Court Masque and Political Culture* (Cambridge: Cambridge University Press, 2008), chap. 2, 34–62, and, among several Web-based reconstructions, John R. Wolcott, "*Florimène* at the Court of Charles I," www.videoccasions-nw.com/history/flor-imene.

25. Orrell, *Theatres of Inigo Jones*, 28, on Jonson's "Blackness," and Nicols, "Ben Jonson's Masque of Blackness, 1604–05," *Progresses*, 1: 481: "These thus presented, the scene behind seemed a vast sea, and united with this that flowed forth, from the termina-tion or horizon of which (being the level of the State, which was placed in the upper end of the Hall) was drawn by the lines of prospective, the whole work shooting downwards from the eye; which decorum made it more conspicuous, and caught the eye afar off with a wandering beauty. . . . So much for the bodily part, which was of Master Inigo Jones's design and act [art?]."

26. A pinhole camera generally projects an image onto a plane; the lens of a human eye projects an image onto the curved surface of the retina. The difference between the plane and curved surfaces, although often mentioned in scholarship, is a red herring, since the processes that transmit this objectively curved image to the brain are far more complex and less well understood than anything in the two-dimensional geometrical representa-tions of the eye or the pinhole camera.

27. *Le nozze degli dei: favola dell Ab' Gio. Carlo Coppola Rappresentata in musica in Firenze nelle reali Nozze de Serenissimi Gran Duchi di Toschana* (Florence, 1637).

28. Most studies of the masque contain numerous examples; see, in Stephen Orgel, *The Illusion of Power: Political Theater in the English Renaissance* (Berkeley: University of California Press, 1975), figs. 14–16 (from Jones), or those in Nicol, *Stuart Masques*, figs. 35–6, 43–44, 51–52. For Jones, see Percy Simpson and C. F. Bell, *Designs by Inigo Jones for Masques & Plays at Court: A Descriptive Catalogue of Drawings for Scenery and Costumes mainly in the Collection of His Grace the Duke of Devonshire, K. G.* (Oxford: Walpole and Malone Societies, 1924), pls. 65, 193, 247, 258, 300, 355, 365.

29. See Nicoll, *Stuart Masques*, figs. 70–75 esp. fig. 70, sketch of Inigo Jones for the Temple of Diana in *Florimène*.

30. Orrell's solution to these types of drawings and representations is often to argue for two vanishing points, and thus two horizons, one for the upper section, the other for the stage; *Theatres of Inigo Jones and John Webb*, and chap. 7, fig. 25 = Simpson, *Jones*, pl. 243, and discussion, 145–58. This works for certain of his drawings, but not all, and is itself only a technical point bearing on their construction (the scored lines implying such multiple vanishing points are still visible in some of these sketches).

31. Most representations of stages are constructed with central viewpoint (see Nicoll, *Stuart Masques*, figs. 38–44 and numerous others).

32. Many of these sketches seem to avoid architecture and the difficulties it presents: see Nicoll, figs. 64–65. Fig. 39, "A Roman Atrium in 'Albion's Triumph'" (1632), is a perspective drawing presenting a view down a corridor of columns, but there is no portico of columns parallel to the picture plane, and the issue of marginal distortion is thus avoided (Simpson, no. 108).

33. The example is from Pirenne, chap. 8, "The Perception of Ordinary Pictures," 95ff.

CHAPTER 8. TYPOGRAPHICAL ANTIQUITY IN THOMAS FROGNALL DIBDIN'S *TYPOGRAPHICAL ANTIQUITIES*

1. Joseph Ames, *Typographical Antiquities* (London, 1749), rev. William Herbert, 3 vols. (1785–1790). Thomas Frognall Dibdin, *Bibliographical, Antiquarian and Picturesque Tour in France and Germany*, 3 vols. (London, 1821); *Library Companion, or the Young Man's Guide, and the Old Man's Comfort*, 2 vols. (London, 1824); *Typographical Antiquities, or the History of Printing in England*, 4 vols. (London, 1810–19); *Bibliotheca Spenceriana, or A Descriptive catalogue of the Library of George John Earl Spencer*, 7 vols. (London, 1814–23).

2. Nicolas Barker, *Biblioteca Lindesiana* (London: Quaritch, 1977). See the useful, if occasionally Dibdinesque, introduction in Victor E. Neuberg, *Thomas Frognall Dibdin: Selections* (Metuchen, N.J.: Scarecrow Press, 1978).

3. Cf. the stated purposes established by later English bibliographers such as William Blades, *How to Tell a Caxton: with some hints where and how the same might be found* (London: Sotheran, 1870).

4. Paul Needham, *The Bradshaw Method: Henry Bradshaw's Contribution to Bibliography* (Chapel Hill, N.C.: Hanes Foundation, 1988), 8–9. For a practical example, see Henry Bradshaw, "List of the Founts of Type and Woodcut Devices Used by Printers of Holland in the Fifteenth Century" (= Memorandum 3), June 1871, 258–79. See examples in Seth Lerer, "Caxton in the Nineteenth Century, in William Kuskin, ed., *Caxton's Trace: Studies in the History of English Printing* (Notre Dame, Ind.: University of Notre Dame Press, 2006), esp. 341–61.

5. Robert Proctor, *Index to Early Printed Books in the British Museum . . . to the Year 1500* (London: Kegan Paul, 1898). See my discussion in *Abstractions of Evidence in the Study of Manuscripts and Early Printed Books* (Aldershot: Ashgate, 2009), 129–31.

6. Among the more important of such facsimile collections were Konrad Burger, *Monumenta Germaniae et Italiae typographica: Deutsche und italienische Inkunabeln in getreuen Nachbildungen*, 10 vols. (Berlin, 1892–1913); *Veröffentlichungen der Gesellschaft für Typenkunde des XV. Jahrhunderts* (Berlin, 1907–1939); and the facsimile volumes of BMC.

7. In England, the complete catalogue of typefaces and printers was extended to 1558; Frank Isaac, *English and Scottish Printing Types, 1501–58, 1508–58*, 2 vols. (London: Oxford University Press, 1930–1932).

8. See, e.g., *A Catalogue and Specimen of the Typefoundry of John James*, 19–23, included in facsimile in Harry Carter and Christopher Ricks, eds., *Edward Rowe Mores: A Dissertation Upon English Typographical Founders and Founderies (1778)* (Oxford: Bibliographical Society, 1961).

9. Daniel Berkeley Updike, *Printing Types: Their History, Forms, and Use: A Study in Survivals*, 2 vols., 2nd ed. (Cambridge, Mass.: Harvard University Press, 1937); see my critique of Febvre and Martin in *The Myth of Print Culture: Essays on Evidence, Textuality, and Bibliographical Method* (Toronto: University of Toronto Press, 2003), chap. 1.

10. Martin Bormann's edict of 1941 defines Fraktur, standing for the entire class of gothic letters and once the mark of political and racial authenticity, as "Jewish letters"; henceforth only roman letters were to be used and taught in schools. See Peter Willberg, "Fraktur and Nationalism," in Peter Bain and Pau Shaw, eds., *Blackletter Type and National Identity* (New York: Princeton Architectural Press, 1998), 40–49; Bormann's typescript reproduced on 48. For use of blackletter in historical publications in England, see my *Who Is Buried in Chaucer's Tomb: Studies in the Reception of Chaucer's Book* (East Lansing: Michigan State University Press, 1998), 98–102.

11. Michael Twyman, *Early Lithographed Books: A Study of the Design and Production of Improper Books in the Age of the Hand Press* (London: Farrand, 1990), 212–25.

12. William Blades, *The Life and Typography of William Caxton, England's First Printer*, 2 vols. (London, 1861–63); see my *Abstractions of Evidence in the Study of Manuscripts and Early Printed Books* (Aldershot: Ashgate, 2008), 128–29; and Robin Myers, "George Isaac Frederick Tupper, Facsimilist," *Transcriptions of the Cambridge Bibliographical Society* 7 (1978): 113–34. Bradshaw, in 1864, claims these facsimiles "exceed any lithographs which I ever saw." Letter to J. W. Holtrop, in Wytze and Lotte Hellinga, eds., *Henry Bradshaw's Correspondence on Incunabula*, 2 vols. (Amsterdam: Hertzberger, 1966), 26.

13. Dibdin rightly notes that the detail found in sixteenth-century woodblocks is no proof of the technique used to produce them (but it is not clear that this is precisely what Landseer means).

14. "This may account for the tardy appearance of the first Copper-Plate impressions in this country, executed by means of a roller—which are supposed to be the frontispiece to 'Galennus De temperamentis' printed at Cambridge in 1521 . . . and the cuts in 'Raynalde's Birth of Mankind,' 1540. Of one of these latter the following is a fac-simile—which, although printed from a wooden block, [for the convenience of press-work] will be found to exhibit a very faithful character of the original" (xxiv–xxv).

15. Ames's "A Specimen of Caxton's Letter" is designed by Ames, and cut by G. Bickham. Cf. Dibdin's "Fac-simile of the French and English Editions of the History of Troy printed by Caxton (a facsimile of the Recuyell), designed and cut by "Bart. Howlett" (Plate VII). Pl. IX (Caxton 3 and 4) is cut by "Js. Basire"; others are unattributed.

16. The dimensions of initials are thus included in the bibliographical descriptions in BMC and even in the more spare descriptions in *Gesamtkatalog der Wiegendrucke*.

17. See Updike, *Printing Types*, 2:188–219; Chap. 4 above.

18. "Olden time" is in blackletter.

19. See also, the illustration of Coutances, with the Roman aqueduct (in semi-ruins) featured more prominently than the cathedral in the far distance (1:408).

CONCLUSION: PRINT CULTURE REDIVIVUS

1. Dennis K. Renner, from J. R. LeMaster and Donald D. Kummings, eds., *Walt Whitman: An Encyclopedia* (New York: Garland, 1998), printed in the Whitman Archive. I assume "superior literary standing" refers to "superior standing" among "literary historians."

2. Gay Wilson Allen, *The New Walt Whitman Handbook* (New York: New York University Press, 1975), 158.

3. Justin Kaplan, ed., *Walt Whitman: Poetry and Prose* (New York: Library of America, 1982).

4. I thank my former student, Janelle Herrick, for calling to my attention the problems discussed here.

PRINCIPAL WORKS CITED

꩜

Ackermann, James S. "Leonardo's Eye." *Journal of the Warburg and Courtault Institutes* 41 (1978): 108–13.

Aguera y Arcas, Blaise. "Temporary Matrices and Elemental Punches in Gutenberg's DK Type." In Kristian Jensen, ed., *Incunabula and Their Readers*. London: British Library, 2003. 1–12.

Allen, Gay Wilson. *The New Walt Whitman Handbook*. New York: New York University Press, 1975.

Ames, Joseph. *Typographical Antiquities*. London, 1749.

Amico, Moneti E. "Giacomo Sardini, patrizio lucchese, erudito e bibliografo." In *Miscellanea in memoria di A. Gallo*. Florence: Olschki, 1956. 47–78.

Andersen, Kirsti. *The Geometry of an Art: The History of the Mathematical Theory of Perspective from Alberti to Monge*. New York: Springer, 2007.

Andrew, Malcolm, et al. *The General Prologue*. Variorum Chaucer II, 1. Norman: University of Oklahoma Press, 1993.

Antonetti, Martin. "Typographic Ekphrasis: The Description of Typographic Forms in the Nineteenth Century." *Word and Image* 15 (1999): 44–45.

Audin, Maurice. *Histoire de l'imprimerie: radioscopie d'une ère, de Gutenberg à l'informatique*. Paris: Picard, 1972.

Baatz, Christine. "'A Strange Collection of Trash'? The Re-Evaluation of Medieval Literature in Thomas Percy's *Reliques of Ancient English Poetry* (1765)." In Barbara Korte, Ralf Schneider, and Stefanie Lethbridge, eds., *Anthologies of British Poetry: Critical Perspectives from Literary and Cultural Studies*. Amsterdam: Rodopi, 2000. 105–24.

Bain, Peter, and Pau Shaw, eds. *Blackletter Type and National Identity*. New York: Princeton Architectural Press, 1998.

Barker, Nicolas. *Biblioteca Lindesiana*. London: Quaritch, 1977.

———. "Reflections on the History of the Book." 1990. Rpt. in *Form and Meaning in the History of Books: Selected Essays*. London: British Library, 2003.

———. "Typography and the Meaning of Words: The Revolution in the Layout of Books in the Eighteenth Century." In Giles Barber and Bernhard Fabian, eds., *Buch und Buchhandel in Europa im achtzehnten Jahrhundert.* Hamburg: Hauswedell, 1981. 127–66.

Bechtel, Guy. *Gutenberg et l'invention de l'imprimerie: une enquête.* Paris: Fayard, 1992.

Benson, Larry D., ed. *The Riverside Chaucer.* Boston: Houghton Mifflin, 1987.

Blades, William. *How to Tell a Caxton: with some hints where and how the same might be found.* London: Sotheran, 1870.

———. *Life and Typography of William Caxton.* 2 vols. London: J. Lilly, 1861.

Blake, N. F. "Aftermath: Manuscript to Print." In Jeremy Griffiths and Derek Pearsall, eds., *Book Production and Publishing in Britain, 1375–1475.* Cambridge: Cambridge University Press, 1989. 403–32.

Blodgett, James E. "Some Printer's Copy for William Thynne's 1532 Edition of Chaucer." *The Library* ser. 6, 1 (1979): 97–113.

Boghardt, Martin. "Partial Duplicate Setting: Means of Rationalization or Complicating Factor in Textual Transmission." *The Library* ser. 6, 15 (1993): 306–31.

Bradshaw, Henry. "List of the Founts of Type and Woodcut Devices Used by Printers of Holland in the Fifteenth Century." Memorandum 3, June 1871. In *Collected Papers.* Cambridge: Cambridge University Press, 1889. 258–79.

Braudel, Fernand. "Histoire et sciences sociales: la longue durée." 1958. Rpt. in *Écrits sur l'histoire.* Paris: Flammarion, 1969. 41–84.

Brooks, Cleanth, ed. *The Percy Letters.* Vol. 7, *The Correspondence of Thomas Percy and William Shenstone.* New Haven, Conn.: Yale University Press, 1977.

Brown, Horatio. *The Venetian Printing Press: An Historical Study based upon Documents for the most part hitherto unpublished.* New York: G. P. Putnam's Sons, 1891.

Burger, Konrad. *Monumenta Germaniae et Italiae typographica: Deutsche und italienische Inkunabeln in getreuen Nachbildungen.* Berlin: Reichsdruckerei, 1892–1913.

Butler, Martin. *The Stuart Court Masque and Political Culture.* Cambridge: Cambridge University Press, 2008.

Butlin, Martin. "Is This a Private War or Can Anyone Join In? A Plea for a Broader Look at Blake's Color-Printing Techniques." *Blake: An Illustrated Quarterly* 36 (2002): 45–49.

———. "William Blake, S. W. Hayter, and Color Printing." From *Blake: An Illustrated Quarterly.* www.rochester.edu/college/eng/blake.

Carter, B. A. R. "Perspective." In Harold Osborne, ed., *Oxford Companion to Art.* Oxford: Oxford University Press, 1970. 843–51.

Carter, Harry. *A View of Early Typography, up to About 1600.* Oxford: Oxford University Press, 1969.

Catalogue of Books Printed in the XVth Century Now in the British Museum. 13 vols. London, 1908–.

Clair, Colin. *A History of European Printing.* London: Academic Press, 1976.

Corsten, Severin. "Die Drucklegung der zweiundvierzigzeiligen Bibel: Technische und chronologische Probleme." In *Johannes Gutenbergs zweiundvierzigzeilen Bibel: Fak-*

simile Ausgabe nach dem Exemplar der Staatsbibliothek Preußischer Kulturbesitz Berlin. Munich: Idion, 1979. *Kommentarband.* 35–67.

———. "Ulrich Zells früheste Produktion." *Gutenberg Jahrbuch* 2007. 68–76.

Crotch, W. J. B., ed. *The Prologues and Epilogues of William Caxton.* EETS, OS, 176. London, 1928.

Damisch, Hubert. *The Origin of Perspective.* 1987. Trans. John Goodman. Cambridge, Mass.: Harvard University Press, 1994.

Dane, Joseph A. *Abstractions of Evidence in the Study of Manuscripts and Early Printed Books.* Aldershot: Ashgate, 2009.

———. "A Ghostly Twin Terence (Venice, 21 July 1475; IGI 9422, 9433)." *The Library* ser. 6, 21 (1999): 99–107.

———. "Linear Perspective and the Obliquities of Reception." In Sandra P. Prior and Robert M. Stein, eds., *Reading Medieval Culture: Essays in Honor of Robert W. Hanning.* Notre Dame, Ind.: University of Notre Dame Press, 2005. 428–53.

———. *The Myth of Print Culture: Essays on Evidence, Textuality, and Bibliographical Method.* Toronto: University of Toronto Press, 2003.

———. *Who Is Buried in Chaucer's Tomb? Studies in the Reception of Chaucer's Book.* East Lansing: Michigan State University Press, 1999.

Dane, Joseph A., and Alexandra Gillespie. "The Myth of the Cheap Quarto." In John King, ed., *Tudor Books and Readers.* Cambridge: Cambridge University Press, 2009. 25–45.

DeRicci, Seymour. *Catalogue raisonné des premières impressions de Mayence (1445–1467).* VGG,8–9. Mainz: Gutenberg Gesellschaft, 1911.

Derolez, Albert. *The Palaeography of Gothic Manuscript Books, from the Twelfth to the Early Sixteenth Century.* Cambridge: Cambridge University Press, 2003.

De Vinne, Theodore. L. *The Invention of Printing: A Collection of Facts and Opinions Descriptive of Early Prints and Playing Cards, the Block-Books of the Fifteenth Century, the Legend of Lourens Janszoon Coster, of Haarlem, and the Work of John Gutenberg and His Associates.* New York: F. Hart, 1876.

Dibdin, Thomas Frognall. *Bibliographical, Antiquarian and Picturesque Tour in France and Germany.* 3 vols. London, 1821.

———. *Typographical Antiquities, or the History of Printing in England.* 4 vols. London, 1810–19.

Dugaw, Diane. "The Popular Marketing of 'Old Ballads': The Ballad Revival and Eighteenth-Century Antiquarianism Revisited." *Eighteenth-Century Studies* 21 (1987): 71–90.

Duggan, Hoyt N., and Robert Adams. The Piers Plowman Electronic Archive. Ann Arbor: University of Michigan Press; Cambridge, Mass.: Medieval Academy, 2000–. www.iath.virginia.edu/seenet/piers/.

Dziatzko, Karl. *Gutenbergs früheste Druckerpraxis.* Berlin: Asher, 1890.

Eaves, Morris, Robert N. Essick, and Joseph Viscomi. The William Blake Archive. www.blakearchive.org/

Eisenstein, Elizabeth. *The Printing Press as an Agent of Change.* 2 vols. Cambridge: Cambridge University Press, 1979.

Elkins, James. "Did Leonardo Develop a Theory of Curvilinear Perspective, Together with Some Remarks on the 'Angle' and 'Distance' Axioms." *Journal of the Warburg and Courtault Institutes* 51 (1988): 190–96.

Enschedé, Charles. *Technisch Onderzoek naar de Uitvinding van de Boekdrukkunst.* Haarlem: Bohn, 1901.

Essick, Robert N., ed. *William Blake: Songs of Innocence and of Experience.* San Marino, Calif.: Huntington Library Press, 2008.

Essick, Robert N., and Joseph Viscomi. "Blake's Method of Color Printing: Some Responses and Further Observations." *Blake: An Illustrated Quarterly* 36 (2002): 49–64.

———. "An Inquiry into William Blake's Method of Color Printing." *Blake: An Illustrated Quarterly* 35 (2002): 74–103.

Febvre, Lucien, and Henri-Jean Martin. *L'Apparition du livre.* Paris: Michel, 1958. Trans. David Gerard. *The Coming of the Book: The Impact of Printing 1450–1800.* London: Verso, 1976.

Field, J. V. "Alberti, the Abacus, and Piero della Francesca's Proof of Perspective." *Renaissance Studies* 11 (1997): 61–88.

———. *Piero della Francesca: A Mathematician's Art.* New Haven, Conn.: Yale University Press, 2005.

Folson, Ed, and Kenneth M. Price, eds. Walt Whitman Archive. www.waltwhitmanarchive.org.

Frangenberg, Thomas. "The Angle of Vision: Problems of Perspectival Representation in the Fifteenth and Sixteenth Centuries." *Renaissance Studies* 6 (1992): 1–45.

Fuhrmann, Otto W. "The Gutenberg Donatus Fragments at Columbia University, One of the Oldest Mainz Imprints." *Gutenberg Jahrbuch* 1954. 36–46

Füssell, Stephen. *Gutenberg and the Impact of Printing.* 1999. Trans. Douglas Martin. Aldershot: Ashgate, 2003.

Galloway, Andrew. "Reading *Piers Plowman* in the Fifteenth and the Twenty-First Centuries: Notes on Manuscripts F and W in the Piers Plowman Electronic Archive." *JEGP* 103 (2004): 232–52.

Gaskell, Philip. *A New Introduction to Bibliography.* Oxford: Oxford University Press, 1972.

Glomski, Jacqueline. "Seventeenth-Century Views on Early Printing." *The Library* ser. 7, 2 (2001): 336–48.

Greg, Walter W. "The Rationale of Copy-Text." *Studies in Bibliography* 3 (1950–51): 19–36.

Groom, Nick. *The Making of Percy's "Reliques".* Oxford: Clarendon Press, 1999.

Hammond, Eleanor Prescott. *Chaucer: A Bibliographical Manual.* New York: Macmillan, 1908.

Hellinga, Wytze, and Lotte Hellinga. *The Fifteenth-Century Printing Types of the Low Countries.* 2 vols. Trans. D. A. S. Reid. Amsterdam: Hertzberger, 1966.

Herbert, William. *Typographical Antiquities*. 3 vols. London, 1785–1790.

Hessels, Jan Hendrik, trans. *The Haarlem Legend of the Invention of Printing by Lourens Janszoon Coster. Critically examined by Antonius van der Linde*. London, 1871.

———. "Typography." 1911. *Encyclopedia Britannica*. www.1911encyclopedia.org.

Ing, Janet Thompson. *Johann Gutenberg and His Bible: A Historical Study*. New York: Typophiles, 1988.

Isaac, Frank. *English and Scottish Printing Types, 1501–58, 1508–58*. 2 vols. London: Oxford University Press, 1930–1932.

Ivins, William M., Jr. *On the Rationalization of Sight*. 1938. Rpt. New York: Da Capo Press, 1973.

Johnson, A. F. "The Classification of Gothic Types." 1929. In *Selected Essays on Books and Printing*, ed. Percy H. Muir. Amsterdam: Van Gendt, 1970.

———. *Type Designs: Their History and Development*. 1934. 3rd ed. Norwich: Andre Deutsch, 1966.

Juchoff, Rudolf. "Wandlungen des Gutenbergbildes." *Zentralblatt für Bibliothekswesen* 57 (1940): 202–14.

Kane, George. *Chaucer and Langland: History and Textual Approaches*. Berkeley: University of California Press, 1989.

Kane, George, and E. Talbot Donaldson, eds. *William Langland's Piers Plowman: The B-Version*. London: Athlone, 1975.

Kaplan, Justin, ed. *Walt Whitman: Poetry and Prose*. New York: Library of America, 1982.

Kapr, Albert. *Johann Gutenberg: The Man and His Invention*. 1996. Trans. Douglas Martin. Aldershot: Ashgate, 1996.

Kemp, Martin. "Leonardo and the Visual Pyramid." *Journal of the Warburg and Courtauld Institutes* 40 (1977): 128–49.

———. *The Science of Art: Optical Themes in Western Art from Brunelleschi to Seurat*. New Haven, Conn.: Yale University Press, 1990.

Laire, Franciscus Saver. *Specimen historicum typographiae romanae xv.saeculi*. Rome, 1778.

Leonardo da Vinci. *The Notebooks of Leonardo da Vinci*, ed. Jean Paul Richter. 1883. Rpt. New York: Dover, 1970.

Lerer, Seth. "Caxton in the Nineteenth Century." In William Kuskin, ed., *Caxton's Trace: Studies in the History of English Printing*. Notre Dame, Ind.: University of Notre Dame Press, 2006. 325–70.

Lindberg, David. "A Reconsideration of Roger Bacon's Theory of Pinhole Images." *Archive for the History of Exact Sciences* 6 (1970): 214–23.

———." The Theory of Pinhole Images from Antiquity to the Thirteenth Century." *Archive for the History of Exact Sciences* 5 (1968): 154–62.

Linde, Antonius van der. *Geschichte der Erfindung der Buchdruckkunst*. 3 vols. Berlin: Asher, 1886.

Lounsbury, Thomas R. *Studies in Chaucer*. 3 vols. New York: Harper, 1892.

Lowry, Martin. *Nicholas Jenson and the Rise of Venetian Publishing in Renaissance Europe*. Oxford: Blackwell, 1991.

Maittaire, Michel. *Annales Typographici ab artis inventae origine ad annum md.* The Hague, 1719.

Manly, John M., and Edith Rickert. *The Text of the Canterbury Tales.* 8 vols. Chicago: University of Chicago Press, 1940.

Martin, Henri-Jean. *Pour une histoire du livre, XVe–XVIIIe siècle: cinq conférences.* Naples: Bibliopolis, 1987.

McGann, Jerome J. "The Rationale of Hypertext." In *Radiant Textuality: Literature After the WorldWide Web.* New York: Palgrave, 2001. 38–74.

McKenzie, D. F. "Typography and Meaning: The Case of William Congreve." In Giles Barber and Bernhard Fabian, eds., *Buch und Buchhandel in Europa im achtzehnten Jahrhundert.* Hamburg: Hauswedell, 1981. 81–126.

McKerrow, Ronald B. *An Introduction to Bibliography for Literary Students.* Oxford: Oxford University Press, 1927.

[McLeod, Randall]. "Enter Reader." In Paul Eggert and Margaret Sankey, eds., *The Editorial Gaze: Mediating Texts in Literature and the Arts.* New York: Garland, 1998. 3–50.

———. "FIAT fLUX." In Randall McLeod, ed., *Crisis in Editing: Texts of the English Renaissance.* New York: AMS Press, 1994. 61–172.

McMurtrie, Douglas C., and Karl Schorbach. *The Gutenberg Documents, with Translations of the Texts into English.* New York: Oxford University Press, 1941.

Mish, Charles C. "Black Letter as a Social Discriminant in the Seventeenth Century." *PMLA* 68 (1953): 627–30.

Mores, Edward Rowe. *A Dissertation upon English Typographical Founders and Founderies (1778), with A Catalogue and Specimen of the Typefoundry of John James 1782.* Ed. Harry Carter and Christopher Ricks. London: Oxford University Press, 1961.

Morison, Stanley, and Harry Carter. *John Fell: The University Press and the "Fell" Types.* Oxford: Clarendon Press, 1967.

Mortet, Charles. *Les origines et les débuts de l'imprimerie.* Paris: Picard, 1922.

Moxon, Joseph. *Mechanick Exercises on the Whole Art of Printing (1683–4),* ed. Herbert Davis and Harry Carter. 2 vols. Oxford: Oxford University Press, 1958.

Muscatine, Charles. *The Book of Geoffrey Chaucer.* San Francisco: Book Club of California, 1963.

Myers, Robin. "George Isaac Frederick Tupper, Facsimilist." *Transactions of the Cambridge Bibliographical Society* 7 (1978): 113–34.

Needham, Paul. *The Bradshaw Method: Henry Bradshaw's Contribution to Bibliography.* Chapel Hill, N.C.: Hanes Foundation, 1998.

———. "The Compositor's Hand in the Gutenberg Bible: A Review of the Todd Thesis." *PBSA* 77 (1983): 341–71.

———. "Division of Copy in the Gutenberg Bible: Three Glosses on the Ink Evidence." *PBSA* 79 (1985): 411–26.

———. *The Invention and Early Spread of European Printing as Represented in the Scheide Library.* Princeton, N.J.: Princeton University Library, 2007.

———. "Johann Gutenberg and the Catholicon Press." *PBSA* 76 (1982): 395–456.

————. "The Paper Supply of the Gutenberg Bible." *PBSA* 79 (1985): 303–74.

————. "Paul Schwenke and Gutenberg Scholarship: The German Contribution, 1855–1921." *PBSA* 84 (1990): 241–64.

Nichols, John. *The Progresses, Processions, and Magnificent Festivities of King James the First*. 4 vols. 1828. Rpt. New York: B. Franklin, 1967.

Nicoll, Alardyce. *Stuart Masques and the Renaissance Stage*. New York: Harcourt Brace, 1938.

A Noble Fragment: Being a Leaf of the Gutenberg Bible (1453–1455), with a Bibliographical Essay by A. Edward Newton. New York: Wells, 1921.

Orlandi, Antonio. *Origine e progressi della stampa o sia del-arte impressoria e notizie dell'opera stampate dall'anno m.cccc.lvi. sino all' anno md*. Bologne, 1722.

Orrell, John. *The Human Stage: English Theatre Design, 1567–1640*. Cambridge: Cambridge University Press, 1988.

————. *The Theatres of Inigo Jones and John Webb*. Cambridge: Cambridge University Press, 1985.

Panofsky, Erwin. *Die Perspektive als symbolische Form*. Vorträge der Bibliothek Warburg, 1924–25. Leipzig: Teubner, 1927. 258–330. Trans. Christopher S. Wood, *Perspective as Symbolic Form*. New York: Zone Books, 1991.

Pearsall, Derek. "Thomas Speght (ca. 1550-?)." In Paul G. Ruggiers, ed., *Editing Chaucer: The Great Tradition*. Norman: University of Oklahoma Press, 1984. 71–92.

————, ed. *The Nun's Priest's Tale*. Variorum Chaucer, II, 9. Norman: University of Oklahoma Press, 1984.

Percy, Thomas. *Reliques of Ancient English Poetry*. 3 vols. London, 1765.

Phillips, Michael. *William Blake: The Creation of the Songs from Manuscript to Illuminated Printing*. Princeton, N.J.: Princeton University Press, 2001.

Piero della Francesca. *De prospectiva pingendi*. Ed. G. Nicco Fasola. 1942. Rpt. Florence: Case editrice Le Lettere, 1984.

————. *De prospectiva pingendi*. Facsimile, Parma Biblioteca Palatina, MS 1576. New York: Broude, 1992.

Pirenne, M. H. *Optics, Painting, and Photography*. Cambridge: Cambridge University Press, 1970.

Pollard, Alfred W. *An Essay on Colophons with Specimens and Translations*. Chicago: Caxton Club, 1905.

Proctor, Robert. *Index to Early Printed Books in the British Museum . . . to the year 1500*. London: Kegan Paul, 1898.

Prothero, G. W. *A Memoir of Henry Bradshaw*. London: Kegan, Paul, Trench, 1888.

Renouard, Aug. Ant. *Annales de l'imprimerie des Alde, ou Histoire des trois Manuce et de leurs editions*. 3rd. ed. Paris: Renouard, 1834.

Ruppel, Aloys. *Johannes Gutenberg: Sein Leben und sein Werk*. Berlin: Gebr. Mann, 1939.

Sardini, Giacomo. *Esame sui principj della francese ed italiana tipografiu ovvero storia critica di Nicolao Jenson*. 3 vols. Lucca: Stamperia Bonsignori, 1796–1798.

Schmidt, A. V. C., ed. *The Vision of Piers Plowman: A Critical Edition of the B-Text*. 2nd ed. London: Dent, 1995.

Scholderer, Victor. "The Invention of Printing." 1941. In *Fifty Essays in Fifteenth- and Sixteenth-Century Bibliography*, ed. Dennis E. Rhodes. Amsterdam: Hertzberger, 1966. 156–68.

———. *William Langland: A Parallel-Text Edition of the A, B, C, and Z Versions*. 2 vols. London: Longman, 1995; Kalamazoo, Mich.: Medieval Institute Publications, 2009.

Schwenke, Paul. *Die Donat- und Kalender-Type: Nachtrag und Übersicht*. VGG, 2. Mainz: Gutenberg Gesellschaft. 1903.

———. "Die Gutenbergbibel." In *Johannes Gutenbergs zweiundvierzigzeilige Bibel: Ergänzungsband zur Faksimile-Ausgabe*. Leipzig: Insel, 1923.

———. *Untersuchungen zur Geschichte des ersten Buchdrucks*. Berlin: Hopfer, 1900.

Sherman, William. *Used Books: Marking Readers in Renaissance England*. Philadelphia: University of Pennsylvania Press, 2008.

Simpson, Percy, and C. F. Bell. *Designs by Inigo Jones for Masques & Plays at Court: A Descriptive Catalogue of Drawings for Scenery and Costumes mainly in the Collection of His Grace the Duke of Devonshire, K. G.* Oxford: Walpole and Malone Societies, 1924.

Skeat, Walter W., ed. *The Vision of William Concerning Piers Plowman Together with Vita de Dowel, Dobet et Dobest, and Richard the Redeles, by William Langland*. 2 vols. London: Oxford University Press, 1885.

Snyder, Joel. "Picturing Vision." *Critical Inquiry* 6 (1980): 507–11.

Sotheby, S. Leigh. *The Typography of the Fifteenth Century, being specimens of the productions of the early continental printers, exemplified in a collection of fac-similes from one hundred works*. London, 1845.

Spencer, John R., ed. *Leon Battista Alberti: On Painting*. New Haven, Conn.: Yale University Press, 1966.

Todd, William B. *The Gutenberg Bible: New Evidence of the Original Printing*. Chapel Hill, N.C.: Hanes Foundation, 1982.

Twyman, Michael. *Early Lithographed Books: A Study of the Design and Production of Improper Books in the Age of the Hand Press*. London: Farrand, 1990.

Updike, Daniel Berkeley. *Printing Types: Their History, Forms, and Use: A Study in Survivals*. 2 vols. Cambridge, Mass.: Harvard University Press, 1937.

Veröffentlichungen der Gesellschaft für Typenkunde des XV. Jahrhunderts. Berlin, 1907–39.

Wallau, Heinrich. "Die zweifarbigen Initialen der Psalterdrucke von Joh. Fust und Peter Schöffer." In *Festschrift zum fünfhundertjährigen Geburtstage von Johann Gutenberg*. Leipzig: Harrassowitz, 1900. 325–79.

Warton, Thomas. *The History of English Poetry*. 3 vols. London, 1778–81.

Wehmer, Carl. *Mainzer Probedrucke in der Type des sogenannten astronomischen Kalenders für 1448: Ein Beitrag zur Gutenbergforschung*. Munich: Leibniz, 1948.

Werfel, Silvia. "Einrichtung und Betrieb einer Druckerei der Handpressenzeit, 1446 bis 1820." In Helmut Gier and Johannes Janota, eds., *Augsburger Buchdruck und Verlagswesen*. Wiesbaden: Harrassowitz, 1997. 97–124.

Zedler, Gottfried. *Der älteste Buchdruck und das frühholländische Doktrinale von Alexander de Villa Dei*. Leiden: Sitjhoff, 1936.

————. *Die älteste Gutenbergtype, mit 13 Tafeln in Lichtdruck*. VGG, 1. Mainz: Gutenberg Gesellschaft, 1902.

————. *Gutenbergs älteste Type, und die mit ihr hergestellten Drucke*. VGG, 23. Mainz: Gutenberg Gesellschaft, 1934.

————. *Die sogenannte Gutenbergbibel, sowie die mit der 42-zeiligen Bibeltype ausgeführten kleineren Drucke*. VGG, 20. Mainz: Gutenberg Gesellschaft, 1929.

————. *Von Coster zu Gutenberg: Der holländische Frühdruck und die Erfindung des Buchdrucks*. Leipzig: Hiersemann, 1921.

INDEX

❧

ACKNOWLEDGMENTS

Chapter 4 is reprinted with slight changes from *Eighteenth-Century Life* 29 (2005): 76–96; a somewhat more tangled version of Chapter 5 appeared in *Studies in Bibliography* 51 (1998): 48–62. I thank their editors for permission to reprint here. I thank also for photo permissions the British Library, the Henry E. Huntington Library, the Doheny Library at the University of Southern California, and especially the William Andrews Clark Memorial Library in Los Angeles. I have received help of various kinds from a number of people, including, but of course not limited to, Amelia Kunhardt, Hoyt Duggan, Svetlana Dyananova, Sidney Evans, Percival Everett, Mac Gatch, Penelope Geng, Alexandra Gillespie, the Greens, Paulina Kewes, Seth Lerer, Randall McCloud, Paul Needham, Phoebe Peacock, Margaret Russett, Sandra Prior, my students, and numerous friends from Maine. I also am most grateful to Jerry Singerman and many others at the University of Pennsylvania Press for their help and support.